HOAX SPRINGS ETERNAL

Unlike sleights of hand, which fool the senses, sleights of mind challenge cognition. This book defines and explains cognitive deception and explores six prominent potential historical instances of it: the Cross of King Arthur, Drake's Plate of Brass, the Kensington Runestone, the Vinland Map, Piltdown Man, and the Shroud of Turin. In spite of evidence contradicting their alleged origins, their stories continue to persuade many of their authenticity. Peter Hancock uses these purported hoaxes as case studies to develop and demonstrate fundamental principles of cognitive psychology. By dissecting each ostensible artifact, he illustrates how hoaxes can deceive us and offers us defenses against them. This book further examines how and why we allow others to deceive us and how and why at times we even deceive ourselves. Accessible to beginner and expert alike, *Hoax Springs Eternal* provides an essential interdisciplinary guide to cognitive deception.

Peter Hancock is Provost Distinguished Research Professor, Pegasus Professor, and Trustee Chair in the Department of Psychology and the Institute for Simulation and Training at the University of Central Florida. He also directs the MIT² Laboratory, which researches human factors psychology. He is the author or editor of twenty books, including *Performance Under Stress* (2008); *Mind, Machine and Morality* (2009); and the award-winning historical text *Richard III and the Murder in the Tower* (2009).

ADVANCE PRAISE FOR *HOAX SPRINGS ETERNAL*

"*Hoax Springs Eternal* is not the usual work of skeptical debunking but rather a deeply insightful psychological thriller across the ages and into the human mind to explore how we come to believe not the impossible so much as the historical possible. In each of the stories artfully presented here Peter Hancock shows how evidence is evaluated in the context of the culture and the times in a way that allows us to understand why many people believe such claims. A ripping good read!"
> – Michael Shermer, publisher of *Skeptic* magazine, monthly columnist for *Scientific American*, author of *Why People Believe Weird Things* and *The Believing Brain*

"Hancock reveals just how we are fooled *and* how we often fool ourselves! He illustrates his many insights with fascinating case studies – letting us tag along on one adventure after another: King Arthur's Cross, the Vinland Map, Piltdown Man, the Shroud of Turin, and more. The results are illuminating."
> – Joe Nickell, Investigative Reporter, Fellow of the Committee for Skeptical Inquiry

"Hancock provides an enjoyable and fascinating journey through historical deceptions, exploring the many facets that contribute to people's willingness to be deceived, as well as the characteristics of deception itself. A good read for students of both history and psychology."
> – Mica Endsley, Chief Scientist, United States Air Force

"A fascinating and inimitable look at the psychology of deception through the lens of historical hoaxes. Hancock even includes a checklist for how to create one (!), but doesn't want to make you liable for future hoaxes!"
> – Missy Cummings, Massachusetts Institute of Technology

"A tour de force. A highly readable account of well-known historical artifacts sometimes (or often) characterized as hoaxes, such as the Shroud of Turin and the Piltdown Man, viewed through the lens of the psychology of deception. Hancock the scientist meets Hancock the historical scholar to take the reader through a fascinating tour of the human mind and its strengths and pitfalls, including the mechanisms of 'cognitive deception' involved in belief or disbelief in these artifacts. An engaging, well-researched, and highly entertaining book."
> – Raja Parasuraman, University Professor, George Mason University

"Hancock's *Hoax Springs Eternal* is a thoroughly delightful expedition through history's most infamous and successful hoaxes, from the Shroud of Turin to King Arthur's Cross and Drake's Plate, Piltdown Man, and much, much more. Highly recommended to any student of history, observer of human behavior, or someone just looking for an excellent and entertaining read."
> – Steven Casey, author of *'Set Phasers on Stun'* and Other True Tales of Design, Technology, and Human Error

Hoax Springs Eternal

THE PSYCHOLOGY OF COGNITIVE DECEPTION

Peter Hancock

University of Central Florida

CAMBRIDGE
UNIVERSITY PRESS

CAMBRIDGE
UNIVERSITY PRESS

32 Avenue of the Americas, New York, NY 10013-2473, USA

Cambridge University Press is part of the University of Cambridge.

It furthers the University's mission by disseminating knowledge in the pursuit of education, learning, and research at the highest international levels of excellence.

www.cambridge.org
Information on this title: www.cambridge.org/9781107417687

First published 2015

A catalog record for this publication is available from the British Library.

Library of Congress Cataloging in Publication data
Hancock, Peter A., 1953–
Hoax springs eternal : the psychology of cognitive deception / Peter Hancock.
pages cm
Includes bibliographical references and index.
ISBN 978-1-107-07168-1 (hardback) – ISBN 978-1-107-41768-7 (paperback)
1. Cognitive psychology – Case studies. 2. Hoaxes – Case studies.
3. Deception – Case studies. I. Title.
BF201.H357 2014
153.7′4–dc23 2014020942

ISBN 978-1-107-07168-1 Hardback
ISBN 978-1-107-41768-7 Paperback

A text on the Nature of Cognitive Deception featuring detailed accounts of the Cross, the Plate, and the Stone, the Shroud, the Map, and the Bone. These exemplars illustrate the ways by which humans seek to deceive each other and by which they act to deceive themselves.

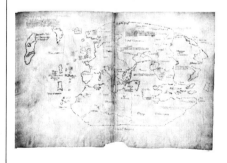

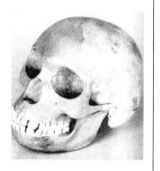

Order and Approximate Purported Dates of Creation

Pre-History   33   6th Century   1369   1440   1579

Alternative Order of Hoaxed Creations

11th Century 14th Century 1860   1908   1920   1930

CONTENTS

PREFACE

This book is about deception. It does not cover all forms of deception but focuses on one particular aspect that I refer to as *cognitive deception*. In this type of deception you are not fooled by some clever sleight of hand. In fact, these cognitive deceptions have been referred to rather as sleights of mind. With cognitive deceptions you are not led into error by some failure or misdirection of your sensory apparatus. In contrast, cognitive deceptions are purposely induced failures of attention, memory, and decision-making capacities. In general, the issue is set before you in a relatively clear and unambiguous manner, and unlike single, one-off events, cognitive deceptions are, by and large, on permanent display. The physical evidence is, in most cases, right in front of you and can be examined repeatedly and even subjected to physical tests and evaluation. These artifacts do not disappear when any particularly skeptical inquisitor approaches. They do not suffer from any sort of Taylor's so-called shyness effects. The objects and entities discussed here do not vanish when a camera or even a mass spectrometer approaches them. Yet important aspects of cognition are involved that induce people into accepting the deception, sometimes even in spite of the results of physical experimentation and examination.

I have framed the present book around a number of stories. Each of the examples discussed exposes different facets of cognitive deception. However, at heart, they have a great deal in common. It is these common elements that form the basis of my discussion of the psychology of cognitive deception, the explorations of which are interpolated between the respective stories. Although each example provides an intriguing case on its own and can be read as an individual study in potential hoax and deception, the purpose here is to take the respective lessons and to weld them into a unified theory of cognitive deception. It is my eventual hope to elaborate that theory beyond cognitive deceptions alone to include other forms such as sensory illusion and motor deception, but that is for the future and not the focus of this text.

I begin with a discussion of deception in general, which seeks to frame the cognitive dimension of deception within a wider context. Much of what is examined here is *not* concerned with establishing whether any particular artifact discussed is or is not a hoax. As I explain, with one specific exception, there remain arguments about the authenticity for each of the examples presented. Rather, the text is about the psychological principles involved in deception and how these general principles derive from an understanding of human behavior in general and how deception is only one specific part of this wider palette of capabilities. I have used a sequence of stories that focus on progressively more famous cases. Are they hoaxes? Herein lies their fascination. For each case can be viewed as true or false, believable or unbelievable, as the readers themselves decide. What I want to achieve is not the imposition of my personal beliefs on the reader, but to allow them to examine the evidence presented and so come up with their own decision. Obviously, as the author, I have had to construct each narrative. However, I have expressly tried to be careful to provide as balanced an account of each as I can. To accomplish this, I have provided extensive text notes as well as a full listing of research references so that if one or several of the stories presented takes the readers' special interest, they can easily follow up for themselves. Nor, of course, do I claim that the current range of example stories are anything but my own personal selection; many other accounts, artifacts, or contentions can be brought to the table of discussion. At the end of each story chapter, I do render my personal opinion, which the readers can then compare to their own persuasion. Perhaps the most important dimension of cognitive deception is the believability of what is offered. In all of the present examples, there is nothing inherently impossible about each story that is being told. Indeed, these have become celebrated cases precisely because they permit both belief and disbelief in almost equal measure. Further, the context of each claim often creates both ardent advocates and strident critics. It is the ability to sustain this partisan conflict that connotes a good hoax, but division is also evident in the case of authentic artifacts. Thus each circumstance serves to reveal as much about our own decision making and belief as they do about the artifacts themselves.

Concerning the dangers created by these partisan allegiances, I begin with a relatively anonymous case about which few, if any, contemporary individuals sustain any heated dispute. It concerns Arthur's Cross. The story of the Cross, which is purportedly a burial token of the quasi-mythical King Arthur, tells us that cognitive deception is no recent invention and argues that its practice and perfection have been pursued now for millennia. However, the commitment of adversarial constituencies heats up with my second story that revolves around Drake's Plate of Brass. It may be a historical fact that such a Plate at one time existed; however, its purported rediscovery in the middle of the last century is a much more disputed contention. Supposedly crafted in 1579, the Plate of Brass bears the assertion that Sir Francis Drake sailed to and then claimed all of California, in the name of Queen Elizabeth I. Of course, the notion that California belongs to the English is, as one might imagine, a much disputed claim. Among other issues, the Plate shows us how important claims are to original land occupation; a concern that is still expressed most evidently in the Near Middle East today, some thousands of years after the beginning of disputation. The historical record is explicit in noting that it was Drake's interactions with the indigenous peoples of that time that provided the foundation for a transfer of sovereignty to Elizabeth I. It was, of course, never made absolutely clear as to why such peoples would voluntarily give up their own sovereignty.

Readers can explore and decide on each of the specific stories presented. Alongside these individual case studies the psychology of cognitive deception is introduced. That is, I first provide the reader with specific cases and then seek to explain these through the application of the principles of cognitive psychology. This sequence is strategic, so that I can provide a scientific and theoretical framework for the subsequent examination of the respective case studies that follow. It will not escape the attention then that each story is presented in a specific sequence so as to illustrate the general principles and themes that are elaborated.

To follow on the first exploration of general principles, the third story is one that very much stirs the cultural and national patriotism of a very animated group. This concerns the Kensington Runestone. Again, this might not be an artifact well known outside the upper midwest of the United States, but in that region it is a very real emblem of Scandinavian pride. It remains a source of great contention and contemporary debate. Nominally dated 1362, the Runestone recounts the voyage, travels, and travails of a small group of explorers, some of whom were attacked and killed by the local tribes. Despite the imminent threat, the expedition somehow had the time to carve a somewhat extensive stone record of their very desperate circumstances. The exhumation of the Stone by a local farmer in the late 1800s caused a stir and debate that continues to this day. Was it a joke? Was it genuine? Farmer Ohman's find continues to intrigue the local populace as I hope the story will intrigue you.

The next story recapitulates many of the motivations seen in the account of the Kensington Runestone. This is the even more celebrated case of the Vinland Map. Based on the same issue of Viking primacy of exploration of North America, the Map purports to show Norse penetration into the American Northeast at around 1440. The motivations of the latter two artifacts prove fascinating, especially in light of the extensive and very real archeological investigation of the L'Anse aux Meadows site in Newfoundland, which does indeed confirm very early Norse settlement in the new world, well before Columbus's more famous journey.

Having presented four case studies and a general framework, I next tackle the processes involved in decision making and seek to explain how people decide whether to believe or disbelieve whatever specific proposition is offered to them. I present two perspectives on decision making and how each impinges on the process of deception. It is through this examination that I begin to flesh out my overall psychological framework for the exploration of cognitive deceptions. While all of the other stories in this text contain dimensions of persistent doubt, the next example, of Piltdown Man, is different. Piltdown *is* a hoax. Very few would disagree with this assessment, but the remaining question here is whodunnit? This fascinating tale shows that even purported "experts" are subject to the self-same propensities toward accepting what they wish to believe, even when contrary evidence is right in front of them. It provides the quintessential case study on how deception is promulgated, accepted, and then perpetuated. But critically, Piltdown also shows the process by which deception is eventually exposed.

The final story revolves around one of the most contentious items in the whole of the western world: the Shroud of Turin. Here we step beyond nationalistic jingoism and enter the world of religious belief. I argue that the self-same motivations are involved here and that this latter story provides striking confirmation about what persuades people to either believe or disbelieve. In the final chapters I reconsider my theoretical formulation in light of these final case studies. Here, I look to refine my eventual position on deception. My argument concludes with the assertion that cognitive deception is an intrinsic part of our human behavioral repertoire and that this capacity is also expressed, to a lesser degree, in other members of the animal kingdom. Thus, in human life as in all life, hoax springs eternal.

This book can be read in a number of ways. For those who are only interested in specific cases, each of the presented stories can be read as self-contained elements. I hope that ardent researchers of each specific artifact will find that the work provides a balanced and informative account. In contrast, readers who are focused only on the general principles of cognitive deception can omit some or even all of the case studies in favor of the more formal chapters that examine the nature of cognitive deception and its links to contemporary cognitive theory. Alternatively, an interested reader might wish to examine one particular section with its focus on specific elements of cognitive deception and the examples thereof in the linked case studies. If I have brewed my potion appropriately, the best way to approach this work is simply to go with the flow and sequentially enjoy each of the elements as they appear. I hope this proves to be an intoxicating libation and not simply "small beer."

I

THE TANGLED WEB

"Oh what a tangled web we weave, when first we practice to deceive!"
Sir Walter Scott [1]

"'It was extraordinary to observe ...', William Henry wrote later how willingly persons will blind themselves on any point interesting to their feelings."
Doug Stewart [2]

INTROCEPTION TO DEDUCTION

Deception is a part of life. Deception can be regarded as one of the essential characteristics that energize the very struggle for life itself [3]. The process of deception permeates virtually all of the animal kingdom [4]. Indeed, the occurrences of, and variations in, the capacities of animals to camouflage themselves and deceive their natural predators had a profound influence on Charles Darwin and the first conceptual development of his theory of evolution. Deception is also something we encounter throughout our personal lives. It is a behavioral characteristic that forms the basis of some of our original cultural narratives. For example, Homer's Iliad, one of the earliest of all human recorded stories, recounts a tale in which the deception of the Trojan Horse plays the central role. The Bible itself proposes that the present form of human existence began with two acts of deception: the first was the Devil's deception of Eve and the second was Eve's subsequent deception of Adam [5]. It is within such religious narratives that we find the first links between deception and sin. As a result, we often conceive of humans involved in deceptions as doing something that is "bad" or even "evil." In general, we have come to consider it wrong to deceive others.

There are, however, cultural differences in such a perception; some groups consider it an obligation to deceive the outsider. A recent and very

FIGURE I.1. A camouflaged stonefish. A highly dangerous species is hidden here from its enemy by the ability to blend against the background conditions [6].

interesting text [7] has suggested that there are evolutionary imperatives to deceive, and that our current mores on deception are simply one transient perspective that time may well change. In the larger animal world, we can see that deception may not be a bad thing at all. Rather, deception often proves to be the difference between life and death and the key to an individual's survival.

With respect to the animal kingdom, most deceptions involve deluding the senses. Instances of these sensory deceptions are one of the major dimensions of the ever-continuing battle between predator and prey. Adaptations that provide camouflage for one organism thus serve to misdirect the actions of specific others. In this enterprise, some animals are spectacularly successful (see Figure I.1). They exhibit capacities that enable them to change their color, shape, and effective size, and in many situations to seek out background conditions that render them virtually invisible. These are indeed wonderful capacities and characteristics and are worthy of extended study in and of themselves [8]. Although our human abilities for deception must have originally been founded upon these basic animal characteristics, the present text is not primarily concerned with such

sensory forms of deception. Rather, the focus here is on more advanced forms of deception that I have termed "cognitive deceptions." These types of deception are almost uniquely human in nature.

Deceptions represented by animal camouflage are designed to fool the senses. These sensory deceptions seek to mislead the perceptual capacity of any searching predator in trying to detect their prey. At the top of the food chain, there is relatively little need for disguise and camouflage. Until human beings invaded their realm, larger animals, such as elephants, had very little to hide from. Nowadays, of course, it is no longer the case that animals at the top of the food chain have nothing to fear. Sadly, whole species of large animals that in the past had no need to resort to deception to survive have now fallen prey to human predators. However, humans prey on each other as well. In this respect, we have cause to fear our own kind. We can see evidence of the need to camouflage ourselves from each other, as expressed most formally in military conflicts. Using the knowledge of intrinsic human sensory capacities, armies over the centuries have generated any number of forms of perceptual camouflage. These range from the personal camouflage of the individual soldier (see Figure I.2) to hiding whole armies from the sight of the enemy [9].

Across the centuries, military camouflage itself has become ever more sophisticated. Advances range from the ability to hide whole cities during the Second World War to the counterintuitive but surprisingly effective naval "dazzle" camouflage [10] that served to render large ships on the high seas extremely difficult to detect. As military detection capacities have progressed beyond the unaided human eye alone, technological forms of camouflage have advanced in turn. For example, in response to the invention and technological refinement of radar, we now have "stealth" airborne and seaborne craft that are purportedly invisible to radar detection. The predator-prey forces that act to fuel innovation through evolution in the natural world exert the same influence in the technological realm of the military arms race.

The antithesis of camouflage is conspicuity. Whereas camouflage tries to perfect the art of remaining undetected, conspicuity represents the active effort to attract attention. Conspicuity research, in addition to taking the negative lessons from the research on camouflage, has looked to benefit from cognitive psychology and what is known of the issue of attention. Conspicuity research involves very important practical topics such as

FIGURE I.2. The military often seek methods to improve sensory deception in order to limit the detection capacities of an enemy [11].

road safety. The same fundamental understanding of the basic processes of human perception and attention are found in both areas of being seen and not being seen. They are two sides of the same coin [12].

Although the forms of the deception I have cited so far involve an interaction between sensory capacities and the higher cognitive abilities of an individual, they are not cognitive deceptions per se. Indeed, cognitive deceptions involve little if any purely sensory misdirection. The item or entity of concern does not hide itself away in any fashion. Rather, many of the forms of cognitive deception discussed in this book actually seek the limelight. They look to make themselves conspicuous and the focus of attention. Colloquially then, we can say that cognitive deceptions do not look to fool the senses but rather to deceive the mind. As such, cognitive deceptions are often bound by their cultural context. Cognitive deceivers therefore need to understand much more about the individual or social group of individuals whom they look to deceive than just their common sensory and perceptual capacities. As a result, *a good cognitive deception proves to be almost as much about the deceived as the deceiver.*

In terms that are more theoretical in nature, cognitive deceptions can be defined as *acts of miscommunication.* This miscommunication may derive from the intentional action of an individual(s) to deceive others.

Equally, however, such miscommunication can arise from problems within the channel of communication between the inadvertent deceiver and the inadvertently deceived. One can think here of a communication channel in terms of one of its most common examples – a telephone call. So, for example, someone might choose to lie to you over the phone, but it is equally possible that the reception may simply be poor and you may well have trouble understanding exactly what the caller said. The latter problem is technically called "noise" in the communication channel, and the nature of this noise effect has been studied extensively for nearly a century or more [13]. Although the noise involved might well be unwanted sound, as in the phone call example [14], technically, noise represents any barrier to clear communication. Thus, smoke drifting across line-of-sight communications such as a semaphore system is still technically considered noise. If the noise (the source of interference) to signal (what is intended to be communicated) ratio in the communication channel is sufficiently high, interpretational failures can well occur independent of any individual's conscious intention to deceive. Think, for example, of a game of Chinese whispers (sometimes also called "telephone"), in which a message is passed around a circle of people and eventually returns in a form very different from the original one.

Given that miscommunication also necessarily involves an original source of reception, it can also occur because of the inability of the person receiving the information to interpret it correctly. So, while the original transmission of source material may be both clear and veridical, and the communication channel both efficient and effective, it might be that the receivers themselves are in some way limited or incapacitated in their act of interpretation. This often leads to frustrating (for some) or amusing (for others) situations in which people delivering the message in turn misinterpret the hearer's incomprehension as the inability to hear the message well. Witness those people who speak louder to try to get their message across to someone who doesn't speak their language! This latter problem of message interpretation can lead to the paradoxical but interesting circumstance in which this incapacity defeats the deceptive intent of the individual or group generating an intentional deceit. For example, one can send a written message that is deceitful in nature, but if the individual receiving it is illiterate, then the goal of the deception is defeated. Such issues are very much the concern of those who would actively seek to deceive others for whatever reason [15].

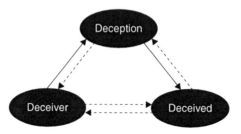

FIGURE I.3. The "Trinity of Deception." Although it might seem that the relationship is simply from the Deceiver to the Deceived via the Deception (the solid arrows), the relationship is actually more complex and interconnected.

THE TRINITY OF DECEPTION

From the foregoing discussion, we can conclude that there are *three essential elements of deception* [16]. These elements are common across all deceptions whether they are based on sensory/perceptual illusions or are primarily cognitive in nature. I have termed these three elements the *trinity of deception*, and these are illustrated in Figure I.3. The first component is the original source of the deception. As noted, this source may be an individual intent on deceiving, or the source of the deception may arise from the environment. For example, we may see a particularly interesting and evocative shape in a cloud, or even the Virgin Mary in a grilled-cheese sandwich, which may appear suggestive but are actually natural phenomena [17]. These sorts of spurious pattern recognitions, or instances of *pareidolia*, happen all the time, sometimes with funny and sometimes with tragic results. Although these "natural" deceptions are informative, the central topic of this book concerns situations in which the deceiver (the source) is an actual individual or group of individuals. Their intentional purpose is to convince others to believe something about the state of the world that is untrue.

We can see here that the purpose of cognitive deception is not solely to confuse others, although this may certainly be a part of the process. *Cognitive deceptions almost always go beyond pure confusion in that they seek to actively inculcate a specific belief in others about the true state of the world.* This belief, of course, turns out to be a false one. This induction of false belief is facilitated by the process known as *apophenia*, which is when one draws cognitive linkages between unassociated items or events. The eventual outcome of this false belief can range from simple embarrassment over being "taken in" to much more serious consequences.

The second component of deception's trinity is the conduit or medium by which the deception is communicated. This medium can be an artifact, a physical entity, but it can equally well be information expressed in the form of spoken or written language. It also can be represented by a person acting as an imposter [18]. In today's world, the medium is often computational in nature and based on information networks like the Internet [19]. The conduits discussed in this book are all physical artifacts, but it is important to recognize that this need not necessarily be the case. As we shall see, the conduit is an essential bridge, since its characteristics must be understood in a shared manner by both the deceiver and the third component of the trinity of deception: the deceived.

The medium itself presumes some common and shared assumptions. For example, you might send a false message, written in a foreign language, which is intended to deceive me in some fashion. However, because I do not speak or read that language, I cannot be led toward the belief that you wish me to adopt via this message. This, of course, is a facile example. In a real-world situation, I would almost certainly endeavor to find a translator and then have to assess the value of that translation itself as well as the content of the message itself [20]. In light of this latter assessment, I would then have to temper my belief about the content of the message and whether to believe it or not [21]. Indeed, my belief might well be swayed by the fact that it *is* in a language I can neither speak nor read. However, one central principle holds: *the deceiver and the deceived must have some common medium through which to interact.* Therefore, the conduit or medium of the message is always an important constraint upon deceit.

The third and final part of the trinity of deception is, as previously mentioned, the deceived. One might easily envisage the deceiver as the active participant and the deceived as the passive recipient in the process of deception. However, this is not necessarily so. Often the deceived individual plays a very active, albeit unwitting, role in the whole process. Many questions emerge as to what degree the deceived "wishes" to, or indeed can, be deceived. Obviously the more the deceiver can co-opt the active participation of the deceived, the more likely the deception is to succeed. Thus, the deceived must frequently prove to be fertile ground in which to plant a false assumption. Often this means that any deception has to address an issue or concern that the eventual recipient is interested in or preferably passionate about. For, as we were warned by Francis Bacon in his observations of the early seventeenth century, "Human understanding... is infused by desire and emotion, which give rise to 'wishful science.' For man prefers to believe what he wants to be true. He therefore rejects difficulties, being impatient of enquiry" [22]. It is a principle to which we shall return. While the world has moved on in a technical sense since Bacon's time, it is clear that certain basic aspects of human nature remain, tragically, very much unaltered.

From the foregoing discussion we can see that a number of constituents are required for a successful deception to occur. The originator of the deception must, through either intentional or inadvertent action, create a message that transmits information about the world that is incorrect in some way [23]. This message must be transmitted through a communication medium, but the overall deception may or may not be facilitated by imperfections in that medium. Here, failures of efficiency in the communication medium can act to mask or even sabotage intentional deception. Conversely, these self-same imperfections can act to facilitate unintentional deception. The origin of the information and its transmission medium are thus necessary but not sufficient conditions for deception, for there must be an individual or group of individuals who receive and interpret this information about the state of the world. The inherent capacities and biases of this person, or group of persons, directly influence the degree to which any deception is successful.

There is one other interesting dimension, and that is the power of numbers and statistical probability. We must emphasize this because, in fact, deceptive messages abound in both the natural world and human society. On a statistical basis, many of these messages will prove completely ineffective and others will be only marginally impactful. However, a proportion of these messages will prove to be totally convincing, at least to some recipients. It is, of course, one of the most interesting elements, and one of the paradoxes, of the science of deception that the most successful deceptions are never discovered. Completely and absolutely effective deceptions are essentially accepted as reality. Intriguingly, in philosophical circles, the question of whether reality itself is actually such a form of deception has been debated now for many centuries [24].

Let us recapitulate here. Cognitive deceptions are not sensory illusions; they have to do with "sleights of mind," not sleights of hand. Cognitive deceptions are not primarily composed of misdirections of the senses, but are much more linked to temporary or permanent degradations in capacities such as memory, attention, and decision making. Cognitive deceptions are incorrect beliefs about the true state of the world. Such misunderstandings may arise because of a person misperceiving natural but confusing signals in the environment, but in human society, they much more frequently derive from the actions of another individual who either intentionally or inadvertently acts to misrepresent reality. While they can be fleeting events, many of the most interesting forms of cognitive deception are on permanent display and challenge us to unravel their story through precise measurement and quiet contemplation rather than through affective response or strident, polemic partisanship.

DECEPTION: FROM THEORY TO PRACTICE

Up to this point, I have been dealing with some of the more formal and technical sides of the issue of deception, setting up some of the major premises that I will consider and develop in later chapters. However, this book is only partly concerned with these scientific dimensions. I also aim to provide a more general level of coverage that is accessible to a wider audience beyond staid academic circles. To that end, I have provided illustrative examples through a series of stories that serve to articulate the central points made in the more formal chapters. Indeed, these stories can be read as stand-alone accounts of the specific items, instances, or objects that have become the source of contention. Of course, these stories could take any number of forms. For example, we might look at cases of state or industrial espionage in which authorities or institutions were fooled in some manner. Examples of these sorts of deception abound [25]. Equally, we might look at deceptions in military maneuvers, marketing scams, or even modern diplomatic activities [26]. As appealing and, paradoxically, popular as these examples are in the contemporary world, my focus here is less on the airing of currently controversial issues and much more on the "classic" forms of potential cognitive deception.

In what follows I have provided a sequence of accounts that are based mostly on physical artifacts. This selection provides a degree of "concreteness" to the illustrative stories chosen. The first of these concerns a cross discovered in what is purported to be the tomb of Britain's legendary King Arthur. As we shall see, local authorities derived much benefit from this discovery. As always, how much money is generated and where it ends up provides interesting and important clues about deceptions, their origins and motivations. The second story revolves around the discovery and potential "ownership" of California. This story of deception proves just how seduced we can be when we see what it is we wish to see rather than what actually is. It is living proof that Francis Bacon's principles still operate today. Armed with these initial observations, I hope the reader will begin to distinguish some of the patterns and threads that make up the psychology of cognitive deception. After these first stories, I return to the more formal elements of cognitive deception seeking to understand how they find their foundations in the science of experimental psychology.

REFERENCE NOTES

[1] Scott, Sir Walter (1771–1832). *Marmion, Canto vi. Stanza 17.*

[2] Stewart, D. (2010). *The boy who would be Shakespeare: A tale of forgery and folly.* Cambridge, MA: Da Capo Press.

[3] Schrodinger, E. (1944). *What is life?* Cambridge: Cambridge University Press. See also more popular treatments such as Macknik, S. L., & Martinez-Conde, S. (2011). The illusions of love. *Scientific American Mind*, January/February, 18–20.

[4] Searcy, W. A., & Nowicki, S. (2005). *The evolution of animal communication: Reliability and deception in signaling systems.* Princeton, NJ: Princeton University Press.

[5] Chaline, E. (2010). *History's greatest deceptions and the people who planned them.* New York: Quid Publishing.

[6] Retrieved from: http://commons.wikimedia.org/wiki/File: Stonefish in the Red Sea (with Flash).jpg. Dukachev, S. S. (2006). Stone fish in the Red sea.

[7] Stevens, M., & Merilaita, S. (2009). Animal camouflage: Current issues and new perspectives. *Philosophical Transactions of the Royal Society B*, 364(1516), 423–427.

[8] Trivers, R. (2011). *The folly of fools.* New York: Basic Books.

[9] There are many examples of this sort of large-scale military deception. Among the more famous ones are the attack by Arminius on the legions of Publius Quinctilius Varus at the Battle of the Teutoburg Forest in AD 9, the surprise attack on the Lancastrian flank at the Battle of Tewkesbury on May 4, 1471, and Wellington's strategy at the Battle of Waterloo on June 18, 1815. These deceptions continue to persist in all forms of modern conflict, as represented by the following examples. Associated military tactics have been specified by Whaley as:
- MASKING consists in erasing attributes in the environment to make the core invisible/not present.
  - *Camouflaging*
- DECOYING consists in creating distractions that take away the attention of the target from the core.
  - *Building cardboard ordnance and displaying it.*
- REPACKAGING consists in modifying attributes of the core so that it is taken for something else.
  - *Simulating highly visible, terminal damage to military equipment.*
  - *Copying the appearance of an enemy weapon.*
- DAZZLING consists in creating confusion, so that identification of the core is made difficult.
  - *Filling the area with smoke, so as to hinder reconnaissance.*

- INVENTING consists in creating (out of nothing) attributes in the environment that hide or support the core.
  - *e.g., Creating false radio broadcasts.*
- DOUBLE PLAY consists in weakly suggesting that a deception is present, for the purpose of having that suggestion discarded.
  - *Having real weapons present where the enemy expects simulated ones.*

See Whaley, B. (1982). Toward a general theory of deception. *Journal of Strategic Studies*, 5, 178–192. Also: P. Johnson, personal communication.

[10] Behrens, R. R. (2003). *False colors: Art, design, and modern camouflage.* Dysart, IA: Bobolink Books. See also Scott-Samuel, N. E., Baddeley, R., Palmer, C. E., & Cuthill, I. C. (2011). Dazzle camouflage affects speed perception. *PLoS ONE*, 6(6), e20233. doi:10.1371/

[11] Retrieved January 6, 2014, from http://www.aboutfacesentertainers.com/face_painters/about_face_painters.htm

[12] For assessment of certain issues in vehicle conspicuity, see Wulf, G., Hancock, P. A., & Rahimi, M. (1989). Motorcycle conspicuity: An evaluation and synthesis of influential factors. *Journal of Safety Research*, 20, 153–176.

[13] See Shannon, C. (1948). A mathematical theory of communication. *Bell System Technical Journal*, 27, 379–423, 623–656. See also Shannon, C. E., & Weaver, W. (1949). *The mathematical theory of communication.* Urbana: University of Illinois Press.

[14] See Szalma, J. L., & Hancock, P. A. (2011). Noise and human performance: A meta-analytic synthesis. *Psychological Bulletin*, 137(4), 682–707.

[15] Montagu, E. (1954). *The man who never was: World War II's boldest counterintelligence operation.* Annapolis, MD: Bluejacket Books, Naval Institute Press. See also Smyth, D. (2010). *Deathly deception: The real story of Operation Mincemeat.* Oxford: Oxford University Press.

[16] In an article by Mitchell entitled, "A Framework for Discussing Deception" (see Mitchell & Thompson, 1986), the formal condition for deception is stated as follows:
  - (i) An Organism (R) registers (or believes) something Y from some Organism (S), where S can be described as benefitting when (or desiring that)
  - (iia) R acts appropriately toward Y, because
  - (iib) Y means X; and
  - (iii) It is untrue that X is the case.

This formal set of descriptions, as we shall see, relates directly to each case of cognitive deception described in the present set of examples.

[17] See, for example, Nickell, J. (2008). Grilled cheese Madonna. *Skeptical Inquirer*, 18(3), 7–8.

[18] Grann, D. (2010). *The Devil and Sherlock Holmes.* New York: Vintage Books.

[19] See Del Giudice, K. V. (2010). *Trust on the web: The impact of social consensus on information credibility.* PhD Dissertation, University of Central Florida, Orlando, FL.

[20] With respect to questions over translation, see Hancock, P. A. (2010). June 13th 1483. *Ricardian Bulletin*, March, 49–50.

[21] See, for example, the discussion of the Zimmerman Telegram: Tuchman, B. W. (1958). *The Zimmerman Telegram*. New York: Ballantine Books.

[22] Bacon, F. (1620). Novum Organum: *The new organon or true directions concerning the interpretation of nature*. Translated by James Spedding (1808–1881), Robert Leslie Ellis (1817–1859), and Douglas Denon Heath (1811–1897).

[23] The term "message" here includes explicit messages such as in books, letters, telegrams, and the like. However, it also embraces intrinsic messages that are "embedded" in items such as those discussed in the present case studies recounted here.

[24] For these and associated discussions, see Russell, B. (1945). *The history of western philosophy*. New York: Simon & Schuster.

[25] See, for example, Masterman, J. C. (1972). *The double-cross system in the war of 1939 to 1945*. Canberra: Australian National University Press; and Hodges, A. (1983). *Alan Turing: The enigma*. London: Burnett Books.

[26] For examples of these, see Joint Publication 3-13.4 (Formerly JP 3–58). *Military deception (MilDec)*. Joint Chiefs of Staff, July 13, 2006.

WEBSITES

http://www.fas.org/irp/doddir/dod/jp3_13_4.pdf
http://news.muckety.com/madoff
http://www.guardian.co.uk/

The Cross of King Arthur

The Embodiment of King Arthur in the Isle of Avalon

INTRODUCTION

There are few heroes better known than King Arthur. To the peoples of Celtic origin as well as good and true Englishmen everywhere, Arthur is a figure of immense symbolic significance. He is the monarch who promised to return, and in White's borrowed but immortal phrase, he remains "the once and future King" [1]. As well as being a hero, Arthur is also a mystery, as there are, in reality, two Arthurs. One Arthur is the hero of myth and legend while the other is a very real and important historical figure of the early centuries of British life [2]. The immediate question arises as to which one we are dealing with here: Are we looking at the legend of Camelot with its Knights and Round Table, or is it the chieftain of early British tribes in and around the time of the final withdrawal of Roman control from Britain? Sometimes it is easy to tease apart these two versions of Arthur and sometimes it is almost impossible. The historic Arthur is indeed an intriguing and mysterious individual and certainly worthy of serious academic study in his own right. However, the Arthur of this story is evidently more the one of symbol and myth. It is this mythical dimension, as represented in the stories first told of him by Geoffrey of Monmouth in 1130, that raises him from the rank and file of early British rulers to the status of immortal, national, and indeed international hero [3]. It is somewhat strange then to begin this story of the Arthurian myth with a very clear focus on actual historical events. However, this is what I have done.

A DISASTROUS FIRE

On May 25, 1184, the monks of Glastonbury received a body blow to both their personal and collective religious lives. Today, Glastonbury, a small town in the south of England, is best known for its festival and association with the "new age" spiritual movement. However, throughout its history it has been associated with the origins of Christianity in England. In 1184, virtually the entire sacred Abbey was destroyed by fire. It raged throughout the edifice, burning almost all of the buildings and consuming many precious relics [4]. The fire also destroyed the little Church of Wattles, dedicated to the blessed Virgin, which was purported to be the earliest Christian house of worship in England. Adam of Damerham provides us with the following evocative account of these tragic events:

> In the following summer, that is to say on St. Urban's Day, the whole of the Monastery, except a chamber with a chapel constructed by Abbot Robert (1178–1179) into which the monks afterwards betook themselves, and the Bell Tower, built by Bishop Henry, was consumed by fire. ... The beautiful buildings, lately erected by Henry of Blois, and the Church, a place so venerated by all, and the shelter of so many saints, are reduced to a heap of ashes! What groans, what tears, what pains arose as (the monks) saw what had happened and pondered over the loss they had suffered. The confusion into which their relics were thrown, the loss of treasure, not only in gold and silver, but in stuffs and silks, in books and the rest of the ornaments of the church, must even provoke to tears, and justly so, those who far away do but hear of these things. [5]

From our present perspective, and recognizing that Adam himself was actually writing in 1291, about one hundred years after the event, we can still feel the anguish that this tragic conflagration must have caused for the unlucky inhabitants of the Abbey on that St. Urban's Day now more than eight centuries ago. The cause of the fire was never identified.

Apparently undeterred by this horrendous disaster, the monks set about rebuilding their church and seeking sources of support for their efforts. In this enterprise, the favor and sponsorship of King Henry II was most influential, and the monks received considerable resources and solace from that royal quarter. Also, they searched for and apparently secured a number of replacement relics such as some of the bones of St. Patrick and also the skeleton of St. Dunstan, a former abbot of their own house who had later ascended to the See of Canterbury. In passing, it should be noted that the latter discovery was strongly disputed by the monks of Canterbury, who themselves claim to have exhumed St. Dunstan in 1070. Parenthetically, and perhaps not coincidentally, he was supposed to be disinterred from a grave of great depth with an inscribed lead tablet and a pyramid set over it [6]. These relic acquisitions and allied entrepreneurial activities saw the new Lady Chapel dedicated in 1186, and prospects looked fair for a complete recovery with perhaps even improvements to what had been known as the most beautiful house of worship in the country. However, the Abbey received another setback when on July 6, 1189, King Henry II died and the royal patronage the Abbey had enjoyed was severely diminished [7]. Henry's son and heir, Richard I, had little time for such concerns. Richard I, later more popularly known as the "Lionheart," was the monarch of the English crusades, and the Holy Land is a long way away from Glastonbury [8]. Although losing this vital royal source of support, it appears that the monks of Glastonbury received one last parting gift from Henry before his death. It was one that would prove of incalculable value. According to the historian Gerald of Wales, before Henry died, he sent a vital message to Glastonbury. We do not know the content of this message, but it was rumored that Henry told the monks the secret of the resting place of Arthur, King of the Britons – information that had allegedly been supplied to Henry previously by a Welsh bard or singer [9].

THE DISCOVERY OF THE TOMB

Henry's revelation of the tomb of Arthur must have been a bolt of lightning from a clear sky. Perhaps Henry's message was actually an expression of what he would have liked to have happen. After all, the discovery of Arthur would be a win-win situation in which identification of his tomb would subvert the pressure that the Welsh followers and advocates of Arthur could place on Henry's heir, Richard the Lionheart. It would certainly provide a secure source of income for the Abbey. Regardless of the precise content of Henry's communication, it must have been the main topic of discussion between his Chamberlain, Ralph FitzStephen, in temporary charge of the Abbey, and the incoming Abbot, Henry de Sully, who had been appointed by his uncle, the new King Richard. The physical search for Arthur's tomb most probably commenced a short time after this meeting, possibly in the late summer of 1189. By the early winter of 1191, some two years later, a pavilion (or possibly some white draperies or curtains) were placed around or over part of the cemetery area between two tall pyramids that stood close to the south door of the new church [10]. The pavilion enclosed a hole that had begun to be dug sometime earlier. Its erection suggests that it was about this juncture that the purported grave of Arthur was actually discovered. This general date is backed up by the accounts of both Adam of Damerham and Ralph of Coggeshall, although it should be noted that the latter author thought that Arthur's grave had been discovered accidentally while digging a grave for a monk who just wanted to be buried between the two pillars [11], see Figure 1.1. Not surprisingly, details of the discovery itself are somewhat sparse, but fortunately some accounts have come down to us from various historians in antiquity.

The first was given around 1193 by Gerald of Wales, when he reported:

> Arthur the famous British King is still remembered, nor will this memory die out, for he is much praised in the history of the excellent monastery of Glastonbury, of which he himself was in his time a distinguished patron and a generous endower and supporter…. His body, for which popular stories have invented a fantastic ending, saying that it had been carried to a remote place, and was not subject to death, was found in recent time at Glastonbury between two stone pyramids standing in the burial ground. It was deep in the earth, enclosed in a hollow oak, and the discovery was accompanied by wonderful and almost miraculous signs. It was reverently transferred to the church and placed in a marble tomb. And a leaden cross was found laid under the stone, not above, as is the custom today. But rather fastened on beneath it. We saw this, and traced the inscription which was not showing, but turned in towards the stone: 'Here lies buried the famous king Arthurus with Wennevereia his second wife in the isle of Avalonia.' In this there are several remarkable things: he had two wives, of which the last was buried at the same time as him, and indeed her bones were discovered with those of her husband; however, they were separate. Since two parts of the coffin, at the head, were divided off, to contain the bones of a man, while the remaining third at the foot contained the bones of a woman set apart. There was also uncovered a golden tress of hair that had belonged to a beautiful woman, in its pristine condition and colour, which, when a certain monk eagerly snatched it up, suddenly dissolved into dust.

Gerald of Wales continued:

> Signs that the body had been buried here were found in the records of the place, in the letters inscribed on the pyramids, although these were almost obliterated by age, and in the visions and revelations seen by holy men and clerks; but chiefly through Henry II, King of England, who had heard from an aged British singer that his [Arthur's] body would be found at least sixteen feet deep in the earth, not in a stone tomb, but in a hollow oak. This Henry had told the monks; and the body was at the depth stated and almost concealed, lest, in the event of the Saxons occupying the island, against whom he had fought with so much energy in his lifetime, it should be brought to light; and for that reason, the inscription on the cross which would have revealed the truth, was turned inwards to the stone, to conceal at that time what the coffin contained, and yet inform other centuries.

As Gerald explained:

> What is now called Glastonbury was in former times called the Isle of Avalon, for it is almost an island, being entirely surrounded by marshes, whence it is named in British Inis Avalon, that is the apple-bearing island, because apples (in British aval) used to abound in that place. Whence Morgan, a noblewoman who was ruler of that region and closely related to Arthur, after the Battle of Kemelen carried him away to the island now called Glastonbury to be healed of his wounds. It used

FIGURE 1.1. This is an illustration of the Monks of Glastonbury in the process of excavating the grave of Arthur and Guinevere. The Illustration is by Judith Dobie, of English Heritage, in Rahtz, (1993) [14]. Reproduced with permission © English Heritage.

also to be called in British Inis Gutrin, that is, the isle of glass; hence the Saxons called it Glastingeburi. For in their tongue glas means glass, and a camp or town is called buri. We know that the bones of Arthur's body that were discovered were so large that in this we might see the fulfillment of the poet's words:

Grandiaque effossis mirabitur ossa sepulchris. (When the graves are opened, they shall marvel at the great size of the bones – Publius Vergilius Maro).

The thigh bone, when placed next to the tallest man present, as the abbot showed us, and fastened to the ground by his foot, reached three inches above his knee. And the skull was of a great, indeed prodigious, capacity, to the extent that the space between the brows and between the eyes was a palm's breadth. But in the skull there were ten or more wounds which had all healed into scars with the exception of one, which made a great cleft, and seemed to have been the sole cause of death. [12]

If Gerald's account was the earliest, it has proved reliable over the years since his observations have been largely confirmed by subsequent commentators, although to what degree they actually just copied Gerald is always difficult to establish. Some centuries later in the early 1600s, at the time of transition between the House of Tudor and the House of Stuart, a crucial observation was published by the famous antiquary William Camden [13]. While his written text follows very much upon Gerald's original account, Camden crucially included a pictorial representation of the Cross. First, however, let us read what he had to say in his own words:

I will briefly set downe unto you that which Giraldus Cambrensis, an eie-witnesse of the thing, hath more at large related touching Arthur's Sepulcher in the Churchyard there. When Henrie the Second King of England tooke knowledge out of the Songs of British Bards, or Rhythmers, how Arthur that most noble Worthy of the Britans, who by his Martial prowesse had many a time daunted the fury of the English-Saxons, lay buried here between two Pyramides or sharpe-headed pillars, hee caused the bodie to be searched for, and scarcely had they digged seven foot deepe into the earth but they lighted upon a Tomb or Grave-stone, on the upper face whereof was fastned a broad Crosse of led grosly wrought: which being taken forth shewed an inscription of letters, and under the said stone almost nine foot deeper was found a Sepulchre of oake made hollow, wherein the bones of that famous Arthur were bestowed, which Inscription or Epitaph, as it was sometime exemplified and drawn out of the first Copie in the Abbey of Glascon, I thought good for the antiquitie of the characters heere to put downe. The letters, being made after a barbarous maner and resembling the Gothish Character, bewray plainly the barbarism of that age, when ignorance (as it were) by fatall destinie bare such sway that there was none to be found by whose writings the renowme of Arthur might be blazed and commended to posteritie, a matter and argument doubtlesse meet to have been handled by the skill and eloquence of some right learned man, who in celebrating the praises of so great a prince might have wonne due commendation also for his own wit. For the most valiant Champian of the British Empire seemeth even, in this behalfe only, unfortunate, that he never met with such a trumpetter as might worthily have sounded out the praise of his valor. But behold the said Crosse and Epitaph therein. [15]

Given the little we know of the historic Arthur, the discovery of his grave at Glastonbury is not as implausible as it might at first appear. From early Welsh annals, we learn that Arthur died around 516 AD and that his center of operations has been attributed to the modern day Cadbury Castle, a hill fort located some 12–15 miles east of Glastonbury [16]. The identification of the Cadbury Castle site as Camelot has been attributed to the Elizabethan antiquary John Leland. Other suggested sites for Camelot include the cities of Colchester and Winchester, as well as any number of other competitors, some not necessarily even located in Britain [17]! Some have argued quite vehemently against the Cadbury site being Camelot, and the actual location of Camelot remains as obscure as so much else about the legendary Arthur. However, given Cadbury Castle as one possible site, its physical proximity to the very early establishment of a Christian church at Glastonbury is at least suggestive. Further, given that Glastonbury was effectively an island before more modern drainage reduced the surrounding marshland, the proposition that a famous local chieftain would be buried at the pre-eminent religious site, described as an island, is not impossible to accept.

It appears that the bodies of Arthur and his wife were discovered buried in a hollowed-out log that was reportedly found at the fairly incredible depth of sixteen feet. Adam of Damerham and John of Glastonbury both note that the bodies were in two separate tombs but this might be attributable to their relative location in two separate sections of the log coffin [18]. Prior to the discovery of the skeletons however, the monks had previously found a stone slab buried only seven feet down! After considerable effort they had brought this to the surface. On turning the slab over, they found a leaden Cross set into the stone. The location of the Cross on the underside of the slab has been

FIGURE 1.2. The depiction of Arthur's Cross from page 166 of the 1607 Edition of Camden's *Britannia*. These are the only drawings that we possess and they come from the 1607 and 1608 editions. Even here, there were some variations in the shapes of the letters between the two editions [19]. Reproduced with permission, Georg Olms Verlag AG.

suggested as a strategy to prevent Arthur's enemies from identifying his grave, although it obviously proved only a minor inconvenience to the monks of the early twelfth century. An illustration of the supposed appearance of this Cross is given in William Camden's 'Britannia' and is reproduced in Figure 1.2.

Before Camden's time, multiple writers had reported on the inscription. We have already heard the first account given by Gerald of Wales. The whole sequence in chronological order reads: Gerald of Wales *Liber de Principis Instructione* (circa 1193) wrote "Here lies buried the famous King Arthur with Guinevere his second wife in the isle of Avalon." Later in his *Speculum Ecclesiae* (circa 1216), Gerald repeated himself with a simple change of word order: "Here lies buried the famous King Arthur in the isle of Avalon with his second wife Guinevere." A short time later in the *Chronicon Anglicanum*, Ralph of Coggeshall reports: "Here lies the famous King Arthur, buried in the isle of Avalon." The *Chronicle of Margam Abbey* in Wales, which is sometimes dated in the early 1190s but at other times in the fourteenth century, reports: "Here lies the famous King Arthur, buried in the isle of Avalon." In the 1291 text *"Historia de rebus Glastoniensibus,"* Adam of Damerham records: *"Here lies interred in the isle of Avalon, the renowned King Arthur."* In the mid-thirteenth century, the monks of St. Alban's report in the *"Chronica Majora"*: "Here lies the renowned King Arthur, buried in the isle of Avalon." The more modern historian, John Leland, records in 1542: "Here lies the famous King Arthur, buried in the isle of Avalon," and finally the translation of Camden's drawn cross shown in Figure 1.2 reads, "Here lies the famous King Arthur, buried in the isle of Avalon." All of these are in basic agreement [20]. However, the earliest commentator, Gerald of Wales, is the only one to mention Guinevere's name as appearing on the Cross.

While some modern authors have focused on the various discrepancies between these different reports, the actual notations are really very consistent, especially given the antiquity and the nature of the historical era we are talking about. The difference, for example, between the use of the word "famous" and "renowned" should not overly concern us as a supposed discrepancy and neither should the order in which the translated words occur. Often translation is contingent upon the personal preferences and idiosyncrasies of the individual translator. What remains the major difference is Gerald of Wales' report, which is closest in time to the actual discovery. He records and then later on confirms the presence of the name of Guinevere on the Cross itself. If we accept the word order he reports in his second text, the *"Speculum Ecclesiae,"* the reference to Guinevere *"cum Wenneveria uxore sua secunda"* comes after the phrase *"in insula Avolonia."* Thus, it may just be possible that some part of the Cross that we see in Camden's illustration is actually missing. Perhaps there was a piece at the base of the Cross that, now broken off, had contained the reference to Guinevere? Unfortunately, without possession of the actual Cross itself, this speculation is unlikely to be resolved.

THE REBURIAL OF ARTHUR AND GUINEVERE

After supposedly finding the legendary Arthur, the monks of Glastonbury did surprisingly little with their discovery. There is the suggestion that the actual exhumation took place in the presence of King Richard I on a visit

SITE OF KING ARTHUR'S TOMB.
IN THE YEAR 1191 THE BODIES OF
KING ARTHUR AND HIS QUEEN WERE
SAID TO HAVE BEEN FOUND ON THE
SOUTH SIDE OF THE LADY CHAPEL.
ON 19TH APRIL 1278 THEIR REMAINS WERE
REMOVED IN THE PRESENCE OF
KING EDWARD I AND QUEEN ELEANOR
TO A BLACK MARBLE TOMB ON THIS SITE.
THIS TOMB SURVIVED UNTIL THE
DISSOLUTION OF THE ABBEY IN 1539

FIGURE 1.3. The present-day plaque showing the location of the reburial of Arthur and Guinevere until the destruction of the tomb during the dissolution of the Monasteries by Henry VIII [21]. This memorial seems rather understated considering the popularity of the historical personage in question. Photograph by the Author.

to the Abbey. This conjunction would indeed perpetuate the link between Arthur and the ruling house of England. The bodies may well have been transferred to the recently constructed Lady Chapel whose shell-like remains still stand today [22]. It is also possible they were put in an alternative, temporary resting place. At least to our knowledge, little of importance took place in the years immediately following 1191. We do learn later from the '*Annals of Waverley*' that the bodies were located in the Abbey's treasury in the east range of the church [23]. Whether they were presented for veneration or visited as a source of pilgrimage or inspiration is not known. The next recorded action occurs on April 19, 1278, when Edward I and his wife Queen Eleanor were on an Easter visit to Glastonbury. The king ordered the opening of Arthur's tomb and discovered bones in two coffers, with Guinevere in a slightly better condition than her husband. Plans were made for the reburial at a central and more important location in the rebuilt abbey [24] (see Figure 1.3). The site of the new tomb was just below the high altar, a position that is recognized as the most important in the whole church, as can be seen from the tombs of Edward the Confessor in Westminster Abbey and King Richard I's brother, King John, who is buried in Worcester Cathedral [25]. Both bodies were re-interred in a new, raised black marble tomb, with two lions at each end, a cross at the head, and an image of the king at the foot. On the tomb were two inscriptions reading,

"Here lies Arthur, the flower of Kingship, the Kingdom's glory, whom his morals and virtue commend with eternal praise" and "Arthur's fortunate wife lies buried here, who merited heaven through the happy consequences of her virtue." With the discovered Cross now placed on top of this structure, Arthur and Guinevere would certainly have represented a great attraction to the Glastonbury enclave.

POLITICAL REASONS FOR THE REBURIAL

Edward I's actions that Easter were not those of a disinterested monarch or a remote patron. He had ascended to the throne in 1272 upon the death of his father, Henry III. As a man of action, Edward set himself to the task of conquering the whole of Britain. (Indeed, he is the maligned "Longshanks" of Mel Gibson's historically doubtful film *Braveheart*) [26]. Prior to his Scottish exploits, Edward had set his sights upon Wales. In 1277, he had conducted the first of his campaigns that saw the building of a series of "holding" castles that ringed the troublesome region and allowed Edward to eventually control the whole of what he would create as the "principality" of Wales [27]. However, victory was not to be won by stones alone. Edward realized that he must conquer the symbols of his enemy, their minds as well as their bodies. Thus the honored reburial of Arthur served immediate political purposes. First, it diminished the myth that Arthur would return again when his people needed him most. The idea that Arthur did not die but was transported to some ethereal realm was not as evident in those times as it is today, but Edward was taking no chances. The public reburial helped dissipate this myth and remove one potential tactic from the enemy of invoking the resurrected Arthur's name. And, of course, the burial was obviously in England.

By locating the tomb in Glastonbury, Edward was physically taking Arthur away from the Welsh. If they wanted to receive inspiration at his feet, they would have to travel into Edward's realm, into England to do it. In essence, he hijacked one of their heroes. The case is not as cut and dried as these observations might make it seem. However, from Edward's point of view, this visit to Glastonbury enabled him to neutralize a potential threat while giving his direct patronage to the great house of Glastonbury which received the prestige and attention it craved, see Figure 1.4. Indeed, it may well have been these political motivations that brought the issue of Arthur back onto the king's agenda. The hiatus between the initial discovery of the bodies and their subsequent rich entombment can therefore be explained

FIGURE 1.4. These are the evocative ruins of Glastonbury today. The notice indicating the site of Arthur's tomb (as shown in Figure 3) can just be seen between the two pillars of the great ruined arch.

in part by the changing political necessities of the times [28]. Edward's strategy against the Welsh proved successful. Even here the mythology of Arthur remained important. At Caernarvon, following upon the defeat of *Llywelyn ap Gruffyd*, the victorious Edward received the royal regalia of the principality, amongst which was the nominal crown of Arthur [29]. His small investment of time spent earlier at Glastonbury had now paid a clear dividend. With Wales subdued, Edward was able to turn his attention to concerns in Scotland and France.

DISSOLUTION OF THE MONASTERY AND BEYOND

The Cross, which was supposedly found during excavation of the original burial, was not forgotten. It was placed on top of the tomb, although whether it was permanently attached or not, we do not know. There the Cross remained for the next 261 years. However, in 1539, when Henry VIII grew frustrated at the Catholic Church over its reticence to divorce him from his Spanish wife, Katherine of Aragon, he had his Chancellor Thomas

Cromwell preside over the dissolution of the monasteries, the main houses of worship throughout England [30]. We do not know what happened to the bodies of the purported Arthur and Guinevere. Tied up with the rejection of various Catholic practices, such as the veneration of Saints, the disappearance of the body of Arthur remains a mystery [31]. However, like many other accoutrements of the various religious houses, their loss and destruction are evident and highly frustrating to modern scholars.

There is, however, one subsequent report by Sir John Harrington in the notes to his 1591 translation of *Orlando Furioso* that Guinevere was buried in the Abbey and "within our memory taken up in a coffin, with her body and face in show plainly to be discerned, save the very tip of her nose, as diverse dwelling thereabout have reported" [32]. In this she seems to have had as much post-mortem respect as Queen Katherine Parr, the last of Henry VIII's unfortunate wives [33]. Nothing is noted as to Arthur's body. What we do find is that John Leland reports having seen the Cross in the years immediately following 1539 and it was still extant, sufficient to be drawn and recorded in William Camden's Edition of 'Britannia' in 1607. Whether this was actually the original Cross that was found, however, has been the subject of further contention. It has been asserted that the Cross was located for approximately the next hundred years in the parish church of St. John the Baptist in Glastonbury [34]. The last recorded sighting of the Cross was sometime in the early eighteenth century while in the possession of one William Hughes, an official of Wells Cathedral. Since then, there have been no reliable observations of the Cross, which remains a valuable artifact in itself and thus one that might well still exist in some hidden location today.

MODERN CLAIMS OF REDISCOVERY

Arthur's Cross is a highly contentious artifact. From the historic record, we have every reason to believe that it really existed. Although whether it was made in the mid-sixth century for the burial of Arthur or actually fabricated in the later twelfth century for more pecuniary purposes or perhaps even created to fool those involved in sixteenth-century dissolution of Glastonbury Abbey, we simply do not know. Our uncertainty derives from the fact that we no longer possess the physical artifact. However, we do have an idea of its size, composition, and message and have every reason to believe it survived the dissolution of the Glastonbury monastery and was in existence well into the modern era. What is frustrating is that it is still missing. We want to recover the Cross for what could be a very informative physical examination, but this remains an unfulfilled desire. Given this situation, it is not surprising that some later hoaxers (hoax built on hoax) have tried to fill this vacuum by offering fake crosses of their own.

One modern story concerns a claim in 1981, although whether this year is significant with respect to the reordering of the earlier date of 1189 is unclear. The purported discoverer of the Cross was one Derek Mahoney who claimed he had found it while dredging a lake bed near the Northern line of the London Underground, close to Maidens Brook in the grounds of Forty Hall in Enfield, Middlesex [35]. On the advice of his friend, a student, he took this Cross to the British Museum but allowed the staff only a brief examination. Sue Youngs, a museum employee, had only sufficient time to note that it was exactly 6 7/8 inches tall, precisely the height shown in Camden's original drawing. Mahoney declined to leave his Cross for additional examination. Since the site of the find was actually on public property, the Council of the Borough of Enfield took Mahoney to court to recover the Cross [36]. However, he failed to produce it and was sentenced to two years imprisonment for contempt of court, eventually serving only one year. The assumption was that Mahoney's Cross was a fake. He had previously worked for Lesney Products, a toy manufacturer. As a skilled pattern maker, Mahoney was familiar with the manufacture of detailed model cars fabricated from lead. Furthermore, he had an obvious motive in terms of seeking publicity over an argument with a local estate agent concerning a house sale. As noted, his Cross conformed in length exactly to Camden's specification, although the historian John Leland in "*Assertio Inclytissimi Arturii*" had claimed to handle the Cross some time soon after the dissolution, around 1542, and pronounced it "about one foot" in length [37]. Perhaps Mahoney's Cross was too perfect? We can conclude that Mahoney had means, motive, and opportunity but we cannot say with certainty that the Cross he possessed was a fake. It is sad to report that Mahoney failed to resolve his issues and, suffering from ill health, eventually took his own life [38]. The Cross he supposedly found has not been seen since. The missing Cross raises one other persistent issue – one of testing techniques and their evolution. Who would have conceived of DNA testing 200 years ago to establish identity? Indeed, can we ourselves envisage the test and evaluation techniques that will emerge across the coming centuries? This is why cognitive deceptions based on material artifacts are open to evolving resolution as long as the artifacts themselves can be retained. Sadly, we cannot supply Arthur's Cross on demand and so future physical test configurations will still have only limited impact on any eventual resolution on authenticity. Perhaps other nonmaterial testing techniques may emerge. Such considerations bring us right back to the original question concerning the authenticity of the Cross.

THE VERDICT ON THE CROSS

Is Arthur's Cross a hoax? I can provide here an almost definitive – maybe. As I have emphasized, the primary problem remains the fact that we do not possess the artifact itself. Some hundreds of years ago the Cross disappeared into the mist of time. Therefore, our conclusions must be based on the written and pictorial evidence, not on an analysis of the actual entity itself. A first concern, as has been noted, must be whether the Cross we see in Camden's illustration is actually the Cross that was found. Suggestions have been made that the script shown on Camden's version is nothing like that of the fifth or sixth century but much closer to tenth-century lettering [39]. Thus, when we judge the Cross, we must be cognizant that we are judging Camden's representation. It may not be an exact likeness of the original discovery since it is only the antique form of the letters for which he vouches explicitly. Perhaps the Cross was actually missing a part that originally referred to Guinevere? We cannot, at present, know if this is true either.

The case for the Cross being a hoax, however, is very strong. It is evident that the desperate monks of Glastonbury were *in extremis*. Their beloved house had been devastated. Some six decades earlier in the 1130s, the Benedictine historian, William of Malmesbury, had traveled to the Abbey and noted that the old church of our Lady of Glastonbury had been built by the hands of the original disciples and thus was the "most ancient of all those that I know in England" [40]. But after the disaster all that had gone. Along with the irreplaceable structure, they had also lost the remains of the many saints that had been preserved there. The whole source of their revenue, their magnificence, was now ruined. Just as the monks begin to get back on their feet, their primary patron Henry II dies at the most inopportune of times. Clearly, some positive action was needed. True, they could bring in more saints' bones, but where would they get these and indeed what contemporary major house of worship in the country did not have these?

After Glastonbury's disaster, who would not rather go to Westminster to revere Edward the Confessor, or travel to Bury St. Edmunds, or even more attractive, Canterbury? After all, it was only just twenty years since the death of Thomas a Becket in 1170 [41]. The fame associated with St. Thomas was helping the monks there recover from their own fire of 1174. Trying to beat others in the competition for famous saints' relics held little attraction. Simply having more saints' bones might put them back in the spotlight, but something much more spectacular was needed for preeminence. Therefore, in respect of a hoax, we certainly have one fundamental component: the motive. Indeed, if following the "ends justifies means" strategy, it is possible that the monks of Glastonbury could salve their conscience with the knowledge that it was all for a good cause anyway and God "helps those who help themselves." With Barber, we might conclude that

> the circumstantial evidence seems strong enough for us to say that there is not much doubt that the coffin and its contents, or at least its connection [through the Cross] with Arthur, were produced by the monks in order to raise the money for the rebuilding of the Abbey, which forgery or no, it certainly did. Nor need all medieval monks be regarded as better in this respect than their secular contemporaries. (pp. 132–133) [42]

If the motive is evident, the opportunity is equally clear. The monks could and did control access to the area in which the nominal grave had been found. If the idea for a hoax had been Henry's, this might explain the hiatus between the communication of later June 1189 and the putative discovery a little over two years later. The hoax took time to prepare. Perhaps this was also Henry's last act of earthly revenge. After the death of Thomas Becket at the hands of the king's own knights who chose to rid their sovereign of that "troublesome priest," Henry himself could have expected little veneration at Canterbury [43]. Perhaps by endowing and supporting the monks of Glastonbury he could revive its claim to primacy among all Christian locations in Britain. Henry may have thought it fine sport for a hoaxed relic to be the object of worship and to 'cock a snook' at Canterbury at the same time. Perhaps in this, one of his last acts on Earth, he tried to tip the scales in Glastonbury's favor. On the other hand, perhaps he did actually know the location of Arthur's tomb. Unfortunately, we shall probably never know.

Whatever Henry's motivation, to accomplish a hoax the monks needed time to set up the discovery. Would they have the skills to accomplish this? That is, would they have the means? The answer again is almost certainly yes. Indeed, one could invert the question and ask whether anyone else at that time could have fabricated such a hoax. The answer to this latter question is most probably not. It is true that some artisan may have been able to make a memorial cross, but virtually no one else could control the site of the "find." Thus, the impetus for the discovery of the grave of Arthur was certainly strong, and all the tools and access were at hand to create both the Cross and the grave itself. As to the bodies – it was a cemetery after all. But why choose Arthur?

Almost immediately the answer to this latter question presents itself. Not only is this simply the return of the king; one now has a secular as well as a religious motivation. Pilgrims and the income from them were one thing, but there was stiff competition for pilgrims from religious establishments both at home and abroad. And we must remember that this is the time when pilgrimages to Jerusalem were slowly becoming a real possibility, especially for the rich. Who among those rich pilgrims will be going to see St. Dunstan when a visit to the Holy Sepulchre itself is now at least a feasible alternative [44]? No, the discovery of Arthur was a very shrewd move, for it brought together hero worship beyond the cloister and tapped into a new segment of the overall pilgrim market. Also, we must never forget geography. Glastonbury sits at the confluence of several traditional cultures. The Celtic peoples, who make great claim on Arthur even today, are a scant few miles away across the Bristol Channel. The traditionally independent Cornish reside further down the peninsula, and yet Glastonbury is not too far from the power of Wessex or the environs of London to discourage visitors from the more easterly parts of England and even northern France. Perhaps a shadow of this geographical advantage is still reflected in the current popularity of the Glastonbury Festival [45]. Thus we have means, motive, and opportunity, combined with royal and ecclesiastical justification. Surely this is a heady brew and one in which the idea, not of a hoax exactly, but let us express it rather as the assisted rediscovery of King Arthur in "Avalon," might well have proved almost overwhelming.

If the case for a hoax is very strong, what facts can we set against such a proposition? One trenchant observation that has been made previously is that if these monks were so subtle and clever as to fabricate a hoax, why did they not take much more immediate advantage of the so-called discovery? Indeed, the historical record does indicate that not much happened immediately following the events of 1191. However, this question cuts both ways. If the discovery was of the real Arthur, then the records indicate that the monks were sadly lax in their exploitation of a true gold mine. Perhaps they took a long-term view of the proposition and had decided to let the idea "mature" a little over time, anticipating that the patina of age would later prove stronger support for authenticity. More recently, the author Geoffrey

The discovery of Prince Arthur's Tomb by the inscription on the leaden Cross

FIGURE 1.5. This is a second depiction of the scene of discovery with a greater emphasis on the Cross itself. Image Courtesy of the British Museum.

Ashe has asserted that modern archeological exploration has confirmed that the monks did indeed dig where they said they did. This is a necessary form of confirmation but not one that adds up to much evidence for the actual discovery of the true Arthur [46].

One further notion that has been advanced to bolster the discovery as being real is that the various reports of the find did not universally agree, the argument being that if the monks stage-managed the whole process, see Figure 1.5, then we would have seen clear unanimity in the accounts of the discovery. However, as I have shown through comparison of these various accounts, I find such reasoning specious. First, the respective accounts are very similar in their content; as noted earlier, the only fundamental difference is the reference to Guinevere. Secondly, it is difficult if not impossible to establish the manner in which each successive commentator has, or has not, borrowed from any or all of his predecessors. We must remember that these publications were also centuries before the advent of copyright and so copying or straight plagiarism were quite common and accepted practices. Indeed, in the days of handwritten material and irregular spelling, grammar, and syntax, it would be somewhat suspect if all accounts were exactly the same.

SUMMARY AND CONCLUSIONS

During the rebuilding process of Glastonbury Abbey following the great fire of 1184, an important grave was either discovered accidentally or as a result of a purposive search. Although the coffins were reportedly found in a hollow log at a depth of 16 feet, it was reportedly only some 7 feet down that a stone slab was encountered into which, incised into the reverse side, was a leaden Cross. It was this Cross that identified the burial as that of King Arthur. Despite being treated with respect and interred in part of the rebuilt Abbey confines, it was almost ninety years later that these remains were placed at a prime location in the newly rebuilt Monastery Church. Part ceremony, part politics, the allegedly discovered Cross was placed on this new resting place for Arthur and Guinevere. Here it stayed almost 300 years until Henry VIII's frustration at the Pope's intransigence over his divorce led to the destruction of this and many other houses of worship [47]. The Cross apparently survived the destruction and was recorded pictorially by the antiquary William Camden in 1607. Evidence for its existence continued after Camden's recording. However, the Cross has not been seen for some time [48]. It was this disappearance that generated some attempts at another hoax in modern times.

We end up with three questions. First, was the original Cross really a hoax? Like many of the cases considered in this book and beyond, the answer lies very near the 50 percent threshold. Indeed, if the issue were clear, these would not be celebrated cases! The evidence of the lettering itself suggests a much later date of its creation than Arthur's sixth-century death. However, does this mean that the artifact would not be, in itself, of tremendous intrinsic value today? The answer here is most definitely no; rather, it would be a wonderful item to possess and research. The second question concerns whether Camden's illustration and text is correct. It is unlikely Camden aimed at providing a perfect representation in terms of size, but the text is consistent with the earlier observations of other commentators.

Further, in the absence of any veridical discovery, it is all we have in pictorial form. Arthur's Cross served as the vital artifact in identifying himself and his wife as opposed to some merely important but anonymous individuals. Without the Cross, the monks had what could have been claimed simply as an interesting burial. It was the Cross that made it Arthur's burial site. It returned the Once and Future King to Glastonbury at the time when the monarch and the monastery most needed him. We should not be so anachronistic as to discount the idea that human beings of a millennia ago had the same desires and wishes we ourselves exhibit today [49]. Perhaps one day we may recover the Cross itself and be able to finally distinguish the provenance of this most valuable artifact. It may well demonstrate that hoaxes are by no means a modern invention.

And what of Glastonbury today? Do people still have that incentive to champion Arthur and his local legend? Well, the good news to report is that Glastonbury is doing very well. Despite being a ruin, the Abbey draws an extensive number of visitors, and the fame of the Glastonbury Festival has grown worldwide [50]. New Age culture is certainly alive and well around Wearyall Hill, and legends such as the Glastonbury Thorn and the Isle of Avalon bring people to the town and the overlooking hill of Glastonbury Tor even in difficult financial times. Whether Arthur was ever in Glastonbury, much less buried in the precincts of its Abbey, cannot and perhaps might never be known for certain. However, it is undoubtedly the case that Arthur still weaves a magic that draws people today to this unique Somerset location. Hoax or not, the legend of Arthur exerts very real effects in the world today. Of course, one of the great legends associated with the great King of the Britons is that one day he has promised to return. Hope springs eternal.

REFERENCE NOTES

[1] White, T. H. (1958). *The once and future king*. London: Collins. See also: Neilson, F. (1944). Glastonbury in Legend and History. *American Journal of Economics & Sociology*, 4(1), 9–23. Such is the power of the legend that when the one-time Earl of Richmond, Henry Tudor, ascended to the throne of England after defeating Richard III at the Battle of Bosworth and realizing that his claim to the throne was tenuous, he named his first son Arthur. Prince Arthur would have ascended to the throne, as opposed to his younger brother Henry VIII, but he died in 1502 and is now buried in Worcester Cathedral close to the borders of Wales. A few feet away from Arthur lies King John, the brother and successor of Richard I (the Lionheart).

[2] Wood, M. (2005). *In search of myths & heroes*. Berkeley: University of California Press.

[3] See, for example, Geoffrey of Monmouth. (1966). *The History of the Kings of Britain* (L. Thorpe, Trans.). London: Penguin Books.

[4] See http://www.glastonburyabbey.com/history.php

[5] Adam of Damerham. (1291). *Historia de rebus Glastoniensibus*. Ed. T. Hearne. 2 vols. Oxford, 1727.

[6] The Glastonbury claim of St. Dunstan is not unexpected given that he was a resident of the area and subsequently rebuilt the church there looking to restore former glories. Eventually Dunstan became Archbishop of Canterbury, and the claim by the monks of Glastonbury for the subsequent possession of his body were refuted in 1508 when Archbishop Wareham established his remains in the Canterbury tomb. See http://www.newadvent. org/cathen/05199a.htm

[7] See Barber, R. (1996). *The Devil's crown: A history of Henry II and his sons*. Conshohocken, PA: Combined Books.; and Warren, W. L. (1973). *Henry II*. Berkeley: University of California Press.

[8] See, for example, Gillingham, J. (2002). *Richard I*. London: Yale University Press.

[9] For the observations of Gerald of Wales, see Giraldus Cambrensis (c. 1193). *De principis instructione liber*. (Ed: G. F. Warner, 1964 Kraus Reprint of 1873 Edition. London: HMSO). See also http://www.britannia.com/history/arthur/ cross.html

[10] Nitze, W. A. (1934). The exhumation of King Arthur at Glastonbury. *Speculum*, 9(4), 355–361. And see "Two Accounts of the Exhumation of Arthur's Body." Britannia.com. Retrieved December 11, 2009.

[11] See "Arthur's Cross: Discovery of the Cross." Britannia.com. Retrieved December 11, 2009. See also William of Malmesbury. (1992). *The Antiquities of Glastonbury*. Facsimile reprint, Llanerch, Felinfach: J.M.F. Books.

[12] Giraldus Cambrensis. (c. 1193). *De principis instructione liber*. (Ed. G. F. Warner). 1964 Kraus Reprint of 1873 Edition, London: HMSO.

[13] Camden, W. (1607). *Brittania*. London: George Bishop, (1970 Georg Olms Verlag, Hildesheim).

[14] Rahtz, P. (1993). *Glastonbury*. London: English Heritage.

[15] Camden, *Brittania*. A somewhat more recent version of the discovery process has been presented by S. Turner (1841) in *The History of the Anglo-Saxons*. Philadelphia: Carey & Hart Philadelphia. The precise quotation reads:

> The king communicated this to the abbot and monks of the monastery, with the additional information, that the body had been buried very deep to keep it from the Saxons; and that it would be found not in a stone tomb, but in a hollowed oak. There were two pyramids or pillars at that time standing in the cemetery of the abbey. They dug between these till they came to a leaden cross lying under a stone, which had this inscription, and which Giraldus says he saw and handled – "Hic jacet sepultus inclytus Rex Arthurus in insula Avallonia." Below this, at the depth of sixteen feet from the surface, a coffin of hollow oak was found containing bones of an unusual size. The leg-bone was three fingers

(probably in their breadth) longer than that of the tallest man then present. This man was pointed out to Giraldus. The skull was large, and showed the marks of ten wounds. Nine of these had concreted into the bony mass, but one had a cleft in it, and the opening still remained; apparently the mortal blow.

Giraldus says, in another place, that the bones of one of Arthur's wives were found there with his, but distinct, at the lower end. Her yellow hair lay apparently perfect in substance and colour, but on a monk's eagerly grasping and raising it up, it fell to dust.

The bones were removed into the great church at Glastonbury, and deposited in a magnificent shrine, which was afterwards placed, in obedience to the order of Edward I, before the high altar. He visited Glastonbury with his queen in 1276, and had the shrine of Arthur opened to contemplate his remains. They were both so interested by the sight, that the king folded the bones of Arthur in a rich shroud, and the queen those of his wife; and replaced them reverentially in their tomb.

The circumstances of Arthur's funeral could be known only from Welsh traditions. Giraldus has left us one of these: "Morgan, a noble lady, proprietor of this district and patroness of the Abbey, and related to Arthur, had the king carried, after the battle of Camlan, to the island called Glastonbury to heal his wounds." The same facts are alluded to by Jeffry, in his elegant poem, which entitles him to more literary respect than his history, and which contains more of real British traditions.

The pyramids or obelisks that are stated to have marked the place of Arthur's interment, long remained at Glastonbury. They had images and inscriptions, which have not yet been understood, but which do not seem to relate to Arthur. A sword, fancied to have been his caliburno, was presented by Richard the First, as a valuable gift, to the King of Sicily.

[16] Ashe, G. (1981). A certain very ancient British book: Traces of an Arthurian source in Geoffrey of Monmouth's History. *Speculum*, 56, 301–323.

[17] Camden, *Britannia*.

[18] Turner, S. (1841). *The History of the Anglo-Saxons*. Philadelphia: Carey & Hart.

[19] Camden, *Britannia*.

[20] The contrary position that these observations do differ in some meaningful way has been expressed at http://www.britannia.com/history/arthur/cross.html

[21] Abbey Guide. (undated). *A guide to Glastonbury and its abbey*. Bristol, UK: Elworthy & Son.

[22] Bond, F. B. (1920). An architectural handbook of Glastonbury Abbey with a historical chronicle of the building. *Central Somerset Gazette*.

[23] Luard, H. S. (1865). *Annales Monasterii de Waverlia*. RS 36.2

[24] http://www.britannia.com/history/arthur/cross.html Retrieved December 31, 2009.

[25] Warren, W. L. (1998). *King John*. New Haven, CT: Yale University Press.

[26] In his 2007 book, *An Utterly Impartial History of Britain*, John O'Farrell opined that *Braveheart* could not have been more historically inaccurate, even if a "Plasticine dog" had been inserted in the film and the title changed to *William Wallace and Gromit*. See http://en.wikipedia.org/wiki/Braveheart#Historical_ inaccuracies. For the present purposes it is especially interesting that the script-writer of *Braveheart*, Randall Wallace, protested that it was based on a highly doubtful earlier poem by one Blind Harry. His comment here spoke volumes: "Is Blind Harry true? I don't know. I know that it spoke to my heart and that's what matters to me, that it spoke to my heart." The film's director, Mel Gibson, opined that although there were obvious historical impossibilities, the version presented was more "cinematically compelling." As we shall see, many things happen when people let wishful thinking ascend over knowledge and facts.

[27] Morris, J. E. (1996). *The Welsh wars of Edward I: A contribution to medieval military history based on original documents*. Conshohocken, PA: Combined Publishing.

[28] Morris, op. cit.

[29] Morris, op. cit.

[30] Starkey, D. (2009). *Henry VIII: Man and monarch*. London: British Library.

[31] See Hancock, P. A. (2009). *Richard III and the murder in the Tower*. Stroud, Gloucestershire: History Press.

[32] Ariosto, L. (1962). *Orlando Furioso*. (J. Harrington, Trans.). London: Centaur Press.

[33] http://www.englishmonarchs.co.uk/tudor_18.htm. Retrieved December 31, 2009.

[34] http://www.britannia.com/history/arthur/cross.html.Retrieved December 31, 2009.

[35] Gillam, G. (n.d.). The King Arthur Cross rediscovered? http://www.britannia. com/history/cross.html.

[36] Gillam, The King Arthur Cross rediscovered?

[37] Leland, J. (c. 1544). *Assertio Inclytissimi Arturii*. London: Wolfe, Distaffe Lane.

[38] Young, M. J. (2001). *London's Camelot*. http://www.britainexpress.com/Myths/ londons-camelot.htm.

[39] D'Art, A. (2004). *Glastonbury Abbey and King Arthur's grave*. http://www. aisling.net/travel/UK-glast/glast5-grave.htm. Retrieved December 31, 2009.

[40] Newell, W. W. (1903). William of Malmesbury on the antiquity of Glastonbury. *Transactions and Proceedings of the Modern Language Association of America*, 18(4), 459–512.

[41] Abbott, Edwin A. (1898). *St. Thomas of Canterbury: His death and miracles*. London: Adam & Charles Black.

[42] Barber, R. (1973). *The figure of Arthur*. Totowa, NJ: Rowan and Littleford.

[43] Harvey, J. H. (1976). *The Plantagenets*. Sutton, Surrey: Severn House Publishers Ltd.

[44] Edbury, P. W. (1996). *The conquest of Jerusalem and the Third Crusade: Sources in translation*. Chichester, UK: Ashgate.

[45] See http://www.glastonburyfestivals.co.uk/

[46] Ashe, G. (1985). *The discovery of King Arthur*. New York: Henry Holt. Here (p. 176) Ashe cites the 1963 explorations by Ralegh Radford as support of this contention.

[47] Leland, J. (1907 [c. 1550]). *The itinerary of John Leland*. (Ed. L. Toulmin Smith). London.

[48] Gillam, The King Arthur Cross rediscovered? op cit.

[49] Hancock, *Richard III and the murder in the Tower*, op cit.

[50] See http://www.glastonburyfestivals.co.uk/op cit.

CASE 2

Drake's Plate of Brass

The Original English Claim to California

"For those who believe, no proof is necessary.
For those who don't believe, no proof is possible."
Alfred North Whitehead

DRAKE'S CIRCUMNAVIGATION

Historically, the first circumnavigation of the Earth is attributed to a Portuguese seafarer named Fernao de Magalhaes, more recognizably known as Ferdinand Magellan. His vision of completely circling the world eventually became a reality after he secured royal sponsorship for his journey. He departed from Spain on August 10, 1519, with 5 ships and a total of 232 crew members. Only one of those ships, with a crew of just eighteen individuals, completed the voyage. It had taken three years and twenty-seven days, returning eventually to Spain on September 6, 1522. Unfortunately, Magellan himself was not one of those very few survivors. He had been killed in a battle with natives in the Philippines on April 27, 1521. The honor of being the first to survive a circumnavigation was thus attributed to the Master of the one remaining ship, Juan Sebastian del Cano. However, despite this fact today, it is still Magellan's name that is associated with this benchmark of exploration. With the evident record of danger and death suffered by this expedition, there was, understandably, no great encouragement to follow in Magellan's wake [1].

Yet the spirit of exploration persists, and during the five decades that followed Magellan's achievement, the notion of glory once again superseded the evident danger. It was thus amid the maelstrom of political maneuvering of the mid-Elizabethan era that the English seafarer Francis Drake [2] left England on December 13, 1577, with approximately 164 companions collected in a 5-ship flotilla. Drake's expedition obviously suited Elizabeth I's posturing with respect to Spain and its ruling monarch King Phillip, her half-sister Mary's widower. Fifty-five years after the return of Magellan's expedition, Drake set off on his own attempt to circle the globe.

As with Magellan's earlier experience, Drake's company encountered similar rates of attrition. Eventually, the remaining members of the latter expedition returned to England two years, nine months, and fourteen days later. However, unlike Magellan, Drake himself personally survived the voyage and thus became the first expedition leader to circumnavigate the globe successfully [3]. Despite the praise and reward that we would naturally expect such an accomplishment to attract, the full account of Drake's adventures was not published until some half a century later owing to policy issues of "national security," a concern that still resonates in our own times. Of course, five decades after the expedition, Drake himself and most everyone who accompanied him had followed Magellan on that one final voyage common to us all. He was long dead.

DRAKE IN AMERICA

In 1628, the complete account of Drake's voyage was published by one of his descendants, under the title *The World Encompassed.* However, observations on his voyage had been included by Hakluyt in an earlier text entitled *Famous Voyages.* These texts are thought to depend largely on the observations of one Francis Fletcher, the chaplain on Drake's expedition [4]. Today, we can partly confirm the truth of these accounts by comparing the observations that are made, for example, with those recorded in contemporary Spanish archives. These corroborations confirm that Drake was where he said he was, when he said he was. In particular, we can place him off the coast of South America, and heading north early in 1579. Because some details of his journey were still a state secret even at the time of this later publication date, some aspects of his voyage remain the topic of mystery and contention even today. Having lost all his companion ships, Drake's own vessel, originally called the *Pelican* but now labeled the *Golden Hind,* was suffering from the hardships of the voyage and was in desperate need of repair.

Drake had sailed north from the coast of modern-day Mexico, away from potential Spanish interference, and proceeded up the west coast of the present-day United States of America. He is thought to have reached a latitude of 48 degrees north, although the precise extent of his exploration remains contentious even today [5]. Turning about, he sailed south to a location that also remains the topic of extensive debate [6]. What appears in the original record of the voyage is that on June 17, 1579, Francis Drake

FIGURE 2.1. Section of the c. 1595 Broadsheet map of Jodocus Hondius showing the Pacific and Indian Ocean portions of Drake's circumnavigation. Note the location of Drake's California anchorage and the Portus Plan, where the latter is shown in more detail in Figure 2.

and his remaining crew beached their one remaining ship at some location on the west coast of America to careen – repair the ravages that the voyage had wreaked [7]. They built some form of fortified encampment in which they spent a number of weeks. While some were busy with ship repairs, others took an opportunity to explore the local area. They met and made reasonably peaceful relations with the local population of indigenous peoples. One clue we have as to Drake's point of anchorage is the so-called Portus Plan. It is an inserted vignette from the circa 1595 Broadsheet map of Jodocus Hondius, which sought to trace Drake's path around the world. This is shown in Figures 2.1 and 2.2. Although such inserts are often meant to be illustrative only, it is the shape of this harbor and its similarity to specific sites on the west coast of the United States that has intrigued historians as well as acting as a guide in the search for Drake's landing site [8].

FIGURE 2.2. The Portus Plan in detail. The vignette from the c. 1595 map of Jodocus Hondius purporting to show Drake's anchorage. Specific enough to be suggestive but matching no candidate site exactly, the Portus Plan has been a source of both information and frustration. [9]

The text of *The World Encompassed* specifies a latitude of 38' 30" for this harbor, and Hakluyt's earlier *Famous Voyage*s also reported this approximate 38 degree latitude. Further, Drake's Plate itself, on which the present chapter is focused, has been used to support different potential locations. Wherever Drake's anchorage actually was, we are told that on July 23, 1579, or thereabouts, Drake and his men left their 'conuenient and fit harborough' and headed out and off across the Pacific Ocean on the longest sea leg of their journey. As they took one last glance backward at the North American continent, they could probably just make out the marker they had set up to record their presence there [10].

RIGHT AND TITLE TO THE KINGDOM

Drake's voyage was one primarily of discovery, but it was also an Elizabethan enterprise. Thus Drake sought to take as much advantage as he could of the various situations presented to him. One aspiration he had was to claim new lands for his Queen. *The World Encompassed* describes the area around their West Coast landing place as an area that:

[t]he Spaniards never had any dealing, or so much as set a foot in this country; the utmost of their discoveries, reaching only to many degrees Southward of this place. [11]

The implication of this statement is clear. What Drake was to lay claim to were virgin territories over which the Spanish had no possible rights. To confirm his claim on these lands for Elizabeth, Drake made sure that just prior to leaving his anchorage he met with the local inhabitants and their chiefs and concluded what he asserted was a transfer of sovereignty.

Before we went from thence, our General caused to be set up, a monument of our being there; as also of her majesty's, and successors right and title to that kingdom, namely a plate of brass, fast nailed to a great and firm post; whereon is engraved her graces name, and the day and year of our arrival there, and of the free giving up, of the province and kingdom, both by the king and people, into her majesties hands: together with her highness picture, and arms in a piece of sixpence current English money, showing it self by a hole made of purpose through the plate: underneath was likewise engraved the name of our General &c. [12]

To seal this deal (although how the natives derived any profit from this transaction is difficult to see), Drake had erected the aforesaid marker that recorded the pact and essentially secured nominal title to the possession of the lands that compose the modern-day west coast of the United States, primarily present-day California. The text is explicit in terms of the content of the bargain and the appearance of the marker itself. We can confirm that there are text references to the rights of the Queen (Elizabeth) and to the lands (kingdom) thereabouts. Also, since Drake was halfway around the world and could not know the state of Elizabeth's health or even whether she was still alive, the Plate cleverly establishes the claim on the land not only for the present queen but for her successors in perpetuity. The marker itself is also noted to contain the date of the expedition's arrival, some reference to the free "giving up" of the land, as well as Drake's name as Captain General of the expedition [13]. In addition to this content material, some physical characteristics of the marker are also reported. It is made of what the voyagers would recognize as brass, it has a configuration such that it could be "fast nailed" to a post, and there was a hole in it sufficient to show a contemporary Elizabethan "sixpence" piece. We are not told any other details as to the specific size, shape, or appearance of the "Plate of Brass" except for its attachment to a post [14].

THE MODERN-DAY REDISCOVERY

When Drake and his men departed on July 23, 1579, they could look back on the harbor that had been their home for five weeks. There were the remains of the fortified stockade that they had created and the marker symbolizing their presence and their claim on the land they were leaving. As they sailed off into the Pacific, the Plate itself disappeared into history. For a period of 357 years we have no certain knowledge or information as to what happened to Drake's Plate. Some, perhaps even many, would argue we still do not know the real Plate's eventual fate. However, everything changed in the summer of 1936 when a young Californian store worker named Beryle Shinn had a flat tire. With this apparently chance event, the material representation of Drake and his claim came shimmering back to life [15]. Shinn's account of discovery reads:

> In the summer of 1936 I was traveling south on highway 101 from San Rafael and when coming down the ridge approaching Greenbrae one of my tires was punctured. Veering to the side of the road I stopped my car. On the ridge above was a likely picnic spot. I climbed under a barbed wire fence and climbed to the top of the ridge. There an extensive view presented itself. To the east was Point San Quentin and upper San Francisco Bay bounded on the southwest by the Tiburon peninsula. Below was the tidal estuary of Corte Medera Creek. Approaching an outcrop of rock near the top of the ridge I picked up rocks and rolled them down the hill. As I pulled a rock from the soil I saw the edge of a metal plate which was partly covered by the rock. When I pulled the plate free from the ground I noticed that it was about the size to repair the frame of my automobile. So when I returned to my car I took it along and tossed it in. Several months later I thought of repairing the frame. While handling the plate I noticed that it seemed to have some inscription on it. I scrubbed it with a brush and soap and noted a date 1579, near the top of the plate. This interested me, so I showed it to a few of my friends, but none could make out what it was until one, a college student, deciphered the word Drake and suggested that the metal plate be shown to Dr. Herbert E. Bolton of the University of California. This was done and Dr. Bolton discovered that it was Sir Francis Drake's Plate of Brass. [16]

Shinn's first reaction was certainly not one of any great excitement. He merely threw the plate into his car and thought nothing more of it for several months. The college student Shinn referred to was a fellow co-worker at Kahn's Dry Goods Store in Oakland, and being a student at the University of California, he suggested taking the plate there. In early February 1937,

FIGURE 2.3. The location of the finding of the Plate by Beryle Shinn. The actual find was made at the base of the rock in the center of the photograph. From: California Historical Society documents.

Shinn found his way to Professor Herbert E. Bolton [17]. Given that the Plate was one of the most important of early Californian artifacts, it would seem almost inevitable that Shinn and his Plate would eventually meet with Dr. Bolton. By that time, the sixty-seven-year-old Bolton was arguably the outstanding living historian of early California. Indeed, the discovery of the Plate fulfilled his dream that he had communicated many times to the students in his history classes. And now, here it was, his dream embodied and held in his own hands. But for how long? Bolton was not going to lose this chance and was quick to contact Allen L. Chickering, then-president of the California Historical Society. Bolton needed to persuade Chickering of the importance of the find and to acquire it from Shinn before others became aware of it and began a potential bidding war.

On Sunday, February 28, 1937, Bolton, Chickering, and Shinn returned to the site of the find that today lies somewhere close to the modern-day intersection of Eliseo Drive and Corte Toluca in the Greenbrae-San Quentin area (see Figure 2.3). On their return journey, a sum of $2,500 was mentioned for the Plate as well as the buyers assuming any risk associated with fraud. On the next day, a Monday, Shinn reclaimed the Plate, indicating that he wanted to show it to a relative. Although he was supposed to bring it back on Tuesday, he failed to appear, and Wednesday and Thursday also brought no sign of Shinn or his Plate. When he did return on Friday, the disturbed historians understandably had managed to push the bid to $3,500. The Plate was handed over and thus on Friday, March 5, 1937, the Plate was officially purchased on behalf of the Society and given to the University of California. As pointed out recently by Von der Porten and his colleagues in their important paper on the veracity of the Plate [18], by this action both Bolton and Chickering had essentially tied themselves to the Plate even before any form of formal test and evaluation could be conducted. But who questions the fulfillment of their precious lifelong dream?

A TWIST IN THE TALE

Shinn's find proved to be a lucky one for him. With the money he was paid, he was able to get married and afford a nice honeymoon [19]. The purchasers were also happy; they had secured a unique piece of California history. It was the quintessential win-win situation. A mere month after the transaction had taken place, on April 6, 1937, Bolton announced the find to the world at a lunch meeting of the California Historical Society. Drake's Plate had finally resurfaced. The newspapers had a field day. The attendant publicity must have reached one William Caldeira who quickly came forward to communicate another chapter in the Plate's story. Caldeira claimed he was the one who actually found the Plate some years earlier, in the latter part of 1933.

At the time, Caldeira had been a chauffeur to a Mr. Leon Bocqueraz [20] who, along with a Mr. Anson Blake, was in the habit of going out to the Laguna Ranch in the Point Reyes vicinity for hunting expeditions. As chauffer, Caldeira was detailed to meet the hunters at the termination of their trek, and on this particular day he was parked at the intersection of two ranch roads, about three-quarters of a mile from Drake's Bay in the Point Reyes area. As he was waiting, Caldeira was in the habit of casting about for any unusual or interesting objects that he would bring to the notice of the hunters since both were also members of the California Historical Society. On this particular day he got lucky. He picked up a Plate alongside of the roadway and washed it off in a nearby stream, an action that revealed the letters "DRAK" but little more [21]. Caldeira showed the Plate to Bocqueraz when he returned to the car, but the light was so poor they could make out no more than Caldeira had already seen. It was agreed to examine the Plate in detail when they reached the more conducive surroundings of civilization. Now comes the amazing part. Even though Drake's Plate was perhaps the most prized artifact any California historian could have found, and despite the fact that the story was very well known, and that the letters "DRAK" had been detected on the Plate, Caldeira indicated that they put the Plate in the side pocket of the car door, but by the time they returned home that night, both men had forgotten about it! In his statement, Bocqueraz had noted that he was very tired and gave no indication of having seen any letters on the plate picked up by Caldeira [22].

After this spectacular memory lapse, Caldeira stated that subsequently he had been cleaning out the car some few weeks later during a ferry crossing from Richmond to San Quentin. After having earlier washed it, saved it, and shown it to his employer, he now decided that the Plate was useless and threw it out of the right side of the car in the first meadow west of the junction of the San Francisco–San Rafael and the San Quentin–Kentfield roads not far from San Quentin itself [23]. It wasn't only Caldeira who came forward; several others also claimed to have seen the Plate between this time and Shinn's eventual discovery. One of these, Mr. Joseph Cattaneo, claimed that he had found the Plate where Caldeira claimed he had discarded it and had himself later thrown it away very close to the site of Shinn's discovery [24].

If we are willing to take these accounts at face value, we have a chain of reports by which the Plate left the environs of the nominal Drake's Bay and found its way to the vicinity of the San Quentin Penitentiary by the summer of 1936 for Beryle Shinn to find. However, there is some doubt that Caldeira's find was the Plate that Shinn pulled from the ground. Strong emphasis has been placed on the fact that he found it largely "buried." If we believe all of the reported "finders" of the Plate, its bona fides is tacitly supported by these connected but ultimately untestable accounts (see Figure 2.4). However, this concatenation of contentions further complicates an already complex issue [25].

THE PLATE ITSELF

We have so far seen how Drake himself came to be in this part of the world. We have an account that records the making of the Plate he is purported to have erected. We also have the story of a modern-day discovery and eventual pathway by which it found itself in the possession of the California Historical Society and its current home in Bancroft Library at the University of California. Now, we have to look at exactly what this object

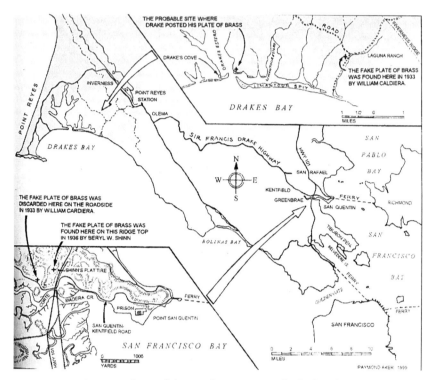

FIGURE 2.4. A comparison of the two locations in which the Plate is claimed to have been found and their relationship to San Francisco Bay and Point Reyes peninsula. Illustration reproduced from the California Historical Society paper of 2002.

is and what efforts have been made to evaluate its veracity. As illustrated in Figure 2.5, Drake's Plate is a small sheet of brass measuring some 7.5 in. by 5 in., although as specified in some of the detailed reports, the Plate is neither a uniform rectangle nor uniform in thickness [26]. At the mid-point of the Plate at the top and bottom are two square grooves presumed to be the places by which it was "fast nailed" to whatever post to which it was originally attached. Similarly, the Plate has a hole at the bottom right, which was presumably meant for the Elizabethan sixpence. In general, the appearance of the plate very much accords with the written record as it appeared in *The World Encompassed*. [27]

We are able to identify some of the words carved into the Plate itself. In particular, we can see the date of the landing and the very prominent name of the expedition leader, Francis Drake. His claim on the new world as "Nova Albion," or New England, is immediately evident.

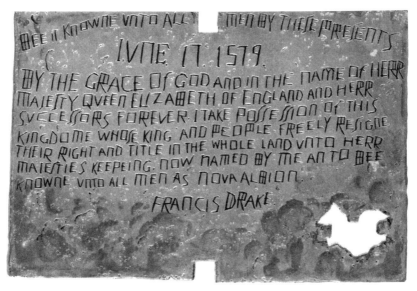

FIGURE 2.5. The "Plate of Brass." This illustration is of a copy in the possession of the Author.

The full text of the Plate of Brass itself reads:

BEE IT KNOWNE VNOT ALL MEN BY THESE PRESENTS.
  IVNE.17.1579
  BY THE GRACE OF GOD AND IN THE NAME OF HERR MAIESTY QVEEN ELIZABETH OF ENGLAND AND HERR SVCCESSORS FOREVER. I TAKE POSSESSION OF THIS KINGDOME WHOSE KING AND PEOPLE FREELY RESIGNE THEIR RIGHT AND TITLE IN THE WHOLE LAND VNTO HERR MAIESTIES KEEPING. NOW NAMED BY ME AN TO BEE KNOWNE V(N) TO ALL MEN AS NOVA ALBION.
  G/C FRANCIS DRAKE. [28]

It was this object that Professor Bolton had declared genuine just one month after securing it. He had publicly "nailed his colors to the mast" and in so doing had implicitly involved both the California Historical Society, which was already involved to the sum of $3,500, as well as the prestigious University of California. Much was already at stake depending on the authenticity of the object Shinn had picked up almost casually, about a year earlier. Acclaim for the Plate was certainly not universal. For example, an expert in Elizabethan literature, R. B. Haselden, recorded his doubts as to a number of aspects of the Plate, including the wording and the spelling [29]. However, these objections were vociferously opposed by those who were now rapidly becoming its de facto champions. Before full acceptance, the Plate had to be subject to scientific testing, and this evaluation process represents the next stage in the Plate's story.

Doubts were still circulating about the authenticity following the initial fanfare of the announcement and the landmark publication of the Society in 1937, with commentaries by Bolton and Watson [30]. To help settle the issue, Bolton as chair of a four-man committee, of which Chickering was also a part, solicited the expertise of Professor Colin Fink, head of the Division of Electrochemistry at Columbia University. In association with his colleague, Dr. Polushkin, a metallurgical engineer, Fink issued a report under the auspices of the California Historical Society in 1938 [31]. Given their respective areas of expertise, these individuals naturally focused on the physical composition of the Plate itself. Commentary on the linguistic content and its matching to existing Elizabethan texts was largely ignored. It has been suggested that this tactic was consciously adopted in order to first assure the antiquity of the metal itself, to ensure its material form. After all, if the metal was of modern manufacture, then analysis of the inscription would prove superfluous and indeed a possible source of embarrassment if the text was authenticated only to find the metal was modern. What the report's authors did conclude, however, was quite startling. Since this report has been discounted and often ignored in more modern times, it is interesting to consider the evidence on which they reached their conclusions, which state:

1. There is no doubt whatsoever that the dark coating on the surface of the plate is a natural patina formed slowly over a period of many years.

2. Numerous surface defects and imperfections usually associated with old brass were found on the plate.

3. Particles of mineralized plate tissue are firmly imbedded in the surface of the plate. This is likewise a very positive proof of the age of the plate.

4. Cross sections of the brass plate show (a) an excessive amount of impurities; and (b) chemical inhomogeneity; as well as (c) variation in grain size. All three of these characteristics indicate a brass of old origin.

5. Among the impurities found in the brass of the plate there is magnesium, which is present far in excess of the amount occurring in modern brass.

6. There are numerous indications that the plate was not made by rolling but was made by hammering, as was the common practice in Drake's time. [32]

It was primarily on these findings concerning the metallurgical analysis that Fink and his colleague concluded that "the brass plate examined by us is the genuine Drake Plate." The nuances between metallurgical and lexical evidence now largely neglected, Bolton had his confirmation, the skeptics were routed, and Robert Gordon Sproul, the president of the University of California, could calm his fears, safe in the knowledge that his institution now possessed one of the greatest historical artifacts in all of the Americas.

PERSISTING DOUBTS

Despite this apparent confirmation of authenticity, doubts about the Plate continued to be voiced. Among these doubts featured continuing issues with the calligraphy and content. In respect to the physical inscription, it is evident that essentially all of the letters are rectilinear. That is, there are very few attempts to create the curvilinear components of letters. Only the letters "s" and "f" show any real evidence of such an effort – the suggestion being that the tool for inscribing these letters had been a straight chisel. Indeed, shortly after the discovery of the Plate, a Berkeley scientist, V. L. Vander Hoof, made another and arguably more refined plate using the same sort of straight-chisel technique [33]. Tongue-in-cheek, this latter Plate recounted the formal annulment of Drake's claim. In addition to several concerns as to how the marks on the Plate had been made, there was clear unease about the way the message was expressed and its comparison with known contemporary Elizabethan tracts. Haselden expressed his concerns early in 1937 and found a number of allies, especially in Dr. Vincent Harlow of Oxford University [34]. Primarily, Harlow's objections were based on word order and expression of titles and rights, which failed to follow Elizabethan precedent. For example, the queen's name normally would have been given the greatest prominence and the date would have followed at the end. Further, the spelling on the Plate was highly consistent, and the interpretation is that it was modern.

Another early commentator, Dr. Robin Flower, Deputy Keeper of the Manuscripts for the British Museum, also commented on the issue of spelling and actual letter forms, especially the crude and atypical nature of B's, P's, R's, M's, and N's [35]. Bolton's response was rational but biased by his own acceptance. He pointed out that word order was not evidence per se, and no one had seen all forms of Elizabethan lettering. In this he was happy to discount negative information. Dr. Denholm-Young of Magdalen College epitomized the doubters because he had "never seen any Elizabethan script like it." It was these observations that inhibited bringing the Plate to larger public attention in the late 1930s.

Slowly, the Plate's initial champions began to fade and die, with both Herbert Bolton and Allen Chickering passing away in 1958. The Plate now had to stand on its own merits and its stature began to diminish as the years passed. The suspicions, expressed now over four decades, coalesced in an edition of Morison's text, *The European Discovery of America*. In chapter 29 of the 1974 edition, entitled "Drake in California," he declared the Plate an outright fraud: "[T]he plate is a hoax perpetrated by some collegiate joker who knew little about Drake except what he had heard from Dr. Bolton" [36]. Spurred on by this and other observations doubting the Plate's authenticity, plans were put in place for subsequent tests on the Plate, although authorities at the Bancroft Library at the University of California were careful to indicate that they had earlier thought of more tests. With Drake's 400th anniversary approaching in 1979, James Hart, the director of the Library, set these tests in progress. It is primarily on the results of these latter tests that the current view of the Plate depends. It is, accordingly, worth looking at what they said in detail.

The focus of the 1977 report, produced under Hart's name, consisted primarily of the metallurgical properties of the Plate [37]. Briefly, the concerns expressed were over the chemical composition of the Plate, whether it had originally been rolled or beaten and whether the Plate itself had been cut by hand or with a large pair of mechanical shears. The central points were that a Plate of certain specific composition strongly implied modern manufacture. A rolled Plate almost certainly meant modern manufacture, and a Plate cut with commercial shears would also indicate recent creation. The outcomes of these three evaluations strongly suggested that the Plate was of modern origin. Subsequent comments on the inscription and its creation are interesting, but it is primarily on the result of these physical evaluations that the opinion on the Plate now turned. The report concluded: "Obviously the evidence [this report] assembled has turned out to be essentially negative."

Before moving on, it is interesting to look a little more at these physical criteria. First, with respect to the chemical composition of the Plate, within measurement error, the composition of the Plate is some 35 percent zinc, 65 percent copper, with minor traces of other elements. The determination that this composition of elements represents modern production is based on the purity and the high percentage of zinc. Comparison with other brass plates of known date does not exclude this percentage composition of zinc; it simply falls on the edge of the distribution of the samples tested in comparison. It should be noted that the collected comparison samples were themselves limited in number. Rolling brass is not necessarily a new process. Indeed, some forms of rolling were apparently in use for the production of coins. However, rolling brass of the width of the Plate had not been observed in the sixteenth century. Thus, evidence of rolling suggests modern manufacture but does not automatically exclude manufacture before Drake's time. Finally, the appendix report by Cyril Smith indicates that the Plate was cut by large commercial shears. Although this conclusion refutes Finks's earlier findings, it depends on analysis of parts of the edge that do not appear to have been hammered, either in manufacture or at some later date. Thus, it is not any one single aspect that proved to be critical but rather a summation of the physical evidence. As one commentator noted, any one aspect shows that it is highly improbable that the Plate is genuine, but when we add together the improbabilities for different and presumably independent sources of information, it shreds the case for authenticity.

The report itself is conservative in its conclusions, definitively not declaring the Plate genuine but stopping short of calling it an outright fraud. Some further tests had been recommended and were subsequently conducted. These included X-ray diffraction and a larger sampling of the composition of medieval brasses. The former is the most relevant since X-ray diffraction can show evidence of rolling, which again supports the idea of modern manufacture. In brief, the test did show this overall propensity and added further weight to the side of the argument favoring the Plate's modern manufacture [38]. Although it should be carefully noted that *none* of these findings represent conclusive evidence of modern fakery, it is the preponderance of this evidence that led to the collective change of opinion regarding the Plate. Apparently, sometime in the 1990s, the Bancroft Library took advantage of the ever-evolving developments in testing capacity to once again test the veracity of the Plate. Although no results were published, it did subsequently lend the Plate to the University Museum of Anthropology to be included in an exhibition entitled "Frauds and Fakes." Today, the Plate

FIGURE 2.6. The author alongside the actual "Plate of Brass" in the Bancroft Library of the University of California at Berkeley. Photograph by Francisca Hancock.

sits in the entry area of the Bancroft Library open to inspection and supported by a friendly and informative staff (see Figure 2.6).

E CLAMPUS VITUS

At the end of the 1977 report, one of the reasons for a degree of equivocation concerned the necessary motive for producing the Plate if it was a hoax. The idea of a student "gag" was aired but the objection was raised that "Since the point of a hoax is to show up the person who is gulled and since no one ever came along to reveal a fraud, defenders of the Plate contended that such lack of revelation was in itself an argument against the idea of a hoax." In essence, since no one benefited publicly from the hoax, there was no hoax. This is spurious reasoning, if it is reasoning at all.

The intervening decades saw little change in the general persuasion concerning the authenticity of the Plate, but it did see the work of a small group of researchers who looked to solve the final mystery of the Plate as to its creation, motivation, and emergence. Their work was published in 2002, in *California History*, the journal of the California Historical Society [39]. The motivation for the modern creation of the Plate, they argue, seems to have been based on the hopes and wishes of Professor Bolton. As noted earlier, he had been telling his students for generations to "keep their eyes open for the Plate"; finding it was his heart's desire. According to their account, a reinvigorated fraternal order named 'E Clampus Vitus' decided to fulfill Bolton's dream. The primary driving force behind the renaissance of this group was Carl I. Wheat, as well as Charles Camp, but another individual who contributed to the renewed Society, one G. Ezra Dane, was identified as one individual behind a plot hatched to deceive Bolton, who incidentally was a "Clamper" himself.

Originally, the enterprise started as a form of joke among friends, a friendly "joshing" of a colleague, essentially a sophomoric joke for older men. Dane recruited a number of fellow members who took on specific tasks. George Barron, the Curator of History at San Francisco's de Young Museum, created the text, which was derived from *The World Encompassed*. Together with another colleague, George Clark, Barron designed the layout and incised the lettering on a plate of commercial brass obtained, purportedly, from an Alameda ship chandlery. The "GC" insignia on the Plate is reported to stand for George Clark not "Captain General" as had been earlier assumed. To ensure the joke would be complete, the letters "ECV" were painted on the back in transparent, fluorescent paint, presumably to be revealed at some intimate dinner of the Society to the great merriment of all!

HOAX OUT OF HAND

Exactly how the Plate reached the location where Caldeira first claimed to have found it we cannot be certain. Was someone in the plot aware of the hunting trips of Bocequeraz and his colleague Blake out to the Point Reyes area? If so, did they "salt the mine" in an area where an ingénue like Caldeira might find the Plate and immediately pass it on to his employer and his companion, who, as members of the California Historical Society, would presumably realize the significance of the artifact immediately? If so, they were to be very much disappointed. It might be that a group of hoaxers would simply find their "plant" gone, not knowing who had taken it or why. It seems that if one went to all the trouble of fabricating such a convincing forgery, the method by which the discovery would be made would have been better thought out.

Shinn appears to be as much an innocent as Caldeira, picking up the Plate in the countryside and not really knowing what he had found, only benefiting later when the contact with Bolton and Chickering had been made. As mentioned earlier, it is not surprising that the Plate eventually found its way to Bolton, but what is surprising is that it appears to have taken a number of years to do so. What were the putative hoaxers doing in the interim? We have no answer to this question. What we do know is that the degree of secrecy maintained by Bolton and Chickering, together with the speed with which they proceeded, apparently did not give anyone "in the know" a chance to warn them before they irrevocably committed themselves to the case for authenticity. The public announcement of April 6, 1937 must have caused consternation among the hoaxers. Now no longer a private joke, public reputations as well as a considerable amount of money were involved. Was there any possible solution?

WARNINGS OF A HOAX

Unable to come right out and reveal the hoax, it appears that a number of individuals tried to provide clues and hints that all was not well with the Plate. One Edwin Grabhorn, another California Historical Society and E Clampus Vitus member, came out with a spoof letter claiming to be a man-ufacturer of brasses [40], while ECV member Charles Camp published an anonymous tract labeled *Ye Preposterous Booke of Brasse*, an evident warn-ing to examine what had been discovered with a skeptical eye [41]. How such warnings were interpreted by Bolton cannot be said. Perhaps he saw them in terms of friendly spoofing of his important find. Gossip as to the perpetration of the hoax continued through the years but perhaps as a form of respect for Bolton and Chickering, as well as the Historical Society and the University, no public announcement of fraud was ever forthcoming. There is also the suggestion that Barron actually hated Bolton and the moti-vation for a hoax might not be the jolly jape that has been portrayed. Again, if this is so, why did Barron never fulfill his revenge? The final conclusion drawn by Von der Porten and his colleagues is that "it was just a 'prank' that got out of hand, created by a 'crazy group' with no objective other than an elaborate joke at the expense of others in their circle." [42] This seems to be the current consensus as we look over the present accounts, especially those on contemporary websites.

A PERSONAL INSIGHT

Not too long ago, I had an opportunity to visit San Francisco, and during that visit had a further chance to investigate the origins of the Plate and its purported etiology as a hoax. I met with a particularly knowledgeable individual in this matter who told me that the hoax was originally meant as an initiation challenge to some prospective new members of E Clampus Vitus. My informant told me that the person who had originally pointed out the source of the hoax was a Dr. Albert Shumate, who himself had been instrumental in the resurrection of the Clampers [43]. Shumate identified the individual who was purported to know most about this deception as G. Ezra Dane. He, like many other members of the local historical community, knew very well of Bolton's preoccupation with and excitement generated by "Drake's Plate." The idea of these prospective members of the Society, or "Poor, Blind, Candidates," was to hoax Professor Bolton by creating the Plate and having him "discover" it on a local field trip which they would help organize.

Following the elation of discovery, the plan was to disabuse Professor Bolton after his momentary triumph, and in so doing earn their "spurs" as Clampers. This was the plan, but unfortunately it went wrong. The hoaxed Plate was spontaneously discovered by William Caldeira who then subsequently discarded it – as previously stated. When the Plate was resurrected by Beryle Shinn, no one from the group of hoaxers was aware of his immediate contact with Professor Bolton, and very soon it was too late to own up without excessive embarrassment all around. Now, very definitively, the issue had changed from one of an insider joke and much personal joshing to a very public affair. It is then understandable that a group of young students, as undergraduates, would not want to embarrass publicly their senior professor. It also looks as though some of the senior individuals involved either knew or suspected a hoax and tried to drop hints to Bolton that all was not as it seemed. However, by this time, it appears that Bolton was wedded to the path of discovery that history now recounts.

THE VERDICT ON THE PLATE

Is the present consensus correct? Is the Plate of Brass sitting in the Bancroft Library a hoax [44] or is it an edict, erected on the orders of Francis Drake on the coast of California now well over 400 years ago? First, there is every reason to believe that Francis Drake accomplished the feats associated with the reports in *The World Encompassed*. Contemporary evidence provides corroboration with what is given in the text. However, there is unfortunately little independent corroboration of Drake's adventures around what is now known as the west coast of the United States of America [45]. But, given the veracity of the rest of the text and, further, given that Drake's remaining ship was most probably in bad need of repair, we have to consider the present case on the presumption that the landing and the erection of the marker are factual events. Of course, the discovery of the Plate of Brass is reinforcing in a circular fashion here. How are we to be sure Drake's account is correct? – well, we have the Plate of Brass. How do we know the Plate of Brass is authentic – well, we have Drake's account. The two provide mutual support. However, if we accept Drake's account of events, do we also have to accept the veracity of the Plate finally brought to the full light of day in that summer of 1936? The answer is that it would be very unwise to assume one necessarily implies the other.

Fortunately, unlike other contentious artifacts such as the Cross of King Arthur, we do still physically possess what is claimed to be the Plate of Brass. Unlike many other claims of the extraordinary, we can still test this item to compare its reality with what it claims to be. As the sophistication of testing has improved, so the case for the authenticity of the Plate has radically diminished. The post–World War II years have seen a veritable explosion of technologies, and the testing capacities available today were not even conceived in the mid-1930s when the Plate first appeared. It is tempting to speculate on what the most modern tests would have to say, but the evaluations of the late 1970s leave little probability of authenticity. The present likelihood of the Plate's authenticity is miniscule and diminishing. If indeed this is not the Plate, there remains the intriguing possibility that some time in the future another version, perhaps the actual Plate itself, may emerge. There are many individuals with metal detectors on the coasts of California, and hope springs eternal.

All successful hoaxes succeed because, at least to some degree, they fulfill the hopes and aspirations of those who embrace them. Drake's Plate of Brass is a wonderful example of this principle in that it embodies the long-held desire of one particular individual, and perhaps the collective aspirations of others, to find a specific historical artifact. It was one that, based on written accounts, anybody would have every reason to believe existed. If we ignore the claims of the indigenous peoples at the time of Drake's visit, the Plate is of interest as more than just a historical artifact. Indeed, the Plate represented incontrovertible evidence of the primacy of English occupation and temporary colonization, and so it lends evidentiary credence to the proposition that the lands of California around the San Francisco Bay area were actually first claimed by the English. That this would be important in an Elizabethan world is evident; that this might still be important in a twenty-first-century world is a proposition to which I return in a later chapter.

Is the Plate a hoax? I think the answer is almost certainly yes, although the final decision I leave to the reader. Was this a hoax that got out of hand? Were these enthusiastic youths directed by a couple of older individuals who got tangled in the web of deceit when the enterprise spun out of control? Whatever one decides, we must all admit that the story is a good one and has kept people interested and involved for many decades. In the late 1930s it made Beryl Shinn a small fortune and in doing so fulfilled the dreams of an aging and respected professor. If you have bought this book, the story still continues to generate some revenue even today. Whatever one perceives ground truth to be, the Plate remains a wonderful and intriguing entity. Hoax or not, the physical Plate now has its own place in the history of California. The general message with respect to cognitive deception is that, having launched an enterprise (hoax or not), it will take on a life of its own in the world and may rapidly move beyond the control of any one individual or even a group of individuals. In essence, deceit, as maladaptive information, persists and often proliferates in the environment and may therefore exert unforeseen consequences far into the future. Thus, in the same way as hope, hoax springs eternal.

REFERENCE NOTES

[1] See, for example, Nowell, C. E. (Ed.). (1962). *Magellan's voyage around the world: Three contemporary accounts.* Evanston, IL: Northwestern University Press.

[2] Kraus, H. P. (1970). *Sir Francis Drake: A pictorial biography.* Amsterdam: N. Israel. See also Hague, J. D. (1908). The Drake medal. *Bulletin of the American Geographical Society, 40*(8), 449–469.

[3] Drake, F. (1628). *The world encompassed by Sir Francis Drake: being his next voyage to that to Nombre de Dios Elibron, Classics series, Issue 16 of Works issued by the Hakluyt Society.* Adamant Media Corporation.

[4] See Kelsey, H. (1998). *Sir Francis Drake: The queen's pirate.* New Haven, CT: Yale Nota Bene Book, Yale University Press.

[5] See *California Historical Quarterly* (1974), 53(3), whole issue.

[6] See, for example, the undated pamphlet; "Nova Albion" Printed for the "Silverado Squatters" (Allen, E. W., Dickinson, E. D., Farquhar, F. P., Grabhorn, E., Kent, A. H., Merner, G. D., Moss, M. W., Sweetland, E. J., and Wheat, C. I.), in the author's possession. See also Oko, A. D. (1964). Francis Drake and Nova Albion. *California Historical Society Quarterly*, 43(2), 1–24. See also Heizer, R. F. (1947). *Francis Drake and the California Indians, 1579*. Berkeley: University of California Press; Neasham, V. A., & Pritchard, W. E. (1974). *Drake's California landing: The evidence for Bolinas Lagoon*. Sacramento, CA: Western Heritage Inc.; Power, R. H. (1974). *Francis Drake & San Francisco Bay: A beginning of the British Empire*. Davis: University of California, Davis.

[7] The dates of Drake's residency were recorded as June 17 to July 23; however, this would be in the calendar that preceded our own. In present-day terms, the equivalent period would have been from June 27 to August 2.

[8] Power, R.H.(1974). *Francis Drake & San Francisco Bay: A beginning of the British Empire*. Literary Associates of the University Literary, Davis; Davis, CA.

[9] See http://en.wikipedia.org/wiki/Jodocus_Hondius. See also "Vera Totius Expeditionius Nauticae Descriptio D. Franc. Draci, etc," engraved by Jodocus Hondius the Elder, *Sir Francis Drake' Voyage Round the World: Two Contemporary Maps*.

[10] The argument is one that persists throughout this whole issue of Drake's expedition. Consider, for example, the conclusion of Shangraw, C., & Von der Porten, E. P. (1981). *The Drake and Cermeno expeditions' Chinese porcelains at Drake's Bay, California*, concerning the Point Reyes site. They conclude: "Forty-one years after the first Chinese blue-on-white porcelain sherds were found at Drake's Bay and the question of their sources was posed, the answer can confidently be stated: thirty-three percent of the porcelains were abandoned by Francis Drake in 1579 and sixty-seven percent were lost in the wreck of Sebastian Rodriguez Cermeno's San Agustin in 1595." Like with all the statements about the location of Drake's landing (the cited one here being Limantour Lagoon), you will be able to find some to dispute this assertion. It has been suggested, however, that a consensus is beginning to emerge for this particular site.

[11] Drake, F. (1628). *The world encompassed*. London: Printed for Nicholas Bourne, Royall Exchange.

[12] Drake, op cit.

[13] See *Berkeley Daily Gazette* (1937). Famous Sir Francis Drake "Plate of Brasse" found. April 7. Also, *Oakland Post and Enquirer* (1937). A young man finds one of history's treasures, April 7.

[14] See Haselden, B. B. (1937). Is the Drake Plate of Brass genuine? *California Historical Society Quarterly*, 16(3), 271–274.

[15] The news of the find was widespread but especially noted in Plymouth, England, which had so many associations with Drake; see *Daily Gazette* (1937). Casual find may change history: Record of Drake's landing in America, May 27. See also *Western Morning News* (1938). Map maker in Golden Hind? Question raised at Plymouth. California Brass Plate problem. March 17.

[16] See this text in Starr, W. A. (1957) Evidence of Drake's visit to California, 1579. *California Historical Society Quarterly*, 36(1), 31–34. Also see Hamilton, A. (1937). A lost treasure found. *Los Angeles Times Sunday Magazine*, May 23. There is speculation that Shinn may not have been so dissociated with the Plate as the role of "innocent" finder implies. Who was his fellow teammate on Kahn's baseball team and what was their connection to Berkeley and the Clampers? Could Shinn have been in on it, or was he an unknowing dupe? As James Spitze has noted, there is still much to learn about this part of the story.

[17] Hyman, A. D. (1937). Drake's Plate claiming bay area found. *San Francisco Examiner*, April, 7.

[18] Von der Porten, E., Aker, R., Allen, R. W., & Spitze, J. M. (2002). Who made Drake's Plate of Brass? Hint: It wasn't Francis Drake. *California History*, 81(2), 116–133, 168–171.

[19] *Oakland Tribune* (1937). Drake Plate finder weds on $2000; He never liked history in school. April 7.

[20] For more detail, see Bocqueraz, L. E. (1956). Finding of the Drake Plate. (Oakland). This is a typed transcript of a tape-recorded interview of November 8, 1955, conducted by Willa Baum for the Regional Cultural History Project. University of California Library, Berkeley. And see note 43 in Oko (1964) op cit (p. 22).

[21] For more on Caldeira's story, see Starr, W. A. op cit. Modern opinion has swung away from Caldeira as a reliable source. Some, if not many, now suspect that his story was simply a form of publicity seeking. Interestingly, it may imply a much more involved and potentially conspiratorial role for Shinn.

[22] See the comments in Gale, I. (2003). Drake's 'plate of brasse' proven a hoax. *Point Reyes Light*, February 20.

[23] See also Von der Porten et al. op cit (p. 123).

[24] For an interesting overview, see also Farquhar, F. P. (1957). A review of the evidence. *California Historical Society Quarterly*, 36(1), 22–30.

[25] See Farquhar (1957) op cit (p. 28).

[26] See Cyril Stanley Smith's 1976 Metallurgical Report on "Francis Drake's Brass Plate," *MIT Institute Archives and Special Collections*. Retrieved January 11, 2011 from http://libraries.mit.edu/archives/exhibits/drake/index.html.

[27] See Drake (1628) op cit.

[28] For an early example of the content of the text on the Plate, see the *Oakland Tribune*, April 6, 1937.

[29] Haselden, R. B. (1937). Is the Drake Plate of Brass genuine? *California Historical Society Quarterly*, 16(3), 271–274.

[30] See Bolton, H. E. (1937). Francis Drake's Plate of Brass (pp. 1–16), and Watson, D. S. (1937). Drake and California. In *Drake's Plate of Brass: Evidence of his visit to California in 1579*. San Francisco: California Historical Society. Also see the review in *Times Literary Supplement* (London), May 22, 1937.

[31] Fink, C. G., & Polushkin, E.P. (1938). *Drake's plate of brass authenticated*. California Historical Society, Special Publication No. 14, San Francisco, CA.

[32] Fink & Polushkin (1938) op cit. See also *Berkeley Daily Gazette*, December 6, 1938, and *San Francisco Examiner*, December 7, 1938.

[33] For information on and an illustration of this Plate, see Von der Porten et al. (2002) op cit (pp. 124–125).

[34] For an example of Harlow's work, see Harlow, V. T. (Ed.). (1929). *Voyages of great pioneers*. London: Oxford University Press.

[35] See http://www.worldlingo.com/ma/enwiki/en/Robin_Flower.

[36] Morison, S. E. (1978). *The great explorers: The European discovery of America*. New York: Oxford University Press.

[37] Hart, J. D. (1977). *The plate of brass reexamined*. Berkeley: Bancroft Library, University of California.

[38] Hart, J. D. (1979). The *plate of brass reexamined: A supplementary report*. Berkeley: Bancroft Library, University of California.

[39] Von der Porten et al. (2002) op cit.

[40] Edwin Grabhorn, who published work on U.S. western history, produced a spoof letter purportedly from the Consolidated Brasse and Novelty Company. This letter offered a "special line of brass plates" that were guaranteed to "make your home-town famous." Also see Von der Porten et al. (2002) op cit, and http://en.wikipedia.org/wiki/Drake's_Plate_of_Brass. The only known copy of this letter is currently in the possession of James Spitze.

[41] E Clampus Vitus. (1937). *Ye preposterous booke of brasse*. San Francisco: E Clampus Vitus.

[42] Von der Porten et al. (2002) op cit.

[43] See Shumate, A. (1996). The mysterious history of E. Clampus Vitus. In R. F. Schoeppner & R. J. Chandler (Eds.), *California vignettes* (pp. 39–49), Brand Book, cited in Von der Porten et al. (2002) op cit (p. 168, n. 4).

[44] It seems rather evident that the institution that possesses the Plate (i.e., the Bancroft Library of the University of California at Berkeley) has already concluded that the Plate is indeed a fake, as noted in one of their official press releases (i.e., Maclay, K. Historical journal reports secrets behind infamous 'Drake's Plate' hoax. *U.C. Berkeley News*, February 18, 2003).

[45] But see the work of Shangraw, C., & Von der Porten, E. P. (1981) op cit.

II

THE PSYCHOLOGY OF DECEPTION

ELEMENTS OF DECEPTION

Up to this point, I have provided a general introduction to cognitive deception and recounted two stories in which deception, or at least potential deception, has played a central role. We need now to take a step back from the specific details of each of the respective stories and begin to explore the overall principles involved. To do this, I look specifically to examine the fundamental psychological dimensions that underlie deception. As noted in the more academic chapters that follow, the human aspects of deception have grown from their more general form found in the animal world. We have seen that deceptions in the animal world have their genesis in life's overall struggle for survival. Primitive forms of deception have thus been around since life itself began. Basic forms of deception are largely illusions to confound the senses. While some deceptions are unintentional, the form with which we are centrally concerned here are those of the conscious kind brought about by the intentional mind. Our examination of these forms of deception must therefore focus on the principles of human psychology.

Human beings typically categorize the domain of deception through reference to a variety of different semantic labels. These include terms such as forgeries, practical jokes, impostures, conjuring tricks, confidence games, consumer frauds, military deceptions, white lies, feints, ploys, gambling scams, and psychic hoaxes, together with other associated labels [1]. Obviously, these differing facets of misrepresentation overlap to some greater or lesser extent. In addition to these differing terms, we also tend to class deceptions according to an associated moral judgment. So, while white lies and practical jokes might be considered merely reprehensible, fraud and forgery are considered egregious and criminal activities. In one of the many paradoxes of morality and deception, we might publicly abhor deception as practiced by our enemies but fully expect our own associates to be efficient and effective in exactly the same forms of deceit [2]. To an extent, we can try, intellectually, to separate the principles of deception from its subsequent effects and therefore from our crucial, moral appraisal of that deception. However, as we shall find in several of the stories that follow, deceptions often trigger extremes of emotion both in their practice and in their subsequent revelation. Victims of a fraud, hoax, or even practical joke rarely, if ever, view the incident in a totally impersonal and dispassionate manner.

TOP-DOWN AND BOTTOM-UP

To understand the general principles of deception, we must first try painting the broad picture of how people understand their world. When most people consider this question, they implicitly begin with what is traditionally known in psychology as a bottom-up approach. That is to say, they think their behavior depends on what their senses tell them about the world in front of them right now. Actually, this is quite a reasonable assumption, given that reality is almost always so immediate that its impact frequently overwhelms our pensive thoughts about either the past or the future. Therefore, to a reasonable degree, this bottom-up view is a correct one. Our sensory organs are indeed sending a constant volley of electronic impulses coursing into our brain. *Bottom-up processing* thus describes this phenomenon very well since the bottom is both correct in a spatial sense (the brain being near the top of the body) and in a processing sense (the brain is where most of the integrative processing of stimuli occur). However, important as these bottom-up processes are, most people grossly underestimate the degree to which these incoming sensory signals are modified by, and are contingent on, the information already present in the brain – that is, on the top-down processes.

One of the first modifications to incoming sensory input is achieved through the capacities of attention. In classical psychology, considerable research has been focused on the nature of such attention and how it acts to "filter" the incoming sensory information for subsequent processing [3]. For example, a classic effect in psychology concerns the "cocktail party effect" [4]. Imagine for a moment that you are attending a noisy cocktail party where a number of conversations are going on at once. You may well be listening to a person in your immediate group but you are certainly also aware of the other noise in the background. Suddenly, in an adjacent conversation, you hear your own name spoken. How did you manage to hear this specific utterance? How is it that what one moment ago was just noise has suddenly become the focus of your attention? This question has intrigued experimental psychologists for decades and shows that attention is not some simple all-or-none capacity but is actually a highly complex phenomenon. Indeed, although reality appears so immediate and so simple, its composition is actually very complicated. Therefore, I cannot emphasize enough that the world as we perceive it is actually a *hybrid compilation* of things occurring at the present point in time and experiences we derive from our individual past, as well as our expectations about the future. Some of these memories and their associated effects are particularly influential in the way we experience our moments of present reality.

Of course, most of our past experiences are mere echoes and exert only the slightest of effects. Sadly, for our full understanding of behavior, these respective influences vary as a function of our own specific history as well as the nature of the things we are presently encountering. This makes individual human behavior very hard to predict with any great degree of accuracy. While the incoming sensory-based information is predominantly the bottom-up component, our memory and attentional capacities are more reasonably characterized as the complimentary top-down processes. So, as we try to understand more about deception, we can define the initial bottom-up effects as being *the content of experience contingent upon immediate sensory and perceptual stimulation.* In contrast, top-down influences dictate *the composition of reality as mediated by memory, attention, and expectation.* These two definitions act as guidelines to help us comprehend the nature of psychological reality. For it is only within this world of psychological reality that we can understand how deception exerts its influence.

THE PROCESSING OF COMPOSITE REALITY

My reason for distinguishing in detail the differences between cognitive and sensory deceptions in an earlier chapter should now be clear. As we can see from the definitions given in the preceding section, sensory deceptions are primarily bottom-up phenomena whereas cognitive deceptions are primarily top-down in nature. I place a particular emphasis here on the word "primarily" because, in the fluid and interactive processes of the human nervous system, the flow of information is virtually never unidirectional. So, pure top-down or pure bottom-up processes are each extremely rare. Having established this general principle, the next step is to provide a

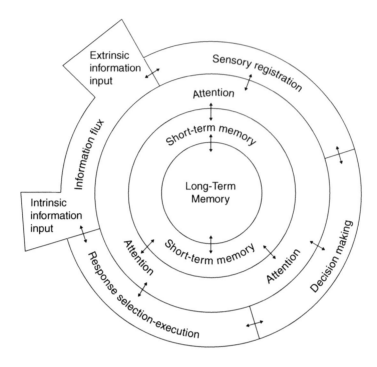

FIGURE II.1. A representation of the interrelationships of components of the human processing system.

working model of such human processing capacities. In graphic form, this model is presented in Figure II.1.

This illustration of human processing capabilities is organized in the form of a circle, mainly because the content of the world we currently perceive is founded, to a major degree, on our own immediate prior actions. So, for example, it is clear that our view of the world changes as we move around in it. From this perspective, we are partly, if not mainly, responsible for what we see, hear, feel, and touch since the content of our present world clearly depends on our own prior self-directed movements [5]. This is another way of saying we partly control the content of our own reality. But crucially, of course, we do not control all of it!

New, unusual, and surprising things often happen in the world. When we come into contact with this novel information, we have to use our prior knowledge and the current context to try to make sense of what we are experiencing. In contrast, when we encounter what we expect – and this, of course, happens most of the time – we have a number of fairly well-learned routines that take advantage of our existing knowledge. Thus, much of behavior is "automated" to the degree that we don't have to consciously "think" about it. And this is a very good thing because thinking requires energy – a lot of energy [6]. Making use of shortcuts and previously stored knowledge and processes is a great way to get around the costly act of cogitation. Such "short-circuiting" strategies work well under most circumstances. The world is indeed regular and predictable, and we, as a species, have undergone extensive evolution to take advantage of these regularities. After all, given that we have survived and thrived so far, we are presumably quite "fit" as a species.

These automatic processes are quite often what we refer to as "unconscious" actions. At one time, some of these unconscious processes were the subject of our active, conscious attention. Remember, for example, when you were first learning to drive and all of the concurrent demands were so overwhelming and confusing. But gradually, most of these skills became "automatic" until there comes a time when, as an experienced driver, you barely think about them at all. Well, think of that learning process now. We possess many processes that our long-distant ancestors have already "automated" for us hundreds of thousands, if not millions, of years ago. We don't have to pay attention to these because we often are not even aware of their presence. They still represent important and effective ways of dealing with the environment but they are running in the "background" as it were, without involving the conscious mind. Virtually no one now alive has ever had to deal with them consciously except in pathological conditions where things go "wrong."

Occasionally, however, these processes do not fit well with the surrounding environment (especially in our new technologically constructed environment, with which they were never designed to cope). For example, remember John F. Kennedy, Jr. and his tragic and fatal aviation accident? Those instrument-based flight conditions represented one of the circumstances in which processes that had evolved to deal with terrestrial conditions were "fooled" because he was up in the air. Humans did not evolve to fly or to operate an aircraft. As with driving, the skills necessary to fly a plane successfully can be acquired, and grow more "automatic" with experience. But for an inexperienced pilot, physiological and psychological processes that work fine on the ground can and often do lead to reactions that generate fatal failures when forced to face unusual flight circumstances.

Fortunately for most of us, these instances are relatively rare, but such exceptions show that "unconscious" processes are far from perfect. Still, we should be grateful for having them. Imagine having to think about each and every step you make, or each and every breath that you take. You simply wouldn't have the time or the energy to think about anything else. In fact, much of our behavior is pre-programmed precisely so we do not have to think about it [7]. But not all of our behavior can be pre-programmed or automatic since there remains much in this world that we do not know and cannot anticipate. We cannot assume that all of our assumptions will be safe, and so the act of thinking has great value.

FROM INFORMATION UNCERTAINTY TO COHERENT BEHAVIOR

With regard to the model presented in Figure II.1, we can begin our journey toward understanding deception by starting from the location labeled "information flux." This one is a big favorite of research psychologists. It simply means that some things we experience (i.e., see, hear, feel, etc.) depend directly on our own behavior, but others do not. In other words, some of the world we can predict while other bits, the surprising bits, we cannot. Nature has perfected the trick of enabling living things to deal with most of the unexpected conditions by using the skills and capacities they have previously developed. Here is where selected capacities like memory and attention come to the fore. Taking advantage of regularities, and thus not having to think about them too much, the processing system can focus its conscious energy on the new, unusual, or ambiguous information. What precisely is it about the conditions that are new or surprising? Do these new and surprising things present a threat, or is there any chance for gain? And precisely how can we take advantage of the opportunities this new information presents?

The aforementioned bottom-up sequence is the first step in sorting out this information flux. What one classical psychologist William James, called the "blooming, buzzing, confusion" of the young child's experience must, even in our own adult world, be parsed into the known and the unknown. Such processes happen very quickly and some can even be performed by the sensory systems themselves (e.g., in the retina of the eye and in the blink of an eye). For example, suppose there was a large truck bearing down on us (it could potentially be a charging rhino, of course; the principle is the same). Now, spending a long time distinguishing the truck's color, model, and make would be a very risky thing to do. Indeed, it might crush us well before we even begin this discovery process. So, rather than trying to capture all that "new" information, characteristics associated with the survival instinct kick in and the perceptual system can use a property called time-to-contact to distinguish when and whether we might be hit. This enables us to get out of the way [8]. Sadly, of course, we are not always successful, and one can argue whether such failures are due to bad genes or bad luck [9].

From the point of view of the model, the outer ring of capacities in Figure II.1 would proceed to act very quickly with little reference to other processes, such as long-term memory. After all, if you are hit by the truck, long-term memory is probably not going to be much use to you for a while, if indeed ever again. But most situations we encounter are, thankfully, not quite so threatening. So, novelties and ambiguities in the information flux can be considered at a little more leisurely pace. To process unfamiliar elements, we now have to focus our attention on them and log them into short-term memory if we are going to perform any transformations and transactions upon them. If they prove to be important or useful, we are liable then to want to place them into long-term memory from where they can be extracted for use later [10].

Extraction at a later point in time is at the heart of this top-down influence. In long-term memory, things are stored neither haphazardly nor in a simple chronological sequence. Rather, the stored information is linked together in a number of functional ways. These ways are largely predicated on the understanding that they need to be used to deal with the future [11]. Putting these processes in the form of a round diagram can make it seem that somewhere in the brain there are some nice little boxes that contain each of these respective functions. This is, however, very far from the truth. Sadly for researchers in human behavior, there are no such boxes, and even the idea of discrete "areas" in the brain that deal with readily identifiable functions has proven to be a proposition fraught with peril [12]. In cognitive deceptions, long-term memories play a critical role. Indeed, these memories can go beyond purely personal ones as some of our long-term memories stem as much from the culture to which we belong as from our own personal history. We are "carriers" of these long-term ideas. A clever deception plays on these forms of cultural long-term memory because we often take the truth of such memories for granted based on the testimony of others we trust, rather than finding out independently ourselves whether or not they are true. What we assume to be the case can sometimes be very wrong, and a cunning deception takes full advantage of such flawed assumptions.

Occurring at the confluence of long-term memory and decision-making capacity, these assumptions can be located at the appropriate point in Figure II.1. However, like all other forms of psychological "box models," missing from this antiseptic representation of the mind is, in truth, its very essence.

In psychology, this essence is described by the general term "energetics" [13]. One of the primary energetic dimensions is emotion and some of its main human expressions are trust and belief. Traditionally, emotion was thought to have relatively little influence on decision making. Recently, however, there has been a dramatic turnaround in thinking on this issue, and so it is to emotion as an aspect of human behavior when dealing with deception that our discussion now turns.

EMOTION AND BELIEF

All deception depends on belief. For deception to succeed, such belief must be sufficiently strong to suppress the more rational and dissociated faculties shown in the processing sequence in Figure II.1. Emotion-laden situations are frequently the site of the triumph of hope over reality. The very best of hoaxes play directly into such desperate aspirations. Deception provides a material foundation for some dearly held hope or belief. It accords with what the individual or group wants to be true and fulfills their wishes in a way that is not obviously contradictory to what is conceivably possible. Thus, emotion-based decision making often features top-down processing, and there is much of wish fulfillment that can be involved in these circumstances. What true Christian and patriot would not want to visit the grave of the legendary King Arthur? What true historian of early California would not have wanted to lay their hands on one of the first European artifacts in the western United States and certain evidence of Francis Drake's visit? In each of the cases we have looked at so far, wish fulfillment has proved to be at the very heart of the act of deception.

All human beings inherit this foible of willing suspension of disbelief, evidenced by the fact that hoaxes and other acts of deception have been occurring throughout recorded history. Thus, we can see that a successful deception frequently uses the inherent hopes, wishes, desires, and beliefs to suppress a person's critical faculties. Indeed, quite often, the greater these hopes, the more the rational abilities to analyze the situation are suppressed. If the deception is powerful enough, the "spell" can never be broken and the vested individuals will never sufficiently activate their critical faculties to be able to rid themselves of the imposed illusion. Thus, there are many cases in which individuals who exhibit even exceptional reasoning abilities in some parts of their life can still divorce themselves from reality sufficiently enough to maintain an illusion in another part of their existence. This argues that hope and desire are very important survival skills, and deception perverts these characteristics in order to be successful.

However, a good deception moves beyond simply playing on an individual's inherent and somewhat passive beliefs. A good hoax presents a mystery, and the better the mystery, the better the hoax. Inherently curious, human beings almost universally love a mystery. The literature of almost all human cultures is riddled with stories of mystery and narratives featuring challenge and resolution. Who were the culprits? What was the reason for their actions? Was the expressed issue ever resolved? *Cui bono?* Such forces are strong drivers of all human interest and attention. Deceptions based on mystery take advantage of the human love of narrative. Indeed, narrative and storytelling are great ways in which humans pass on experience to successive generations. Stories are the source of the collective cultural experience referred to earlier. It is the way for humans to garner critical experience at little cost to oneself. Besides, listening to stories is fun! Mysteries then are some of the most powerful motivations behind hoaxes.

BIFURCATION AND MOTIVATION

One characteristic of the stories I have presented so far – and which also occurs in the stories yet to come – is that they lead to highly divisive expressions of opinion. As I noted earlier, a completely successful deception is never actually acknowledged because it causes no controversy and is accepted as the collective "truth." However, the present stories, like others of their kind, hover around the halfway mark in terms of controversy they generate, with almost equal evidence on both sides of the issue. Advocates and detractors look to emphasize the relative value of the supportive and critical evidence, respectively [14]. This begs the question: When the evidence is so very finely balanced, do we feel compelled to commit ourselves one way or the other? The whole question of commitment can be exacerbated by the tendency of some individuals to think in terms of black or white, the "for us or against us" mind-set [15]. Having once decided which side of the respective fence we are on, it is very difficult then to cross over to the other side or even to sit atop it again. The level of evidence required to change committed minds is very much in proportion to the degree of allegiance a person expresses to an original position. For some minds, no level of evidence is ever sufficient to induce change [16].

Before we proceed to the next series of stories, there is one further dimension we must briefly consider – the motivation of the deceiver. Motivations for deception, in general, include the full range of the human foibles; greed, revenge, spite, and jealousy among them. Each of these is an expression of the energetic facet of human behavior. A hoax is often a way to get even with another individual or a group of individuals by taking something of value from them or by lording one's superiority over their gullibility. This something can range from their dignity to their belief in their position in the world, some other form of resource, or, most prosaically, their money. Deception thus often proves to be a "Robin Hood Syndrome" with a twist of malice: it provides the deceiver with a sense of fulfillment and goal achievement, however inappropriate that goal might appear to others. In a sense, deception has one of the same fundamental motivations as laughter – that is, the discomfiture of authority. Of course, a hoax may well live longer than does its perpetrator. Sometimes this suits the hoaxers, but sometimes they yearn for the exposure of their work. The same form of motivation, perhaps amplified to a much greater degree of maladaptation, can be seen in some cases of serial murder. As you read the next two stories, I invite you to consider the perpetrators and their motivations. We shall advance to the question of deciding on potential cognitive hoaxes after the stories that follow.

REFERENCE NOTES

[1] Hyman, R. (1989). The psychology of deception. *Annual Review of Psychology*, 50, 133–154.
[2] The brilliantly effective surprise attack on Pearl Harbor by the Japanese on December 7, 1941 is termed "the day that will live in infamy" in the United States. The long-range Doolittle Raid on the Japanese home islands on April 18, 1942, is, in contrast, considered a triumph of military strategic planning.
[3] James, W. (1890). *Principles of psychology.* 2 vols. New York: Henry Holt: New York; also Broadbent, D. E. (1958). *Perception and communication.* London: Pergamon Press.
[4] For the classic work on this, see Cherry, E. C. (1953). Some experiments on the recognition of speech, with one and with two ears. *Journal of Acoustic Society of America*, 25(5), 975–979.
[5] In general, the notion of the importance of self-directed motion in understanding behavior comes under the general term "ecological psychology." The foundation of this movement is often associated with the eminent psychologist James J. Gibson; see Gibson, J. J. (1979). *The ecological approach to visual perception.* Boston: Houghton-Mifflin.

[6] See, for example, the argument in Hancock, P. A. (2010). The battle for time in the brain. In J. A. Parker, P. A. Harris, & C. Steineck (Eds.), *Time, limits and constraints: The study of time XIII* (pp. 65–87). Leiden: Brill.

[7] There is even evidence that the control of the stepping motion is hardwired into human babies so they do not have to learn this critical skill from scratch. See Forssberg, H. (1985). Ontogeny of human locomotor control I. Infant stepping, supported locomotion and transition to independent locomotion. *Experimental Brain Research*, 57, 480–493.

[8] For a general overview of the area, see Hancock, P. A., & Manser, M. P. (1998). Time-to-contact. In A. M. Feyer & A. M. Williamson (Eds.). *Occupational injury*. London: Taylor & Francis; more recently, see Smith, M. R. H., Flach, J. M., Stanard, T. W., & Dittman, S. M. (2001). Monocular optical constraints on collision control. *Journal of Experimental Psychology: Human Perception & Performance*, 27(2), 395–410.

[9] Raup, D. M. (1991). *Extinction: Bad genes or bad luck?* New York: W. W. Norton.

[10] Schacter, D. (2001). *The seven sins of memory*. New York: Houghton-Mifflin.

[11] Hancock, P. A, & Shahnami, N. (2010). Memory as a string of pearls. *Kronoscope*, 10, 77–82. See also: Hancock, P. A. (2010). The battle for time in the brain. In J. A. Parker, P. A. Harris, & C. Steineck (Eds.), *Time, limits and constraints: The study of time XIII* (pp. 65–87). Leiden: Brill. Also see Schacter, D. L., & Addis, D. R. (2007). The ghosts of past and future. *Nature*, 445, 27.

[12] Fodor, J. A. (1983). *Modularity of mind*. Cambridge, MA: MIT Press.

[13] Freeman, G. L. (1948). *The energetics of human behavior*. Ithaca, NY: Cornell University Press.

[14] For an example of this form of bifurcation, see Hancock, P. A. (2001). The polarizing plantagenet. *Ricardian Register*, 26(4), 4–7.

[15] See Hendrick, H. W. (2010). *It all begins with self*. Salt Lake City, UT: Millennial Mind Publishing.

[16] The same process often occurs in legal cases, with each side seeking to support their own interpretation of events. Nominally, the "truth" is supposed to emerge from the advocacy provided by each side. In reality, the only thing usually to emerge is a winner, since the legal system seems strangely but frequently concerned not with objective truth, but rather only with the persuasion in favor of the truth as one of the sides sees it. Thus a skillful attorney can overcome a poor case, and vice versa.

The Kensington Runestone

The Vikings in Minnesota – For Sure, For Sure

THE SETTING OF THE RUNESTONE

The small settlement of Kensington is situated in the west-central part of Minnesota, some 23 miles from Alexandria, which is the largest local town. Minnesota, like several other north-central states of the United States, has a predominantly immigrant population largely of Scandinavian and northern Germanic ancestry. Even today, intrinsic cultural influences remain obvious, from institutional names to the specialties of the local diet [1]. Various claims have been made as to the different dates of initial occupation, but the generally accepted era is around the late 1860s [2]. Indeed, the first government survey of this particular region was made in 1866, although settlers began to move into the locality of Douglas County around 1858 when Minnesota first became a state [3]. Like many lands of the Mississippi headwaters, the prairie around Kensington is agriculturally fertile, but not every immigrant was lucky enough to secure a prime section. Some of the rolling hills are predominantly rock and stone rather than soil and are often surrounded by marshlands and overrun by stunted woods. Such land was still available in 1890 when a thirty-six-year-old immigrant of Scandinavian descent named Olof Ohman [4] decided to grub his farm from this section of Minnesota, rather than trekking west to the still open plains of the Dakota Territory.

FINDING THE RUNESTONE

Olof Ohman took up occupancy in 1890 and his property was specifically designated as the SE 1/4 section 14, of Solem Township, of Douglas County, in the state of Minnesota. Figure 3.1 provides a rough map of Ohman's holding [5]. Eight years after he first occupied the property, he was still in the process of clearing and improving the land. In the late

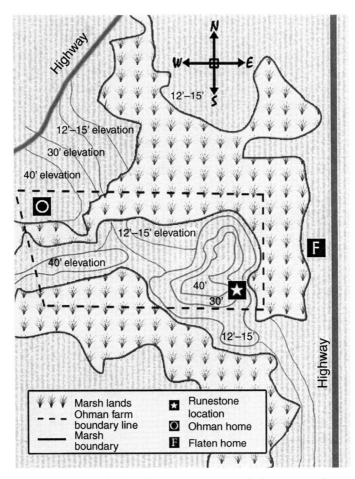

FIGURE 3.1. A sketch of the Ohman property and the surrounding vicinity. Illustration by Richard Kessler (after Holand). © Peter Hancock.

summer and early fall of 1898, he was engaged in such efforts on the portion of his property opposite his house and farm buildings. On or about November 8th of that year, he discovered a stone clasped in the roots of a large aspen tree [6]. The stone, with the inscribed side facing down, was "flipped over with the tree as it fell" [7]. To give an idea about how long the stone might have been in the ground, the girth of the toppled tree was estimated to be some 8–10 inches in diameter, and the height was approximately 18 feet. Ohman's son Arthur, who was about eight years of age at the time, confirmed that many people inspected this find while the stone was still entangled in the tree's roots [8]. Among these individuals were the Flaten family, whose farmhouse was actually nearer to the discovery site than Ohman's own home. In addition to the three Ohmans and Nils Flaten, two other locals, Roald Benson and Samuel Olson, witnessed the first moments the runestone saw daylight [9]. Five of these individuals later signed affidavits as to the circumstances of discovery, including Ohman himself, his son Edward, and Nils Flaten. Landsverk's book (1961, pp. 62–69) gives Arthur Ohman's own personal account of the find:

> I am completely certain that no one in the Ohman or Flaten families could have, desired to, or actually did have any part in a forgery. My Father was absolutely honest. Everyone in the community knew and acknowledged this. He was not a man for practical jokes, hoaxing, or scheming. Furthermore, how could he possibly have covered up such a hoax with his own family and friends even if he had wished to do so? My Father could not possibly have carved the inscription. He was not ever more than a fair stonemason. He did not even own stonemason's chisels until considerably after 1898.... none of us ever expected or dreamed that it would ever become such a controversial issue. [10]

THE PHYSICAL APPEARANCE OF THE STONE

What Ohman had unearthed was an irregular, rectangular slab of greywacke measuring roughly some 30-by-15-by-6 inches in size and weighing a total of just under 202 pounds. A picture of the stone as it appears today is shown in Figure 3.2 [11]. Originally, it seems that farmer Ohman had taken little notice of the stone when he first unearthed it. Apparently some little time later it was another of his sons, Edward, who had brought his father some refreshment out into the field and was either poking at the stone with a stick or brushing it with his cap when he observed some markings. After digging some dirt out of the scratches, he called his father and others to take a closer look [12]. Physically, the runestone appears to resemble a somewhat smallish tombstone, and the part with the carving appears to have been designed to stand above the ground with the rest of the unmarked stone embedded in it. It was reportedly found at a slanting angle, with one end almost protruding from the ground and the runes that Edward had observed facing downward [13].

On closer examination there appeared to be several lines of markings on the stone and it was these that had intrigued young Edward and are shown in detail in Figure 3.3 [14]. There is no evidence that any of the initial discoverers

FIGURE 3.2. Farmer Ohman's find, the Kensington Runestone. Photo courtesy of the Minnesota Historical Society.

were able to tell what these markings meant, and a generally acceptable translation only appeared sometime after this initial disinterment.

The following is now generally accepted as the translation of what is written.

> Eight Goths [Swedes] and Twenty-Two Norwegians upon an exploring journey from Vinland very far west. We had camp by two Skerries, one day's journey North from this Stone. We were fishing one day. When we returned home, we found ten men red with blood and dead. AVM save us from the evil. We have ten men by the sea to look after our vessel fourteen days journey from this island. Year 1362. [15]

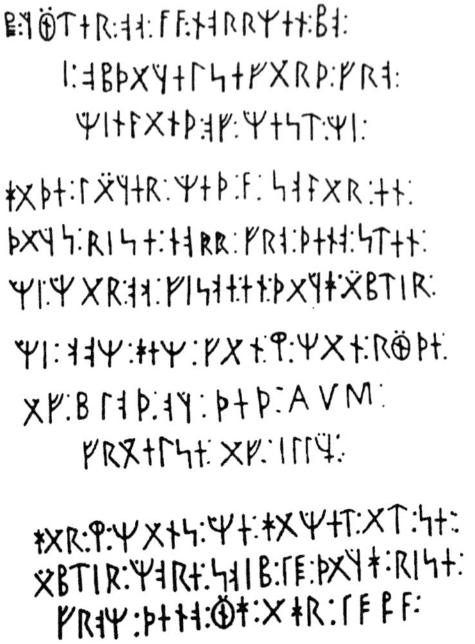

FIGURE 3.3. The inscription on the Kensington Runestone. Image by the Author.

THE STORY ON THE STONE

It is worth taking a little time here to consider the story the stone purports to tell. The date is probably its most startling feature – prominently displayed and given as an exact number, 1362 AD, rather than referencing the year of some king's reign or of the expedition itself. Indeed, it squarely places this exploration 130 years before Christopher Columbus began his transatlantic voyage. Reading back into the inscription, it implies the stone was set up on an island. However, Ohman's discovery was in the middle of a vast plain; how was this conundrum to be explained? Had the slightly higher ground of the discovery previously been an island, or had the stone been moved there? Further, which sea was fourteen days' journey away and how far was a day's journey to such people anyway? Where was Vinland? And how far west was it? Was it west of the discovery, or was the discovery west from it? Why Swedes and Norwegians? Why in this proportion? Where were the skerries (small rocky islands), and did the death of the ten men take place at the skerries or the present site? What happened to the men? Were they attacked by the local inhabitants of the time, or was this rather a virulent attack of the plague? Does the inscription AVM actually mean *Ave Virgo Maria* (save us, Virgin Mary) [16]? Having found, presumably, one-third of their party dead, why would anyone in much potential danger sit down and immediately begin to carve a Runestone monument? More generally, why did they have come to this region and did any members of this putative expedition ever return to their homeland? Allied to these questions are issues of whether there is any corroborating evidence from any other source beside the stone itself [17].

As is clearly evident, the inscription itself raised any number of questions, and while it is very specific about some aspects such as the date, the numerical composition of the party, and the days traveling between various points, it is curiously silent on other specifics such as who led the expedition, who carved the Stone, under whose mandate they were exploring, what had they hoped to find, and the like. For authentication purposes, one cannot invoke the issues of time and accuracy with respect to some parts of the inscription only to contradict them with respect to others, although several commentators have done just this. If the expedition had time to carve the story that appears, surely they could have named some, if not all, of the individuals who died if the Stone was intended to serve as a commemorative monument. As we have seen, there is plenty of physical space left on the Runestone for more words to be included. Thus, the combination of certain exact information (i.e., the critical date) combined with frustrating omissions (e.g., the sponsor of the voyage) argues that the story on the stone is meant to intrigue and not exhaustively inform. Any expedition looking to use the stone as a claim of both presence and possession would, as Drake's Plate does, surely be more specific. If the carver of the Runestone had sufficient time at this dreadful juncture to sit down and recount the horrible and bloodthirsty story it communicates in stone, why did that individual not possess the time to provide a much more extended litany of specific details that would have proved unequivocal? This combination of fact and omission tends, to some degree, to argue against the authenticity of the discovery.

FOLLOWING THE DISCOVERY

All these questions were very much in the future for those who had witnessed the discovery and seen the stone moved to the buildings that composed Ohman's farmstead. Arthur then confirmed that his brother had taken special interest in the carved symbols after the stone was brushed and washed [18].

The cleaned stone was seen by more witnesses, among them Hans Moen, a local shoemaker. After a "few days" the Stone was taken to Kensington and exhibited in a local bank or store as an object of general interest [19]. However, as the writer Blegen noted, no one photographed the Stone at the site of the find or even later when it was exhibited in the town [20]. In fact, the record is problematically silent about the immediate two months after the find.

What follows is a simplified account of a potentially much more complex sequence, and anyone wishing to make a special study of the Runestone is encouraged to begin with Blegen's text, especially his chapter on "Documents and Puzzles" that tries to provide a complete account of these various convolutions [21]. At some juncture when the stone was in Kensington, a copy of the inscription was made by a Mr. John Hedberg and sent to Sven Turnblad, the publisher of a Swedish-language newspaper in Minneapolis [22]. The editor, thinking the symbols were Greek, sent it to the University of Minnesota to be translated. Personnel at the University recognized the inscription as runic and forwarded the copy to Olaus Breda who was a professor of Scandinavian Languages at Minnesota. Breda perceived it to be a curious mixture of Swedish, Norwegian, and English words and thought that even though it was likely a hoax, it still merited further study [23]. Breda provided an initial translation but could not decipher the numerals, and although his translation was similar in content to the one presented earlier in this chapter, it was nowhere near as complete or as evocative, as the readers can see for themselves if they ignore the numbers, especially the date "1362."

In February 1899, the stone was shipped to Professor George Curme, an expert in old German at Northwestern University in Chicago [24]. Together with his assistant, John Steward, Curme examined the stone and provided a number of evolving translations but finally concluded, largely on linguistic grounds, that it was "ungenuine." Meanwhile Professor Breda in Minneapolis had independently solicited the opinion of Ludvig Wimmer of Denmark and Sophus Bugge of Norway, experts on runic inscriptions. These experts pronounced the inscription a fraud [25]. The Runestone itself was back from Chicago and returned to Ohman, who stored it within his farm buildings. In the spring of 1899, some efforts were made to excavate in the area around the location where the Runestone was found. Unfortunately, nothing further of interest was discovered. The Runestone now seemed destined for a fate of quiet obscurity and the oblivion of old newspaper clippings about local oddities. A catalyst was missing, but this was soon rectified.

ENTER THE RUNESTONE'S CHAMPION

From the early summer of 1899 to the late summer of 1907, the Runestone gradually faded into obscurity. The picturesque story later told was that it had formed the step to Ohman's granary door, an assertion that was later flatly contradicted by both of Ohman's sons [26]. However, somewhere in the farm buildings the stone might well have stayed, except for an enterprising young scholar named Hjalmar Rued Holand. I think it is safe to say that if it were not for Holand and his extensive championing of the stone, we would probably know very little of this artifact today [27]. Holand himself descended from immigrant Norwegian stock. He had previously been engaged in research on immigration to and the Norwegian settlement of the upper United States as a scholar at the University of Wisconsin. The story of how the stone first came to Holand's notice is rather unclear; several versions have appeared over the years. One story is that he chanced upon it during his tour of the local area looking for cultural oddities. A second version of events, also from Holand's own pen, reports a more deliberate trip with a viewing of the stone as the expressed purpose in mind. In his book, Blegen tracks down a much earlier 1899 newspaper article by Holand in the Chicago *Skandinaven*. This article suggests a clear interest on Holand's behalf in both runestones and the primacy of Norwegian heritage in the discovery of America, a full eight years before Holand even arrived in Kensington [28]. Such an observation must temper our understanding with respect to Holand's motivations and his subsequent actions. The suggestion that his was just a chance encounter with the Runestone must be treated with significant caution.

It is hard to distill a man's thoughts, but from his initially expressed doubts about the Runestone prior to his visit, Holand certainly had his "conversion on the road to Damascus," or in this case on the road from Kensington. One of the first things Holand needed to do was secure the stone for himself. Again, we enter murky waters as to exactly what went on between farmer Ohman and scholar Holand. One can well imagine a good, old-fashioned Scandinavian bargaining session, which is exactly what Holand reports in his autobiography [29]. Holand asks Ohman what he will take for the stone; Ohman replies, "How much will you give?" Holand offers five dollars and Ohman suggests ten. After some further haggling, Holand describes Ohman magnanimously concluding: *I think you are as poor as I am, so you can have the stone for nothing.* Stirring though this picture of the grizzled farmer and young researcher is, such an account does not seem to accord with any other record. Holand had told others that he had bought the stone for twenty-five dollars while Ohman denied ever giving the stone to Holand for his

personal possession, but rather indicated that he lent the stone to Holand
as an exhibit for the Norwegian Society of Minneapolis or the Minnesota
Historical Society; it is again unclear which [30]. Over the years that followed, Ohman and his sons continued to assert their ownership.

Having secured possession of the stone, Holand himself did at one time
look to make a significant financial profit from it [31]. Whether or not we
now have another stereotypical case of the city slicker making a bit of a
fool of his country cousin is not clear. What is evident is that Holand went
ahead and declared the runestone genuine, and, from January 1908, began
what can only be called a crusade to establish and cement the authenticity
of the stone and thereby its implication of the primacy of America's discovery by the Scandinavians. Holand had found his life's focus. He sought
to establish a degree of provenance for the stone through his identification
of the potential link to the Paul Knutson expedition authorized by King
Magnus in 1354 [32]. Nominally this was a voyage to reestablish Christianity
in Norse settlements, but Holand argued that some members of the expedition had proceeded on to Kensington, eventually returning to Norway
around 1364. Like other intriguing linkages that Holand sought to establish,
this one suffers from a lack of corroborative evidence. It cannot logically be
excluded as a remote possibility, but it certainly does not represent the order
of evidence that generates any strong confidence in the stone's authenticity.
Holand also sought to use linguistic arguments, the putative identification
of other Norse artifacts in America, the association with other mysterious
structures such as the Newport Tower in Connecticut [33], and an undy-
ing personal conviction to fight what was for him the good fight. Until his
death in 1963, at the age of ninety-one, Holand published and republished
material in support of the stone's authenticity. He debated and responded
to detractors and championed it at every turn. Today, the essential question
still remains: Was he right, was it wishful thinking on his part, was he simply deluded, or could he have been the deluder?

TESTING THE STONE

The Runestone had slumbered for almost a decade, but it was in for a rude
awakening. Around the end of the first decade of the twentieth century, a
sequence of pronouncements was made concerning the stone, some unfa-
vorable but none totally dismissive [34]. While individual researchers came
and left, Holand proved to be the one continuous thread throughout the

story. The persistence of the Runestone's claim came, in part, from its divide-and-conquer characteristic. For example, an expert in geology would object to some aspect of the rock itself but immediately disclaim any knowledge of runic symbols. Investigators who could go to the vicinity of the find took extensive evidence about the discovery itself and the inhabitants there-abouts, but most often they were not geologists. The potential for fraud was considered, but the limited knowledge of such on-site investigators in geology and runology handicapped definitive pronouncements. Runologists did evaluate the stone, but most of the time they were far away, in Sweden or Norway, and worked mostly from copied inscriptions or at best from indistinct photographs. From whatever angle the stone was criticized, it was always possible to find a response. And Holand was always the man to provide it.

It was almost certainly Holand who first persuaded the museum committee of the Minnesota Historical Society to begin an investigation in light of the various observations that had cast significant doubts on authenticity [35]. Here again we encounter one of those strange quirks that seem to bedevil virtually all other cases considered in this book. The committee was composed of well-meaning and intelligent individuals, but their expertise did not lie in the specific fields in question. Note how similar this circumstance is to the consideration of Drake's Plate, where there are experts in metallurgy who cannot follow the calligraphy arguments, and so forth. This is quite common as we see that challenge and authentication take place on several levels, in several dimensions, and in several distinct scientific disciplines. Hoax's can thus often benefit from the way in which science itself has become dispersed among specialist disciplines [36]. It seems that the museum committee did its best by soliciting expert opinion concerning the runes on the stone from some of the era's leading authorities. Unfortunately, the committee generally ignored the very opinions it had sought. The chairman relied heavily on Holand's own comments and refutations of any external, critical observations. The effective chairman of the committee, Newton Winchell (the official chairman was Edward Mitchell, but Winchell seemed to do most of the work), was a geologist [37]. Naturally, as a geologist, his central focus was on the physical nature of the stone and the environment from which it came. He did investigate the provenance of the stone quite extensively, visiting Kensington on a number of occasions, but inevitably he had incomplete first-person information and relied heavily on his own impression of Ohman and his neighbors. Unfortunately, geologists by and large are not psychologists, and his personal reflections remained just that.

Winchell also explored the murky issue of the ownership of the stone. Ohman was adamant that he never sold the stone to Holand and only allowed him to have it for a museum, either at the Norwegian Historical Society or perhaps the Minnesota Historical Society. Holand's own accounts, as we have seen, vary considerably. However, Holand was in possession of the stone when, in 1910, he offered to sell it to the Minnesota Historical Society for $5,000! Of this $3,000 was to be in the form of a stipend for work done and $2,000 in payment for the stone itself [38]. Even if he did pay Ohman $5, or even $25, the latter $2,000 still represents a nice return on investment. The Historical Society itself was not slow on the uptake and had representatives visit Ohman who signed his rights over to them for $10, a nominal fee since Ohman's expressed desire anyway was to lodge the stone at the Historical Society in St. Paul, the state capital. Paradoxically, the committee decided, by one vote, to return the stone to Holand who had deposited it with them, stating that they wished to avoid a legal wrangle. Holand then proceeded to take the stone with him to Europe.

The committee issued a report that was favorable to the authenticity of the stone but was concerned enough with a published evaluation by Illinois philologist George Flom to temporize their conclusions to some degree [39]. They amended their earlier opinion with the following resolution: "Resolved, that this Committee regards the genuineness of the supposed Kensington Runestone as not established, but that they deem the preponderance of evidence to be in favor of the Stone." The report subsequently came under a great deal of criticism. Flom himself considered it unworthy of a response. Later, Wahlgren, a major writer on the Runestone, showed that part of the report was actually written by Holand himself, who could by no stretch of the imagination be considered a disinterested scholar, or for that matter even an official member of the committee. Such was the concern that the Executive Council of the Minnesota Historical Society refused to endorse the report, and despite the subsequent misuse of the museum committee's report by ardent proponents of the stone, no official pronouncement of the Minnesota Historical Society judged the stone genuine [40].

THE WILDERNESS YEARS

Despite the apparent approval by the museum committee, but most probably because of the denial by the upper echelons of the Minnesota Historical Society, the Runestone failed to gain a foothold with professional historians and only continued with popular recognition, predominantly because of Holand's crusade. Each attack on the stone was met with his riposte. There was a sequence of continuing critiques from commentators such as Larson and Quaife, and Holand met each one of these publications with a clear counterattack [41]. As the years went by, Holand faced new critics whose comments became progressively more difficult to reject. The evident accusation of a hoax by Wahlgren was followed by a most insightful commentary by Blegen, the latter being published soon after Holand's death. However, in all these conflicts, Holand himself was not without allies; Tanquist and Landsverk provided a strong defense of the Runestone [42]. Over the century since its discovery, the tide of opinion, both the experts and the public, has swayed back and forth, oscillating between absolute denial and unequivocal support.

A MODERN REVIVAL

Modern times have seen works generally more supportive of the Runestone. In two texts, Robert Hall, an emeritus professor of linguistics from Cornell University, has argued that the text is indeed authentic [43]. Naturally, Hall focuses on the character and content of the carved runes themselves and engages in much confirmation bias in an attempt to demonstrate that possibly such runes were symbols contemporary with the purported age of the inscription.

"Confirmation bias" is a well-known phenomenon in psychology, in which an individual searches for and emphasizes those facts and observations that support the positive case. They are somewhat less assiduous in searching for and discussing evidence contrary to their own hypothesis [44]. Certainly, extensive expert knowledge in Norse runes would be very helpful in adjudging the value of Hall's fundamental assertions, but alas, few modern specialist scholars seem to find the topic of sufficient interest to provide an informative response. Hall's opinion is simply embodied in the full title of his book, *The Kensington Rune-Stone is Genuine*. There is no wishy-washy temporizing here! He is not alone in this persuasion, and Hall cites his indebtedness to Rolf Nilsestuen whose own book, *The Kensington Runestone Vindicated* [45], is even more direct. In the latter work, Nilsestuen directs his most virulent attack at Erik Wahlgren and Wahlgren's highly critical text.

If one wishes to get a flavor of just how emotive discussion of the Runestone can be, Nilsesturn's chapter on Wahlgren will prove a ready example [46]. Much is made in this and other works about the character of farmer Ohman and what he could and could not have known or accomplished in light of his native intelligence and degree of formal schooling. Of course, all such opinions have to be predominantly speculation and thus cannot represent empirical evidence per se, but as for feeding an already raging emotive contretemps, such assertions provide heady fuel. The persistence of this argumentative side can be seen in the article by Whitaker and the response by several outraged readers [47]. Whitaker is as certain in his dismissal as proponents such as Hall are in their advocacy.

One of the more recent treatments of the issue has been by Alice Kehoe who provides a welcome departure from the argument over whether or not the stone is "real." Rather, she uses the controversy as a vehicle to explore evidence in which she asks the reader to think "holistically" about the question [48]. Neither an outright advocate nor a hard-line debunker, Kehoe provides a useful introduction to the controversy and the various motivations that underlie it. Her conclusion, that we cannot simply dismiss the Runestone as an evident hoax, is certainly justified.

The story of the Runestone, however, is never static for long. One of the more recent evaluations of the Runestone has been conducted by Barry Hanson and Scott Wolter [49]. Hanson is a chemist who hired Wolter's American Petrographic Services of St. Paul, Minnesota, in association with members of the University of Minnesota-Duluth's Geology Department, to evaluate the physical features of the stone using tests such as reflected and transmitted light microscopy, as well as scanning electron microscopy and energy-dispersive analysis. Interestingly, these were among the first modern scientific tests conducted, and this was an important step in the history of the stone. The group concluded that the stone was carved into a tombstone-shaped form at the same time the runes were carved. According to Wolter, their results indicated that the Runestone was buried after it was carved for decades at least and possibly for centuries. While not definitive proof, the weight of this evidence seems against a more modern dating of the carving of the runes. Thus, while for many years the general persuasion was one of disbelief, perhaps in our modern time, the pendulum is beginning to oscillate back toward a more favorable interpretation. In the section that follows I examine one other interesting factor that might support the possibility of authenticity. This concerns the geographical nature of the possible exploratory expedition and the way in which our common conception of the mapping of the world might influence our opinion.

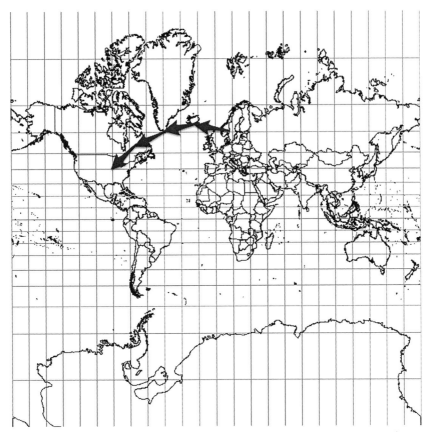

FIGURE 3.4. Mercator's projection of the world showing the common conception of the geography of the land masses of our planet.

STRAIGHT-LINE EXPLORATION

When we consider the proposition of an expedition exploring the inner reaches of northern Minnesota and emanating from the countries of Scandinavia, we can easily be trapped by our perception of the world in the form derived from Mercator's projection, as illustrated in Figure 3.4. Using this projection, if we impose a straight line between the nominal origin of the expedition in Scandinavia and its purported destination in Kensington, it appears that the intrepid explorers had to cross the whole of the Atlantic Ocean and a large part of the eastern portion of the North American continent to get to central Minnesota. From this perspective, it seems a long and

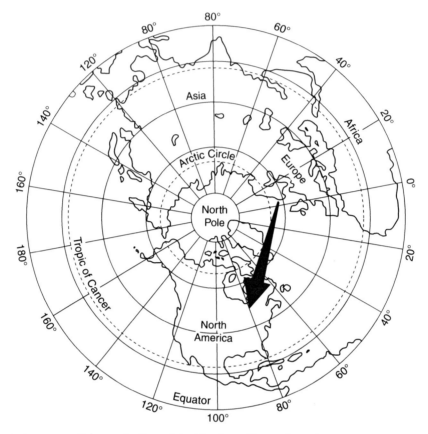

FIGURE 3.5. Polar projection of the Northern Hemisphere showing the straight-line projection of the possible path of the expedition in polar coordinate space.

daunting journey involving distances that would pose challenges even to modern yachtsmen and land trekkers.

However, if we look to see the world from a different perspective and use a polar projection, as shown in Figure 3.5, a different vision is presented to us. As is now evident, the longest sailing challenge in this whole journey is the initial crossing from the port of origin somewhere on the Scandinavian coast to Iceland. This was a journey frequently undertaken by these peoples, and modern-day historians confirm the occurrence of such journeys well before the fourteenth century [50]. There is also solid evidence of follow-up voyages to Greenland and the upper coast of modern-day Canada, as is also discussed in a later chapter on the Vinland Map. From Iceland to the tip of Greenland is virtually the same challenge as from Greenland to the coast of North America. Similarly, if transport by ship were the way they traveled, then entry into and passage across modern-day Hudson Bay would leave such individuals relatively close to the region in which the stone was found. It is also of more than passing interest to note that almost a straight line on a polar projection from upper Minnesota to parts of modern-day Norway can include intersection with both the tip of Greenland as well as Iceland.

My central point is not to demonstrate that any group actually did accomplish this journey. Rather, it is to say that there are no inherent, undefeatable barriers to their being able to do so. In fact, one of the great attractions of the Runestone is this ever-present, reasonable possibility. Indeed, this dimension of reasonable possibility is a reflection of the 50/50 idea that was proposed earlier as a common characteristic of each of these polemic examples, and by extension many of the other most highly disputed artifacts we possess and research.

Scandinavians would later, in the nineteenth century, certainly find themselves in the upper Midwest, occupying an area whose climate and constitution is not unlike that of their homeland is not in dispute. This migration and subsequent occupation of lands similar to their homeland are also not happenstance. Thus we have no fundamental argument with the fact that Scandinavians of one generation or another created the stone. Nor is there great contention over the fact that Scandinavians occupied both the origin and destination of the purported journey that the stone describes. So, what the contention really comes down to is not a matter of culture, nor indeed a matter of space. It is all a matter of time.

THE VERDICT ON THE STONE

In the general scientific community, the stone is largely considered an oddity, an interesting quirk in history. Even if it were true, however, it would not alter the collective consciousness by much, since pre-Columbian times, Norse presence in North America has been more than adequately established by the finds at L'Anse aux Meadows as reported by Ingstad [51]. However, in the world of Scandinavian culture, the stone generates much polarization. It has its strong supporters and evident detractors, and the following observations by the radio personality, Garrison Keillor, reflects the general persuasion that the stone is a modern hoax:

> Now in the historical society museum in the basement of the town hall, it sits next to the Lake Wobegon runestone, which proves that Viking explorers were here in 1381. Unearthed by a professor Oftedahl or Ostenwald around 1921 alongside County Road 2, where the Professor, motoring from Chicago to Seattle, had stopped to bury garbage, the small black stone is covered with Viking runic characters which read (translated by him): "8 of (us) stopped & stayed awhile to visit & have (coffee) & a short nap. Sorry (you) weren't here. Well, that's about (it) for now." Every Columbus Day, the runestone is carried up to the school and put on a card-table in the lunchroom for the children to see, so they can know their true heritage. It saddens Norwegians that America still honors this Italian who arrived late in the New World and by accident, who wasn't even interested in New Worlds but only in spices. Out on a spin in search of curry powder and hot peppers – a man on a voyage to the grocery – he stumbled onto the land of heroic Vikings and proceeded to get the credit for it. [52]

Ever the social commentator, Keillor adopts the skeptical stance, and it seems the preponderance of opinion agrees with him. However, is this collective perception fair to the stone? My own personal opinion is that it is more likely than not to be a hoax, and if it is a hoax, it is a darned good one. It fulfills the general desire of the local populace, and since it is carved in stone, there are relatively few material tests that can be considered definitive in either proving or disproving its authenticity. This leaves the textual material, which, as we have seen, can be argued over almost without limit. One of the final factors that militate against the Runestone is the absence of a contemporary sponsor for the journey. Any such exploratory expedition must have been on behalf of someone influential, and the purpose of creating what is essentially a news bulletin in stone would not have omitted an explicit claim to the land by such a sponsor. However, this speculation is not evidence, and, in the end, the resolution as to doubtful authenticity should, as far as possible, be decided by evidence.

SUMMARY AND CONCLUSIONS

Carved in the Kensington Stone are the runes that tell the story of a party of Vikings and Norsemen who are represented as exploring the region of central Minnesota some 130 years before Christopher Columbus even set sail, see Figure 3.6. If true, the stone represents certainly one of the most

FIGURE 3.6. This is a large replica in the Runestone Park, Kensington, Minnesota.

important historical artifacts ever discovered in America. In contrast, if it is false, the stone represents a wonderful example of a hoax that continues to be sustained today even though its ingenious perpetrator is long dead. In the former eventuality, historical notions of Amerind exploration may well have to be recast and, to some degree, reexamined. However, given the evidence of the L'Anse aux Meadows finds in Newfoundland, the Kensington expedition would really be expressed now only in the form of an interesting footnote. If it is a hoax, we will have insight into the process of deception perpetrated by rural immigrants, which has remained viable for now well over a century. In either case, the Kensington Runestone has much to offer to scholarship and to the process of skeptical and critical thinking [53].

Investigation of the case of the Kensington Runestone is especially valuable for a variety of reasons. First and foremost, the Runestone represents one of the most controversial historic artifacts of the North American continent. That it might be possible to resolve the mystery is evident from the fact that significant bodies of documentation concerning the Runestone are still held at locations such as the Minnesota Historical Society – resources that have yet to be thoroughly explored and evaluated. Further, since the last major investigations of the evidence [54], there have been significant new insights into Viking exploration [55]. In particular, there is now a window of significant opportunity to investigate differing hypotheses. For example, Landsverk claimed that the remnant of this expedition returned to Bergen in Norway in 1364 and it included one Nicholas of Lynn, an Englishman, a friar and an astronomer who, he claims, invented the astrolabe [56]. In England, Nicholas wrote a book entitled *Inventio Fortunate* [*The successful discovery*] in which he describes a voyage to sub-Arctic parts of America around 1360 [57]. Unfortunately, only references to the book now exist. Perhaps modern scholars can find more than just reference to such text. In addition to historical scholarship, the techniques of modern science are offering new methods through which to glean the truth of the Runestone. Perhaps someday these innovations will permit a more certain pronouncement concerning authenticity.

Finally, we must come to one question that all those who doubt the authenticity of the stone must at least address, if not answer. If it is not genuine, then who perpetrated the hoax and how did they do it? If we lay the blame at the door of farmer Ohman, or perhaps even to neighbor Flaten, the answer is relatively simple, since Ohman certainly, and Flaten probably, could ensure eventual rediscovery of the stone if they themselves had buried it. However, if neither of these individuals were responsible, how would the hoaxer ensure the stone would ever be rediscovered? Indeed, as we have seen, Ohman's farm was a rather poor one compared to many in the area, and a hoaxer could not be sure that such poor land would ever be cleared if the stone was buried before farming began in the area. It might be suggested that the hoaxer created a number of Runestones, relying on chance to bring one to the surface. However, one Runestone might be real but more than one would surely be suspect. Any hoaxer faced this conundrum. But suppose the hoaxer knew that this land would be cleared in years to come. Such information would be privy to very few, and this directly points to Sven Fogelblad, the one-time teacher and minister.

Those who are skeptical about the stone for linguistic reasons often point to Ohman as the forger, and thus almost as much controversy surrounds the character of Olof Ohman as it does the stone itself. However, if I am forced to chose the faker – and in doing so I do not admit the question of authenticity is yet closed – I would point to Fogelblad as a prime suspect, or at least a member of a conspiracy. Readers who wish to delve deeper into this mystery will, if they are not firm advocates for authenticity, surely find their own candidates.

What is so wonderful about the stone is that, unlike some other objects, the medium of the stone itself is all natural. No one seriously suggests that testing the physical material will produce definitive information. The granite was certainly around at the contentious time. Evidence about the physical character of the carved symbols may render insight, and we know the information is at least 100 years old and appears on a stone that has spent at least some time buried or partially buried in the ground. However, as we have seen, as science proceeds, assessment and diagnostic techniques become ever more sophisticated. Perhaps some future techniques will be more definitive here over material cause.

Given the present state of understanding, however, it is overwhelmingly the actual physical carving, the semantic content of the inscription on the stone, and the nature of the stone's recorded discovery that provide the fundamental evidence [58]. Although the actual story recorded on the stone is the subject of considerable discussion, the content of the message is, in and of itself, insufficient to decide the issue of veracity. Thus, present arguments largely revolve around the veracity of the runic symbols that constitute the inscription. In this, the search has largely been influenced by confirmation bias. This is a psychological process, observed in detail by Francis Bacon [59], in which we seek evidence that confirms our prejudice and discount evidence that is contradictory in nature. The modern exposition of this propensity has been eloquently expressed by Nickerson [60]. Further, confirmation bias tends to overemphasize single cases. That is, finding a single matching rune for any of the contentious symbols is taken as evidence of a possibility of veracity. Absence of evidence is given relatively short shrift, while the balancing of such evidence is sadly absent in many commentaries that almost inevitably turn out to be partisan in nature. In some ways the latter situation is not unexpected. After all, if you are not passionate about a particular topic, why are you writing about it in the first place? An essential corollary of deception is the accompanying swirl of passion.

REFERENCE NOTES

[1] Zahl, M. A., & Andrews, J. (2003). Traces of Norwegian influence in the development of social services in Minnesota, USA. *International Journal of Social Welfare*, 12, 154–164.

[2] Blegen, T. (1925). The Kensington Runestone discussion and early settlement in southern Minnesota. *Minnesota History*, 6, 370.

[3] http://www.co.douglas.mn.us/general.htm

[4] See, for example, Pinckney, R. (1995). Minnesota's Vikings. *American History*, 30(6), 22–25, 64–65; and Trow, T. (1998). The "Mooring Stones" of Kensington. *Minnesota History*, 56, 121–128. Retrieved from http://www.kahsoc.org/ohman.htm

[5] The Kensington Rune Stone. Retrieved from http://www.kahsoc.org/runestone.htm

[6]   Einarsson, S. (1933). The Kensington Stone: A study in pre-Columbian American history. *Speculum*, 8, 400.

[7]   Blegen, T. C. (1968). *The Kensington Rune Stone: New light on an old riddle.* St. Paul: Minnesota Historical Society.

[8]   See, for example, Flom, G. T. (1910). The Kensington Rune Stone. *Transactions of the Illinois State Historical Society*, 105–125. Retrieved from http:// newport-tower.org/html/history.html

[9]   See Nielsen, R., & Wolter, S. F. (2006). *The Kensington Rune Stone: Compelling new evidence.* Lake Superior Agate Publishing.

[10] Landsverk, O. G. (1961). *The Kensington Runestone: A reappraisal of the circumstances under which the stone was discovered.* Glendale, CA: Church Press.

[11] Holmen, W. P. The Story of the Kensington Runestone. Retrieved from http:// kensingtonmn.com/runestonepg.html

[12] Flom, G. T. (1910). *The Kensington Rune-Stone: A modern inscription from Douglas County, Minnesota.* Springfield: The Illinois State Historical Society.

[13] Runes Alphabet of Mystery: North American Rune Stones. Retrieved from http://www.sunnyway.com/runes/americanstones.html

[14] See *The Legacy of the Kensington Runestone*. Kensington, MN: Runestone Museum, Kensington, and also Wahlgren, E. (1958) *The Kensington Stone: A mystery solved.* Madison: University of Wisconsin Press.

[15] The translation presented here follows Wahlgren. See Wahlgren, E. (1958) *The Kensington Stone: A mystery solved.* Madison: University of Wisconsin Press.

[16] The nature of the abbreviation "AVM," if indeed it is an abbreviation, has been much discussed and disputed. Recent commentators, such as Massey and Massey (2004), have, on the basis of the representative lettering and the actual carving itself, argued in favour of authenticity (see http://home.att. net/~phaistosdisk/mystery.PDF). Like much else, the topic remains a source of much continuing contention. See also Yzermans, V. A. (1964). Our Lady of the Runestone. *Marian Era*, 5, 73–75.

[17] See Friedrich, O. (1993). *The great ice sheet & early Vikings in mid-America.* Elam, IA: Author. Also, for example, see evidence of various finds, such as the certification of a find by the Reverend D. C. Jordahl (1912), in the possession of the author. Also the statement of T. A. Jensen (1930), made on July 18.

[18] Blegen, T. C. (1968). *The Kensington Rune Stone: New light on an old riddle.* St. Paul: Minnesota Historical Society.

[19] See Nielsen, R., & Wolter, S. F. (2006). *The Kensington Rune Stone: Compelling new evidence.* Lake Superior Agate Publishing.

[20] Blegen, T. C. (1968). *The Kensington Rune Stone: New light on an old riddle.* St. Paul: Minnesota Historical Society.

[21] Blegen, T. C. (1968). *The Kensington Rune Stone: New light on an old riddle.* St. Paul: Minnesota Historical Society.

[22] Olsson, N. W., & Hammerstrom, L. G. (2001). *Swedes in Twin Cities: Immigrant life and Minnesota's urban frontier.* Minneapolis: Centre for Multiethnic Research.

[23] Blegen, T. C. (1964). Fredrick J. Turner and the Kensington puzzle. *Minnesota History*, 39, 133–140.

[24] See *The Minneapolis Journal*, February 24, 1899.

[25] Blegen, T. C. (1968). *The Kensington Rune Stone: New light on an old riddle*. St. Paul: Minnesota Historical Society.

[26] Like many of the stories associated with the Runestone, this one has grown out of picturesque myth rather than established reality.

[27] For early works on the Stone by Holand, see Holand, H. R. (1909). Runestenen fra Kensington. *Skandinaven*, January 11, 1908; Holand, H. R. (1909). An explorer's stone record which antedates Columbus: A tragic inscription unearthed in Minnesota, recording the fate of a band of Scandinavian adventurers. *Harper's Weekly*, 53(October 9), 15; Holand, H. R. (1909). The Kensington Stone's Language and Runes. *Symra*, 5, 209–213. (A reply to Gjissing, 1909).

[28] See Blegen, T. C. (1968). *The Kensington Rune Stone: New light on an old riddle*. St. Paul: Minnesota Historical Society.

[29] Holand, H. (1957). *My first eighty years*. New York: Twayne Publishers.

[30] The issue of possession was a somewhat confused and occasionally bitter contention.

[31] From correspondence of the Minnesota Historical Society, originals held at the MHS in St. Paul, MN, copies in possession of the author.

[32] See *The Legacy of the Kensington Runestone*. Kensington, MN: Runestone Museum.

[33] See, for example, Holand, H. R. (1962). *A pre-Columbian crusade to America*. New York: Twayne Publishers.

[34] See works by reporters such as: Anderson, R. B. (1910). The Kensington Runestone Fake. *Wisconsin State Journal* (February 7), 8; Larson, C. (1916). The Kensington Rune Stone: Ancient tragedy. In C. Larson, *History of Douglas and Grant counties Minnesota: Their people, industries and institutions* (Vol. 1, pp. 72–122), Indianapolis, IN: Bowen; Schaefer, F. J. (1910). The Kensington Rune Stone. *Acta et Dicta*, 2, 206–210; Skordalsvold, J. J. (1913). The Kensington Stone and "the Learned Ones." In N. H. Winchell Papers (147.D.6.5 (B), Folder B16.M56b), Minnesota Historical Society, St. Paul, MN.

[35] Minnesota Historical Society. (1915). The Kensington Runestone: Preliminary Report to the Minnesota Historical Society by the Museum Committee. *Collections of the Minnesota Historical Society*, 15, 221–286.

[36] And see the discussion on science and the unity of knowledge in Wilson, E. O. (2000). *Consilience: The unity of knowledge*. New York: A. A. Knopf.

[37] Minnesota Historical Society. (1915). The Kensington Runestone: Preliminary Report to the Minnesota Historical Society by the Museum Committee. *Collections of the Minnesota Historical Society*, 15, 221–286.

[38] From the correspondence of the Minnesota Historical Society, originals held at the MHS in St. Paul, MN, copies in possession of the present author, and see note [31] to this chapter.

[39] Flom, G. T. (1910). The Kensington Rune Stone. *Transactions of the Illinois State Historical Society*, 105–125.

[40] Minnesota Historical Society. (1915). The Kensington Runestone: Preliminary Report to the Minnesota Historical Society by the Museum Committee. *Collections of the Minnesota Historical Society*, 15, 221–286.

[41] See, for example, Larson, L. M. (1921). The Kensington Rune Stone. *Wisconsin Magazine of History*, 4, 382–387; Larson, L. M. (1936). The Kensington Rune

Stone. *Minnesota History*, 17, 20–37; Quaife, M. M. (1934). The myth of the
Kensington Rune Stone: The Norse discovery of Minnesota, 1362. *New England
Quarterly*, 7, 613–645; Quaife, M.M. (1947) The Kensington myth once more.
Michigan History, 31, 129–161.

[42] See Landsverk, O. G. (1969). *Ancient Norse messages on American Stones*.
Glendale, CA: Norseman Press; Landsverk, O. G. (1974). *Runic records of the
Norsemen in America*. New York: Twayne Publishers.

[43] See Hall, R. A. (1982). *The Kensington Rune-Stone is genuine*. Alexandria, VA:
Hornbeam Press; and Hall, R. A. (1994). *The Kensington Rune-Stone: Authentic
and important*. Lake Bluff, IL: Jupiter Press.

[44] Klayman, J. (1995). Varieties of confirmation bias. *Psychology of Learning and
Motivation*, 32, 385–418.

[45] As a parenthetical aside, I think one should always be somewhat wary of texts
with titles such as "Runestone vindicated" and "Runestone genuine." Under
such strictures, one is hardly likely to get a balanced argument, although as
I have noted, these sorts of authors never seek to hide their opinion. Such
feverish advocacy is perhaps even more evident in cases involving religious
persuasion.

[46] Nilsestuen, R. (1994). *The Kensington Runestone vindicated*. Lanham, MD:
University Presses of America; but see Wahlgren, E. (1958) *The Kensington
Stone: A mystery solved*. Madison: University of Wisconsin Press. The attack
on Wahlgren reads: "Wahlgren was so driven by a compulsion to destroy the
record of Norse explorations in North America before Columbus that he
wrote a 228-page book attempting to discredit the entire body of evidence,
including the reputation of Hjalmar Holand and anyone who gave testimony concerning the discovery. His "solution" is based, not on evidence,
but on misinformation; unfounded suspicion; innuendo; ridicule, especially
of Hjalmar Holand; numerous philological errors; misinterpretation of the
statements of others; unwarranted conclusions; and a shameful lack of either
human decency or common sense."

[47] For this particular sequence, see the original article: Whittaker, J. (1992). The
curse of the Runestone: Deathless hoaxes. *Skeptical Inquirer*, 17, 59–63, and the
various responses that prompted subsequent replies by Whittaker, J. (1993).
Reply to Criticisms. *Skeptical Inquirer*, 17(3), 335–338.

[48] Kehoe, A. B. (2005). *The Kensington Runestone*. Long Grove, IL: Waveland
Press.

[49] See Nielsen, R., & Wolter, S. F. (2006). *The Kensington Rune Stone, Compelling
New Evidence*. Evanston, IL: Lake Superior Agate Press.

[50] Fitzhugh, W. W., & Ward, E. I. (Eds.). (2000). *Vikings: The North Atlantic saga*.
Washington, DC: National Museum of Natural History and Smithsonian
Institution Press.

[51] Ingestad, A. S. (1971). Norse sites at L'Anse aux Meadows. In G. Ashe (Ed.),
The quest for America (pp. 175–196). New York: Praeger Press. See also
Ingstad, H., & Ingstad, A. S. (2000). *The Viking discovery of America: The
excavation of a Norse settlement in L'Anse aux Meadows, Newfoundland*.
St. John's, Newfoundland: Breakwater Books.

[52] Keillor, G. (1985). *Lake Wobegon days*. New York: Viking.

[53] A relatively new article by Sprunger provides further insights and dimensions into the Runestone issue by contrasting Holand with one of his chief opponents, J. A. Holvik; it is a highly recommended read. See Sprunger, D. A. (2000). J. A. Holvik and the Kensington Runestone. *Minnesota History* (Fall), 141–154.

[54] See Hall, R. A. (1994). *The Kensington Rune-Stone: Authentic and important.* Lake Bluff, IL: Jupiter Press; Nielsen, R. (1988/1989). New evidence which supports that the Kensington Runestone is genuine. *Epigraphic Society Occasional Publications*, 18, 110–132; and Nilsestuen, R. (1994). *The Kensington Runestone vindicated*. Lanham, MD: University Presses of America.

[55] See, for example, Haywood, J. (1995). *The Penguin historical atlas of the Vikings.* London: Penguin.

[56] Landsverk, O. G. (1961). *The Kensington Runestone: A reappraisal of the circumstances under which the stone was discovered.* Glendale, CA: Church Press.

[57] See DeCosta, B. F. (1881). *Inventio Fortunata: Artic exploration with an account of Nicholas of Lynn.* Paper read before the American Geographical Society. And see entry in Google Books.

[58] For a most interesting discussion on lost civilizations and messages in stone, see Lepper, B. T., Feder, K. L., Barnhart, T. A., & Bolnick, D. A. (2011). Civilizations lost and found: Fabricating history. *Skeptical Inquirer*, 35(6), 48–54.

[59] See Bacon, F. (1863 [1620]). *Novum Organum.* Boston: Taggard & Thompson.

[60] Nickerson, R. S. (1998). Confirmation bias: A Ubiquitous phenomenon in many guises. *Review of General Psychology*, 2(2), 175–220.

CASE 4

The Vinland Map

The Visual Evidence for the Norse Claim of the Discovery of America

THE MAP AND ITS INTRINSIC CLAIM

Ensconced deep in the Beinecke Rare Book and Manuscript Library of Yale University in New Haven, Connecticut, resides a small parchment map upon which faint ink lines delineate an early representation of the world. In the top left-hand corner of this map is an irregularly shaped island that is referred to in the associated text as "Vinlanda Insula" [1]. It is this notation that has provided its popular name: "The Vinland Map." A representation of this map is shown in Figure 4.1. Even a cursory glance at this illustration immediately communicates the fact that, to the left of the centerfold, the map shows Western Europe, Iceland, Greenland, and then further west what appears to be an island beyond Greenland. This is often what is purported to be the coast of North America. We can add to this spatial representation a claimed date of creation of the map around 1440 AD [2], and when we put these two facts together, it becomes clear that what the map appears to represent is the discovery of America by someone presumably from Europe prior to Christopher Columbus. As with almost all of the other examples in this text, the first and most prominent question that is always raised is whether this is an authentic artifact or whether it is a much later creation and thus a hoax. If it is a hoax, was it an intentional one? Or could it possibly have been a personal and private creation in the form of an exercise that, through a sequence of unforeseen circumstances, resulted in an unintentional hoax? If it is an authentic artifact, what are the ramifications for history and especially the respective claims of primacy in respect to European expansion into the New World? As with each of the accounts presented here, as Damon Runyon would say, "a story goes with it."

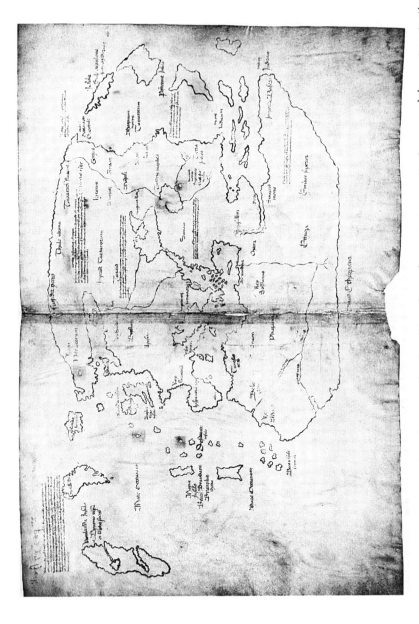

FIGURE 4.1. The Vinland Map. Note how the text is distributed but shows the greatest concentration around the most contentious site. From: Vinland Map; Hystoria Tartarorum. Image courtesy of the Beinecke Rare Book and Manuscript Library, Yale University, New Haven, Connecticut [3]. Note also the two large scale but mythical islands that appear in mid-Atlantic about which little contention seem to have arisen.

THE PROBLEM OF PROVENANCE

What we would really like from the Vinland Map is a timeline of its ownership that traces its history back through the ages until around 1440 AD, its proposed date of creation [4]. Ideally, we would like to see a mid-15th-century equivalent of a "bill of sale" that identifies the map's creator and its transfer of ownership to an original purchaser. It would also be nice if this catalog of events were recorded in contemporary documentation such that we could follow this path of existence right up to the present time. Alas, such documentation is missing almost altogether, and although its absence is certainly not a fatal blow to the authenticity of the map, the lack of even a more recent provenance has been a cause of both concern and frustration. However, before we are tempted to dismiss the claims of the Map out of hand, we should also remember that missing or impoverished provenance is true for many, if not most, historical documents that claim such an early date of creation. In this respect, the Vinland Map is neither unique nor unusual.

If we cannot follow the history of the Map from its creation forward, the alternative is to work from the present and go backward in time. The map itself has been at Yale University at least from 1965 when that institution announced its acquisition, bound together with a tract referred to as the *Tartar Relation* and the four books of Vincent of Beauvais's *Speculum Historiale* (*The Mirror of History*) [5]. The whole compilation had been acquired for the university from a New Haven rare book dealer, one Laurence Claiborne Witten II. Further, it was eventually reported that the acquisition was made through the purchase by, and donation of, the philanthropist Paul Mellon [6]. As a Yale alumnus, he was generous enough to present the Map to his alma mater. It was Witten who had recombined two of the items together since he had acquired them, apparently sometime in September 1957 [7]. These respective items were the Vinland Map and the *Tartar Relation*, which had cost the reputed price of $3,500 [8]. The *Speculum Historiale* had been added in by Witten a little later in a tripartite compilation whose unity was crucial to the whole question of authenticity. Today, the Map is insured for $25 million, although upon whose valuation it is difficult to ascertain [9].

ANNOUNCING THE MAP

The announcement of the Vinland map to the world stage was, to all appearances, a carefully stage-managed production. Clearly, after Yale had acquired

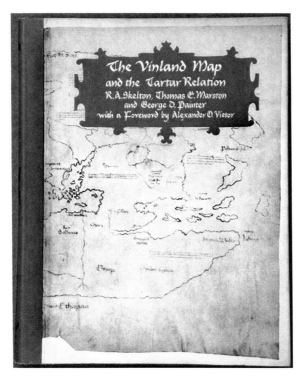

FIGURE 4.2. The 1965 text by Skelton, Marston, and Painter that announced the Map and championed its authenticity [10]. From Permission with Yale University Press.

the Map, they rightly decided to go to significant lengths to establish whether or not it was the genuine article before any public unveiling. Whether by happenstance or as a result of an unfortunate but conscious decision, the announcement itself was made on October 9th 1965 [11], perhaps even symbolically on the eve of Columbus Day, a national holiday in the United States [12]. The joyful celebration by the Yale administration of their acquisition and the authenticity was buttressed by the opinion of three well-known scholars: Skelton, Marston, and Painter in a text entitled *The Vinland Map and Tartar Relation*, the cover of which is shown in Figure 4.2 [13]. There must have been a significant print run of this text since, despite its bulk, one can easily obtain cheap secondhand copies to this day. Not only was there scholarship involved in its production; there was a clear aspect of public promotion.

As may well be imagined, the announcement caused a significant stir not only within the United States but across the globe. In his popular book *Iberia*, James Michener noted the antipathy to Yale University throughout

Spain as a result of their announcement of the Map [14]. He commented that the Spanish in general view Columbus as one of their own, and in the Beinecke Library files there is a record of a short, sharp exchange between Michener and some of the Yale faculty with respect to his comments and observations. Michener's reply was that he was merely conveying the Spanish sentiment of condemnation of the New Haven school; but perhaps this was not too arduous a task for a Harvard alumnus!

Within the closeted world of cartographic studies, this emerging evidence was thought to provide direct visual confirmation of the reality of Norse exploration of North America. This visual confirmation went beyond the intrinsic ambivalence of the Norse sagas in which fact and fiction appear to be so readily and frustratingly intermingled. Here, half a century before Columbus's journey, was a direct visual representation on the map of the Norse voyages beyond Greenland to the previously mythical but now very real Vinland. Even more crucially, the names of the valiant and well-known explorers, Bjarni and Leif Eriksson, were specifically inscribed on the map [15], the very same ones from these early stirring stories of exploration. In a piquant way, one is saddened that Haljmar Holand, of the Kensington Runestone fame, had died only two years before this announcement. One senses that he certainly would have been brimming with pride and a keen advocate for the authenticity of the Map, although sadly for him there is no reference to any Viking exploration of 1362 in the textual information of the Vinland Map.

When the axis of the historic and cartographic worlds is edged slightly off kilter by an announcement such as the one made by Yale, it generates a standard set of responses. Some embrace the new perspective that is generated, while others hold hard to the traditional version of things. Such polarized reactions depend on the hopes, aspirations, and prejudices of those involved [16]. At the same time, some scientists and historians rightly leap into action to further explore and evaluate the physical, psychological, and social aspects of what is being claimed. Of particular concern was the account of the Map's origin and this revolved around its recent discovery and its subsequent purchase.

PULLING ON THE HISTORICAL THREAD

When we left the history of the Map, it had been acquired for Yale from the New Haven bookseller Laurence Witten [17]. But how did the Map come into Witten's possession? This proves to be a story in and of itself. A recent popular television program on the Map, entitled "The Viking Deception," indicated that Witten had bought the Map from another dealer in the rare book trade, one Enzo Ferrajoli de Ry, a former Italian Army officer. In his statement on this sequence of events, Witten provides a slightly different version. In September 1957, he had been on one of his regular trips to Europe where he had been in search of inventory for his business [18]. One stop was in Geneva where he visited an old friend and colleague, one Nicolas Rauch [19]. It was at a meal that they were having with Ferrajoli that the topic of the Map was first broached. Witten expressed an interest in seeing the Map, but Ferrajoli stated that he had returned the Map to its owner since he had been unable to establish its authenticity. Witten then stated that Ferrajoli subsequently arranged to take him to meet the owner, and this meeting occurred at the owner's own home [20]. It was there that Witten claimed to purchase the Vinland Map and the *Tartar Relation* "on the spot" (Witten, 1966). Intriguingly and unfortunately, Witten does not reveal the name of this original owner [21].

He returned with his prize to New Haven and showed it to some individuals who were privy to what he had bought. Among these individuals was Alexander Vietor who was then Curator of Yale's map collection. Vietor asked for right of first refusal if Witten subsequently decided to sell [22]. However, Witten claims he was aware of the problem of authentication, having been informed of the previous attempts by Ferrajoli and another bookseller, a Mr. J. Davis, to have the Map approved by the British Museum. Witten claimed that R. A. Skelton and G. D. Painter of the museum viewed the Map but at the time of that viewing did not arrive at a certain conclusion concerning authenticity [23]. As we shall see, these individuals subsequently had much to do with the later process of authentication for Yale's unveiling. Witten was persuaded that the primary barrier to authentication was that of the holes. These had been created presumably by bookworms over the years, and were evident in the Map as well as the *Tartar Relation*, but it appeared that the positioning of the damage on the two documents failed to match up [24].

It is at this point that we must venture into the rarified atmosphere of startling coincidence. Witten had identified the primary problem of authentication as not being with the Map itself but with the degree that it could be tied directly to the *Tartar Relation*, the account of the travels of a Franciscan friar, one John de Plano Carpini to Mongolia in 1247–1248. This latter text was essentially universally agreed to be an authentic 15th-century document. If this link could be unequivocally established, then the map would be supported as genuine, largely by this process of association. Witten reported that he had surmised that some missing pages would act as the integrating material between the Map and the *Tartar Relation*.

Despite asking Ferrajoli to inquire with the original owner about this, no such material was forthcoming [25]. Without this connection, authentication was unlikely, and Witten withdrew the collected materials from his stock list and gave it to his wife [26].

Then, almost miraculously, Witten received a call from Thomas Marston of Yale who had bought some unrelated manuscripts from a catalog of the Davis and Orioli Company in London. This would be the same Mr. Davis who had originally accompanied Ferrajoli to the British Museum in his earlier attempt to authenticate the Map. Among the latter pages that Martson bought was a fragment of Vincent of Beauvais's *Speculum Historale* [27]. Witten writes that the specific textual format of *Speculum* reminded him of the *Tartar Relation* still in his possession, and he asked Marston if he could take the fragment home for comparison purposes. Receiving Marston's assent, Witten then found almost unbelievably, that the fragment proved to be the very element that connected the two items already in his possession. This addition now appeared to link the Vinland Map conclusively to the *Tartar Relation* and thus establish its authenticity. The news was communicated to Marston that very night, and Vietor was also informed the next day. Of this momentous event, Witten wrote: "As far as I was concerned, the Vinland Map was authenticated then and there beyond any reasonable shadow of doubt" [28]. Unfortunately, as we shall see, others have not been so sanguine about this proposition.

Witten sought to explain this unlikely chain of events by suggesting that the three respective pieces of the whole had, at one time, been together in the library of the still unnamed and anonymous owner and must have become separated when the respective bindings had deteriorated and needed to be replaced [29]. Unfortunately, as we have seen, this supposed owner is not named and the only reference given is to an unsupported observation that the materials had been in the unidentified library for one or two generations. Having managed now to satisfy himself and some others as to the bona fides of the Map, he sold the whole compilation (since Marston had given the critical fragment of *Speculum* to Witten's wife) to an anonymous buyer. As we now know, that generous individual was Mellon who, as a Yale alumnus, was kind enough to donate it to the university [30]. The subsequent announcement of possession and the case for authentication was presented some six years later, as mentioned earlier. In one final statement, Witten sought specifically to dissociate any of his materials with manuscripts that had been stolen from the library of the Cathedral of La Seo in Saragossa, Spain, by citing their incompatibility with any of the descriptions of the items that had been taken. What Witten could not dissociate was the connection via Ferrajoli, who was charged with the alleged felony [31]. While still protesting the bona fides of the Map, he could not place equal confidence now in the bona fides of the individual who first introduced him to the Map.

A PERSONAL PERUSAL

Unlike Arthur's Cross, which is now lost to us, or the highly restricted Shroud of Turin, the Vinland Map, like Drake's Plate, is open for direct inspection. Thus, one sunny day in an early fall found me in New Haven bent on viewing the Map in person. The Beinecke building is itself well worth the visit. It is an imposing concrete shell that houses a set of glass-fronted stacks in which all forms of delight present themselves to the ardent bibliophile. Of course, access to this inner sanctum itself is limited to the librarians alone, but for the price of filling out a small call number sheet, they will bring forth their guarded treasures for brief perusal in one of the most highly monitored rooms that I have ever been in. Who can blame them? Many of their holdings are unique and, like the Vinland Map, absolutely irreplaceable. I personally requested MS 350a and within a short time there in front of me was the Vinland Map itself. Very kindly, the librarians also provided a full-size photo reproduction that, in terms of legibility, is actually a little better than the actual Map itself. The reproduction sits in front of me as I write.

As might be suspected, one's time with the Map is limited because the library wishes to minimize its exposure to light. I was personally very interested in examining the various holes in the Map, as I discuss later. However, one is very aware of being watched at all times, and I was kindly requested to keep the Map flat and not hold it up to the light for inspection. Following my brief examination of the Map itself, I was able to move on to the originals of the *Tartar Relation* and Vincent of Beauvais's *Speculum Historiale*, which, as we now know, each have their very important part to play in the story. Finally, the Yale University library is also in possession of a number of boxes that contain all other materials related to the Map. My last task in New Haven was the inspection of these materials, the vast majority of which I had not previously seen. Most of the boxed materials represented correspondence addressed to Yale personnel concerning the Map and its announcement. Again, the library proved very efficient in taking and delivering my order for photocopies of materials from these latter collections.

Whatever issues there may be in respect of the Vinland Map, there can be no criticism of the way it is made available for study.

ARISTOTLE AND THE MAP

As I sat in Yale's wonderfully lighted facility, I was faced with the question of how to structure my evaluation of the Map so that I could decide on its authenticity for myself. In some other work I had been doing, I had occasion to read the works of Aristotle. So on that day I tried to put myself in his place and to approach the Map as he would. As a result, my personal examination was framed around Aristotle's four forms of cause [32]. These are: (1) material cause (what an object is made of); (2) formal cause (the arrangement or shape of an entity); (3) efficient cause (what is external to the entity that changes or creates it); and (4) final cause (the aim or purpose of an entity). The discussion that follows uses each of these in order. In some sense, each of these builds on the other, and I hope that the reader will feel tempted to use them also in deliberating on the other examples I present in this book. Of course, such use could prove habit forming, and you might find yourself considering a whole range of things based on this interesting approach.

Material Cause

The material cause in this case is certainly contentious because it is the materials that compose the Map itself that render themselves most readily open to analysis. The two primary elements are the physical medium of the material on which the Map is drawn and the ink with which the markings on the Map are made. Regarding the parchment itself, the central issue is, of course, correct dating. The parchment almost certainly meets this criterion, and recent tests have provided strong evidence supportive of this contention. However, finding a blank parchment page of this date does not represent an insurmountable problem, particularly for a specialist. Thus, the age of the page is a necessary but not sufficient criterion for authentication. A later date for the parchment would have disproved the map, but a contemporary dating of the parchment alone unfortunately tells us frustratingly little. In terms of material, what this leaves us with is the ink in which the map has been drawn.

It comes as no surprise that the authenticity of the ink has been at the epicenter of contention over the map. If the ink is of the correct constitution, this is also necessary but again not sufficient evidence. A forger might be clever enough to fabricate the correct constitution of the ink. We would need to know the age of the ink, and even then there is some possibility, albeit slight, that correctly dated ink was put to correctly dated parchment but at some time later than 1440. At this juncture, we have to introduce anatase – one of the three mineral forms of titanium oxide. It was because of this substance that opinion on the map turned in the early 1970s [33]. After Yale's triumphant announcement, the general opinion was one in favor of authenticity, especially for those who did not have time to conduct any detailed investigation and whose primary source was the text by Skelton and his colleagues.

In 1974, the highly respected chemist Walter McCrone and his daughter published an announcement that immediately swung the pendulum of general opinion. A careful reading of their original article indicates that it had been personnel from Yale University who had first approached McCrone's organization and asked for his assessment several years earlier, in 1968. McCrone himself observed that the necessary techniques to accomplish this assessment were not mature enough and only became adequate to the task in 1972. Consequently, his coauthored paper followed this investigation and was published in 1974 [34]. Basically, McCrone found that the ink on the Vinland Map was different from that of either the *Tartar Relation* or *Speculum Historiale*. In that one stroke, the link that Witten had earlier sought to establish in the basic case for authenticity was badly damaged. However, there was more to come when the McCrones concluded: "The inks on the Vinland Map contain as an integral constituent substantial percentages of a pigment, anatase, available in the observed form only since 1920" [35]. It appeared to be the fatal blow – the map was a fake. However, reading further into this paper we find three exculpatory possibilities that kept the authenticity claim alive. They were: (1) anatase was somehow available to the 15th-century creator of the map; (2) a later restorer had inked over the faded original lines in more recent times (this was founded on the observation that the map had been drawn once and then later inked over with the fluid that presumably contained the anatase) [36]; (3) the present map was a copy of an earlier map. As we shall see, option (1) very quickly became the center of the next wave of controversy.

McCrone's claim that the anatase found on the map did not occur naturally and would thus not be available to a 15th-century scribe was almost immediately challenged. Others reported that indeed it was possible that this was a naturally occurring substance and appears in kaolin clays. In 1987, an evaluation by Cahill and his colleagues argued that, in contradiction to the McCrone's findings, anatase was not as prevalent as had earlier been suggested and was completely missing from some of the lines on the map [37]. The latter group concluded that, in combination with the possibility of natural occurrence, the anatase on the map was *not* a smoking gun and that this objection to authenticity was not the fatal one that the McCrone report had implied. The pendulum had swung again, and while radiocarbon dating confirmed the age of the parchment itself, the problem of a later creation on an authentic piece of parchment still remains [38]. Indeed, the argument concerning the physical materials of which the map is composed continues to be pursued to the present. Although it would seem the best avenue of scientific resolution, the material form of the map continues to support the belief of the believers and the skepticism of the skeptics.

One final and most interesting dimension of the material cause here concerns the *absence* of material in the map – the critical holes. It is these infamous holes and the question of how and when such holes were made that are also cause for a great fascination. Of all of the material issues, none is more complex or indeed perhaps more critical than the nature of these holes and how they align within the map itself and, crucially, how they match up to the putatively corresponding holes in the *Tartar Relation* and *Speculum Historale*. Indeed, it was through the original association of these respective holes that proponents first looked to establish the claim to authenticity. From a personal inspection, I resolved that there are five holes on the left side of the map and five holes on its right side. Four of these respective holes appear to correspond to each other when the pages of the map are folded over, as would be the case if and when the map was to be bound in a book. However, one hole on each side of the map does not appear to align with anything on the other side and thus appears to be unique. With respect to the matching holes, the first is in the peninsula that shows modern Sweden and Norway, which is aligned east-west on the map (see Figure 4.1). The second hole is just to the south of the tip of Greenland and has its corresponding partner approximately on the coastline of eastern Asia. The third and fourth matching holes appear in the area of the Atlantic Ocean, the northern of these two appearing off the coast of Ireland and the southern one adjacent to the Bay of Biscay in and among a series of scattered islands. With respect to the holes that have no matching partners, the largest in the whole map is one in the center of Asia, while the unique hole on the left side occurs in what appears to be a smudge to the south of the identified island of Vinlanda (Figure 4.3).

Even on good facsimile representations of the map it is difficult to see these holes clearly and align them unequivocally. Further, on the actual map,

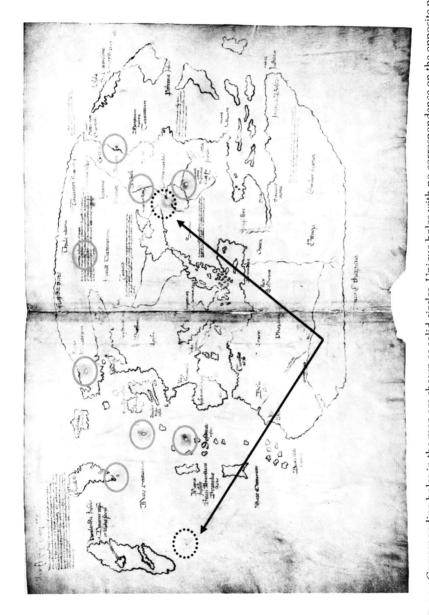

FIGURE 4.3. Corresponding holes in the map are shown as solid circles. Unique holes with no correspondence on the opposite page are as dotted circles (see arrows). All additions to the original image by the Author.

these holes have been covered over with small square patches in some form of crude repair [39]. This makes seeing some of these holes difficult, even with the original map in hand. Two of the separate pairs of the corresponding holes are curiously circular, and one has to be an expert on the way insects consume molds on the surface of books to attest to whether some of the holes in the Map are potentially created by human hands. Again, in the case of artifacts that are not obvious frauds, the determinative science can get very detailed very quickly. What is shown here in the creation of the map, as it is in so many artifacts, is that it is not only what one puts in but what one takes out or leaves out that can prove to be absolutely pivotal.

Formal Cause

If we cannot offer the immediate resolution of the authenticity issue using the science of the materials involved, can we provide some definitive conclusions based on what the map purports to represent? And can we align this with what we know of the history of the era and the probability of the creation of such a map? Here we switch from the subtleties and nuances of analytical chemistry and electron microscopy to the more social and historical investigations of paleo-cartography and medieval history. In its essence, the map provides two components of formal cause: (1) its graphic dimension and (2) its textual information.

Let's deal with the former first. There are, of course, discussions about other drawn elements of the map, but my discussion here necessarily focuses on the island to the very left identified as *Vinlanda Insula* [40]. The first thing to note is that it *is* an island. Strictly speaking, this is an incorrect representation. If the map purports to show the eastern seaboard of North America, then showing it as an island is a mistake. However, with respect to this island-inspired configuration, the Vinland Map is not alone. For example, the Honter map of 1546, which includes South America, also provides an irregular, island-type configuration for North America [41]. The Honter map is also very helpful because it illustrates one of the great problems of trying to authenticate the Vinland Map using formal cause, which is the issue of projection.

We are all so used to seeing the globe from the generally accepted modern projections that it becomes an exercise in imagination to understand that early maps use a whole variety of different projections. The heart shape of the Honter map, shown in Figure 4.4, is only one example of many such variations. All projections have some distortional effect as a result of trying

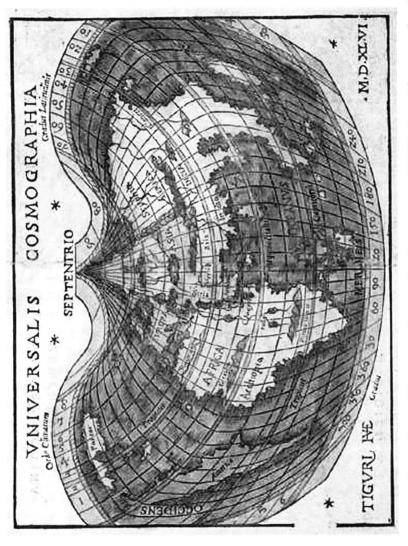

FIGURE 4.4. Heart-shaped map of the world, based on Waldseemüller. The monogram 'HVE' in lower left corner is that of the woodcutter Heinrich Vogtherr the Elder who was specially commissioned by the printer Froschauer. There are a number of editions and undated versions; Honter's block was used to illustrate other works. Honter, Johann. *Universalis Cosmographia*. Tiguri MDXLVI, Zurich, 1546. Image by permission of Barry Rudesman Antique Maps, La Jolla, CA.

to fit a three-dimensional surface onto a two-dimensional representation. However, the nature of that distortion varies as a function of the projection chosen. As a generalization, the degree of distortion most often varies with the distance from the center of the projection. Thus, early maps tend to be quite accurate concerning the known lands, where the maker often places their homeland either close to or in the middle of the map. Unfortunately, this often induces inherent distortions into distant or remote lands placed at the very edge of the map. Such problems occur when we look at the Vinland Map. While the Mediterranean and some parts of Europe are eminently recognizable, as we move away from the middle of the map, landmasses become much less familiar to the modern eye. There is, however, the interesting exception of Greenland, which has been the topic of extensive discussion in the Vinland literature. Much of the contextual argument concerning issues such as the relative position of various known and putatively "new" discoveries are thus based on what form of projection the maker of the Vinland Map employed [42]. Unfortunately, even though many inferences have been made, we do not have this information. Therefore, despite extensive discussion about the various possibilities (and see McCulloch 2005 for detailed observations), the circumstances here are *underspecified*, and thus formally there are too many degrees of freedom to arrive at a definitive conclusion concerning authenticity based on relative positioning of identified landmasses. If the map is genuine, this is indeed understandable. Many early maps left vast blank areas, often labeled "terra incognita" [43], when no certain information was available. Their mapmakers were appropriately honest in expressing their ignorance. If the map is a fake, then the clever fabricator has taken advantage of this fact and has used the inherent underspecification to retain the ambiguity that a good hoax must possess. In this way, uncertainty is very much a strong ally of the aspiring hoaxer.

As well as the formal graphic elements, the Vinland Map contains many captions that themselves can be used to assess the possible authenticity. Such analysis recapitulates the textual consideration that was central to the evaluation of the Runestone. In this realm of controversy, arguments rage over dipthongs (the use of "a" and "e" when adjoined together), virgulas (vertical strokes to indicate inter-sentence pauses), and punctuses (forerunners of the modern-day period) [44]. These arguments rapidly devolve into heated controversies over early textual formats, with some arguing that certain forms are anachronistic and therefore evidence of fraud, while others cite abstruse incidents of what might be similar marks in other early manuscripts. As McCulloch rightly observes, such arguments often rapidly degenerate into picayune punctiliousness. The metaphor that comes most readily to mind is Princess Leia's speech to Grand Moff Tarkin in the original *Star Wars* motion picture, that the more one squeezes, the more that the substance seems to escape through one's fingers. As Fitzhugh recently, and rightly, noted, "the nature of the debate had become so complicated and technical that the general public and most reporters could no longer follow the (scientific) argument, only the spin" [45]. The more detailed one's calligraphic and textual evaluation becomes, the further one appears to be from resolution on the issue of authentication. The Vinland Map does present a basis for possible analysis by material cause. However, when we begin to try to provide a resolution based on formal cause, the textual issues serve more to confuse than resolve. This, then, is a general principle. As we approach the 50% threshold (i.e., 50% real, 50% deception), the science itself becomes less deterministic because such cases force us to the edge of scientific knowledge for resolution. In circumstances of true debate (as opposed to mere apathy), there is a consistent appeal to the imprimatur of science. What is fascinating about some of the present examples is that unequivocal scientific resolution is yet to be achieved. Of course, for nonscientific deliberations, the question of authenticity of some of the present artifacts will live forever, if only in the minds of their unquestioning believers.

There is yet more to consider when we look at the forms of the representations shown on the map. Why, for example, if this map is purportedly derived from Viking sources, is the Scandinavian peninsula depicted as going east-west when both Iceland and Greenland, two lands settled by these explorers, oriented in the north-south direction? Also, why is the critical representation of Vinland shown expressly as an island (see detail in Figure 4.5)? If it purports to show the coast of North America, why is it a representation that does not imply the presence of a whole continent? Arguments have raged over the depiction of Greenland as an island, since the first circumnavigation was not accomplished until much later than the purported date of the map's creation of 1440 [46]. Was it the cartographer's propensity to draw unknown locations as islands? If one were being pedantic – and there are many involved in the debate over the map who appear to be so – one could claim that this does not technically show the discovery of America but some disproportionate representation of yet another island in the Atlantic, as is already represented by the collection of islands in the center of the Atlantic (see Figure 4.3).

With regard to formal cause, some have sought to diffuse the controversy by questioning the informational value of what the map presented. It has been argued that because the Vinland Map provided nothing beyond what could be known from the sagas themselves, the visual representation

FIGURE 4.5. Detail from the Vinland Map showing the critical region illustrated as an island with two extensive inlets. It should be noted that while Greenland is corrrectly shown as an island, the configuration of Vinland, if it is North America, is clearly incorrect as the Island label "Insula" confirms.

on the map rendered no new knowledge. This perspective argues that the map is superfluous to our understanding of early European exploration of the North American continent. Strictly speaking, this is correct since what is shown on the Map could have feasibly been known, in some respects, prior to 1440. However, this argument vastly underestimates the power of pictures. For the Vinland Map is not simply a source of information; it is an icon. In our age of visual ascendency, it presents a single, visual "light-byte." It is a message that all the collected written works of the sagas were unable to accomplish in establishing the primacy of Norse exploration of North America. In this respect, it represents more than a mere informational document and in this we come to the question of motivation and to who actually fabricated the map itself. Here we move to the realm of efficient cause.

Efficient Cause

With respect to efficient cause, or who physically created the map, we are intrinsically asked to believe that the map was created by some 15th-century scribe who had access to information as to the shape of the world and especially the specifically illustrated expedition to central Asia. This is a feasible proposition, and one that was accepted in the early published materials in support of the map's authenticity. Unfortunately, we cannot put a name to this faceless individual, and, in and of itself, this fact engenders some frustration. However, the idea of creating maps was certainly a known pursuit before this juncture, as we can see from examples such as the *Mappa Mundi*. Thus, the making of a map is, in and of itself, no limit on our present day conundrum.

What Seaver has noted, however, is that the Norse, who were the explorers whose actions are at issue here, did not themselves make maps, at least not as of the proposed date of creation [47]. This is an important point that is often overlooked, since it is rightly assumed that other people did make maps. But critically, the Norse explorers whose exploits are illustrated did not *think* in terms that would be amenable to the subsequent creation of a relatively modern, God's eye–view representation of the Earth, even if they were to report their exploits to an external scribe. In his landmark text, *Cognition in the Wild*, the psychologist Ed Hutchins describes the sorts of heuristics that enable the peoples of Polynesia to navigate across vast tracts of the open Pacific Ocean (Hutchins, 1995). Theirs is a comparable case to the Viking explorers. The Polynesians used a variety of naturally occurring environmental cues to guide their passage [48]. It is this form of knowledge, and assumedly similar forms of direct experience, which would be codified and passed on by the Norse. Among these guides and aids, mapmaking and the associated knowledge and observations required to create God's eye–view maps would probably be missing. As a result, it would be very difficult for any articulate 15th-century cartographer to create a representation such as the Vinland Map, even if he had the contemporary explorers alongside him, which he did not. We are left with the options that the map was created by someone for whom mapmaking was a known art and was somehow able to translate Norse sailing recollections into a rectilinear God's eye–view map. Or the Vinland Map is the very first example of such an art in the Viking-dispersed culture. Since the map primarily records the eastward exploration, this latter proposition seems rather unlikely.

One particularly noteworthy thing about the Vinland Map is the extensive text passages written on it. Perhaps most interesting is the fact that *the* most extensive text of the whole of the map itself concerns the exploration of Vinland when the document attached to it is the *Tartar Relation*, which concerns an expedition to Asia [49]. This suggests the possibility that the map is a hybrid. That is, part of the map (and the crucial part showing Vinland) is a more modern set of graphics and text added to an older and perhaps genuine map. However, this seems unlikely. Not only would this have defaced a genuine artifact, which a forger may have been tempted to do; it also implies a very careful forging of the added textual materials and graphics, since the original text is directly adjacent and readily comparable. Up to now, no one has seriously advocated for such a hybrid form of fake.

In regard to a completely modern fabrication, Kirsten Seaver is quite certain of her identification of the Vinland Map as a near-contemporary fake [50]. Equally, she is clear in her identification of the forger. He is Father Joseph Fischer, a Jesuit priest and an author of an interesting text on the early exploration of North America by the Norse [51]. Seaver is explicit in her identification and accomplishes this through a sequence of questions as to who exactly possessed the knowledge, the scholarship, and the potential capacity in the appropriate time window. Establishing these necessary qualifications for creating such deception led Seaver to her conclusion. In identifying Father Fischer, Seaver has a great advantage over others who seek to explain the Vinland Map, for the name gives concreteness to her account, which others lack. For those who think the map genuine, they lack the maker's name, and even tentative identifications are limited at best. For others who also follow Seaver in believing the map a fake, they have often been handicapped by having no identity for their putative forger, although, of course, Ferrajoli would seem to provide an interesting candidate. Today we do not know whose hand created the Vinland Map, and thus equally, we do not have the necessary information to distinguish the creator's motivations. However, as we move on to the final component of Aristotle's four causes, it is to the estimation of this final cause that, in the end, we must turn.

Final Cause

When we look to the final cause, the purpose or goal of the map, we are looking directly at the motivation of the creator(s) and what they were trying to achieve via the presentation of their graphic and textual material. If this is truly an original document, then the individual must have been looking to provide an annotated cartographic representation of the *Tartar Relation* and, in a wider sense, express the known state of the world. Presumably, this was undertaken as an effort to inform and guide other contemporaries concerning what was known of the existing geography of the world. As exemplified in fiction (e.g., Clavell, 1975) and in motion pictures (e.g., *The Sea Hawk*, Curtiz, 1940) such early representations of the world were actually sources of great power [52]. Knowledge concerning the location and configuration of foreign lands was pivotal, not only in trade but also in war. If the Vinland Map is the genuine article, then its 1440 possessor was in a position of both knowledge and power well beyond the vista of most of Europe's temporal and spiritual powers at that time. Its creation is unlikely to have been purely an expression of that power, but its exploitation, toward both east and west, could have rendered great advantage. We do not see such exploitation derived specifically from this map, and thus the absence of any reference to its existence around this time is an issue for those who argue for its authenticity. Of course, as I noted earlier, information about the existence of the North American continent could feasibly have been known and as with all information in any form, its value is relational – that is, in relation to its source and to its user.

If the creation of the map is one of a later date, then the forger or forgers, for reasons of their own, were looking to retrospectively influence the collective perception of history. The latter, like other examples in this text, is very much to do with issues such as precedent, ownership, and the pride and influence of nation and culture. We can be certain about only one thing at this juncture. The map is not a simple fake. If it were merely a simplistic hoax, then the degree of scientific investigation to which it has been subjected would have revealed this fact long ago. Even if our eventual determination is that the map is a fake, we must respect the forger to some degree, whose efforts have defied definitive dismissal now for more than 50 years. Thus, the creator in antiquity or the forger of modern times demands a modicum of admiration even if, in the latter case, we may abhor the act of deception.

Like all forms of communication, the map seeks to persuade. Like all speculation on the motivation of others, explanations of persuasion are replete with the conundrum of what other people can or do know. In her extensive and influential text, which was the basis of the equally influential television program "The Viking Deception," Seaver concludes that as a fake, the map is based on anachronistic, 19th-century assumptions about Viking explorations, and was derived from complex motivations to deceive the ascendant Nazi regime, which was pursuing its purported associations with early Norse culture. She claims that Father Fischer's motivation would have been to "create" a representation that, as a scholar of that era, he may have been able to persuade others "ought" to exist. However, his "intellectual exercise" was confiscated by invading German troops, who seized the college in which Father Fischer had been a teacher. The map might well have been seen as evidence of the theory of Aryan supremacy, which the ascendant Nazi Party espoused. Seaver speculates that this is how, eventually, it found its way into the possession of Ferrajoli, who is described in the "The Viking Deception" as a known fascist and Nazi sympathizer. In respect to the specifics of this claim, Seaver buttresses her case for identification by illustrating some commonalties between the script on the legends of the map and known instances of Father Fischer's hand. However, like all such graphological comparisons, it is replete with a variety of pitfalls concerning selection and confirmation bias [53]. It remains a source of both contention and debate as to whether graphology itself is an art, science, or pseudoscience, and therefore we need further evidence of Father Fischer's authorship before we deliver any final deliberation on the authenticity of the map.

In respect to final cause, we must eventually look to the issue of profit, or as Churchill once noted, we must follow the money. To do this we must recount the trail of ownership and purchase as far as we know it. If the map was a creation in the 20th century by person or persons unknown, then the $3,500 Lawrence Witten paid sometime around 1957 must have been a good return for some blank parchment, a pen and ink, and a degree of imagination. Today this amount would be approximately $40,000 and may be as high as $100,000, depending on the algorithm one uses to complete the calculation. This is certainly a considerable amount and therefore no mean motivation for the creation of a hoax. We do not know what Mellon paid Witten for the Vinland Map and its accompanying texts, but the postulation is that it was some orders of magnitude more than what Witten paid for it. In terms of present value, it is certainly possible that Witten received the equivalent of more than $1 million when he sold the map. This is certainly a powerful motivation; however, there is no current indication that Witten acted as more than a middleman in the process. If it was a 20th-century hoax and the fabricator was living at the time of the acquisition by Yale University, that individual would have been perhaps more than frustrated by the fact that others profited more from their hoax than he/she did. However, such frustrations occur in the world of fine art every day.

THE VERDICT ON THE MAP

Is the map genuine? This is indeed the $25 million question [54]. Inevitably, the owners have an overwhelming impetus to establish authenticity, and this can certainly have profound effects on objectivity. However, it is equally clear that Yale University staff have done their best, at least in more recent years, to try to handle this issue with an appropriate degree of objectivity. It is very clear that the original announcement was designed to establish the map's bona fides and this initial strategy caused a degree of turmoil that persists to the present day. To a most understandable extent, Yale, as an institution of knowledge, tries to keep itself above the pecuniary issues, and it is doubtful whether this artifact would ever come on the market, except in the direst of circumstances. However, the original enthusiasm for authenticity has most recently been replaced by a much more dominant persuasion that the map is a fake. Seaver's recent text strongly suggests that the Vinland Map is a modern production. Further, in the mind of the public, which must have been swayed by the associated television documentary, the tendency to doubt the authenticity must have been strongly increased. However, these various objections have not left everyone convinced. Indeed, some still adhere to the conception that the Vinland Map is an authentic 1440 representation. The great thing about emotive items such as the Vinland Map is that they force you to choose [55]. Although fence sitting is a very popular scientific pastime, and the appeal to the necessity for further research is almost a ubiquitous one, I think the map is a very clever forgery. Contrary to a recent assessment by Rene Larsen, Rector of the School of Conservation of the Royal Danish Academy of Fine Arts, my assessment is based on the totality of my experience with the map, including a personal viewing. I do not claim any one single fact or issue is the sole arbiter of this persuasion. Indeed, to specify such a single reason is to invite almost inevitable debate. However, as with all things, I must also admit that I might well be wrong and that, as with all rational beings, future additional evidence may well sway my opinion, which is never so fixed that it cannot be altered by evidence.

REFERENCE NOTES

[1] Skeleton, R. A., Marston, T. E., & Painter, G. D. (1965). *The Vinland Map and the Tartar Relation* (with an Introduction by Alexander O. Vietor). New Haven, CT: Yale University Press (VMTR). The quote is on p. 124. Reprinted in 1995 with new prefatory essays by G. D. Painter, W. E. Washburn, T. A. Cahill, B. H. Kusko, and L. C. Witten II (VMTR95) [original pagination retained in body]. See also Jacobs, F. (2009). *Strange maps: An atlas of cartographic curiosities. [True or false: The Vinland Map]*. New York: Viking Studio.

[2] Skeleton et al. (1965), p. 3. See also Seaver, K. A. (1997). The Vinland map: A $3,500 duckling that became a $25,000,000 swan. *Mercator's World*, March/April, 42–47.

[3] Vinland Map; Hystoria Tartarorum. Beinecke Rare Book and Manuscript Library, Yale University, New Haven, Connecticut. Available at http://www.library.yale.edu/beinecke/. For a full translation of the text above Vinland, see the excellent text by Garfield, S. (2013). *On the map.* (p. 91) Gotham Books: New York.

[4] Skeleton et al. (1965), p. 3.

[5] Seaver, K. A. (2004). *Maps, myths and men: The story of the Vinland Map.* Stanford, CA: Stanford University Press. The quote is on p. 3.

[6] McCulloch, J. H. (2005). The Vinland Map – Some "finer points" of the debate. Available at http://www.econ.ohio-state.edu/jhm/arch/vinland/vinland.htm

[7] Washburn, W. E. (Ed.). (1971) *Proceedings of the Vinland Map Conference.* Chicago: University of Chicago Press. The quote is on p. 5.

[8] McCulloch (2005). op cit.

[9] McCulloch (2005). op cit.

[10] I possess at least three copies of this text. They can easily be found through any number of differing Web-based vendors.

[11] Washburn (1971).

[12] This date, selected for the convenience of the major figures involved, generated an unintentional insult to the Italian-American community. The timing of the announcement did not go unnoticed!

[13] See Skeleton et al. (1965).

[14] Michener, J. (1968). *Iberia: Spanish travels and reflections.* New York: Random House.

[15] See Babcock, W. H. (1921). Recent history and present status of the Vinland problem. *Geographical Review*, 11, 265–282; Bovey, W. (1936). The Vinland voyages. *Transactions of the Royal Society of Canada*, 27–47; Skeleton (1965), p. 139. Further reference to the Vinland explorations can be found in Sprague-Smith, C. (1892). The Vinland voyages. *Journal of the American Geographical Society of New York*, 24, 510–535, and also the introductory text by Reeves, A. M. (1890). *The finding of Wineland the good.* Frowde: London. The names cannot be seen in the presently embedded illustrations but are clear on larger-scale versions of the map, and of course on the map itself.

[16] Of course, this sequence of announcement, furor, controversy, and the establishment of pro and con camps is certainly not limited to the case of the Vinland Map. Indeed, it might be considered a characteristic process of all such "stunning" announcements as we saw, for example, with the case such as "cold fusion": see Huizenga, J. R. (1993), *Cold fusion: The scientific fiasco of the century* (2nd ed.). New York: Oxford University Press. One related problem is that many serious scientists see the often puerile squabbling that takes place, which often features those with very little knowledge or understanding of the scientific process. There is little benefit to busy research scientists to become embroiled in prolonged debates with certain individuals who are never going to be swayed by the facts, whatever they are.

[17] Seaver (2004), p. 14.

[18] Washburn, W. E. (Eds.). (1971) *Proceedings of the Vinland Map Conference.* Chicago: University of Chicago Press. The quote is on p. 4.

[19] Lonnroth, L. (1997). Untitled. *alvissmal, 7*, 115–120.

[20] Logan, D. (2005) *The Vikings in history.* Padstow, Cornwall: TJ International Ltd. The quote is on p. 92.

[21] Seaver (2004), p. 90.

[22] Washburn (1971), p. 5.

[23] Logan (2005), p. 89.

[24] Logan (2005), p. 92.

[25] Washburn (1971), p. 6.

[26] Seaver (2004), p. 104.

[27] Seaver (2004), p. 108; Dent, J. (2005). *The Viking Deception: The Truth Behind the Vinland Map.* NOVA, WGBH Educational Foundation, calls this a "spectacular coincidence." The degree to which one believes in spectacular coincidences might very well color one's perspective on authenticity. The incident is reminiscent of the sequential Piltdown finds which each answered specific criticisms; and see the later Chapter on Piltdown.

[28] Washburn (1971), p. 7.

[29] Washburn (1971), p. 8.

[30] McCulloch (2005).

[31] Candelaria, L. (2008) *The Rosary cantoral: Ritual and social design in a chantbook from early Renaissance Toledo.* Rochester, NY: University of Rochester Press. The quote is on p. 16.

[32] http://www.philosophypages.com/hy/2n.htm

[33] McCulloch (2005).

[34] Seaver (2004), pp. 180–190. It has been noted that McCrone's assessment was that the likelihood of anatase being found on a true map was equal to: "the likelihood that Nelson's flagship at Trafalgar was a hovercraft."

[35] McCrone, W., & McCrone, L. (1974). The Vinland Map ink. *The Geographical Journal,* 140(2), 212–214.

[36] Seaver (2004), p. 190.

[37] Dent (2005).

[38] Donahue, D. J., Olin, J. S., & Harbottle, G. (2002). Determination of the radiocarbon age of parchment of the Vinland Map. *Radiocarbon,* 44(1), 45–52.

[39] See Baynes-Cope, A. D. (1974). For the scientific examination of the Vinland Map at the research laboratory of the British Museum see Baynes-Cope, A. D. (1974). *The Geographical Journal,* 140(2), 208–211.

[40] The Vinland Map, The Shroud, and Walter McCrone: A Parallel Example of Science in Conflict (Shroud Report), Shroud University. Available at http://shroud2000.com/articlespapers/article-vinlandmap.html

[41] Richard B. Arkway, Inc. *Fine Antique Maps, Atlases, Globes and Voyage Books.* Catalog 54: World Maps c.1200–1700. Available at http://www.arkway.com/pdfs/cot54.pdf

[42] McCulloch (2005). op cit.

[43] http://www.absoluteastronomy.com/topic/terra_incognita

[44] McCulloch (2005).

[45] Fitzhugh, W. W. (2005). *A Saga of Wormholes and Anatase.* Available at http://www.sciencemag.org/cgi/reprint/sci.307/5714/1413.pdf

[46] Dent (2005).

[47] Dent (2005).

[48] Finney, B. (1996). Colonizing an island world. *Transactions of the American Philosophical Society,* 86(5), 71–116.

[49] Grone, G. R. (1974). The "Sources' of the Vinland Map." *The Geographical Journal,* 140(2), 205–208.

[50] Dent (2005).

[51] Fischer, J. (1903). *The Discoveries of the Norsemen in America, with special relation to their early cartographical representation*. New York: Burt Franklin. Translation of 1902 German edition. Herder: London.

[52] See, for example, accounts in fiction such as Clavell, J. (1975). *Shogun*. New York: Dellacorte Press, or some of the more lurid tales given in early film such as Curtiz, M. (1940). *The Sea Hawk*. Warner Brothers.

[53] Such issues can be seen in other high-profile utilizations such as the Lindbergh kidnapping, e.g., Haring, J. V. (1937). *Hand of Hauptmann*. New York: Patterson-Smith. See also Nickell, J. (2005). *Detecting forgery: Forensic investigation of documents*. Lexington: University of Kentucky Press. Garfield, S. (2013) op cit. (p. 102) observes that the *Imago Mundi* review of Seaver's contentions found them ingenious, compelling, but without proof.

[54] Campbell, E. (1974). Verdict on the Vinland map. *Geographical Magazine*, April, 307–312. Garfield, S. (2013) op cit, (p. 102) concluded that: "*The mystery of Vinland shows us the power of maps to fascinate, excite and provoke, to affect the course of history, to serve as the silent conduit to the compelling stories of where we've been and where we're going.*" It is as fitting an epitaph to the Map as any.

[55] As one of the reviewers of this text insisted, there is a third path. That is, one can simply choose to ignore the whole issue. While I agree that this is a path that many often take, this is because they are not deeply vested in the issue. I believe, however, that there comes a time for us when we are vested deeply enough to have to choose. For to live a life where one is never passionate about an issue might appear to be *dolce far niente (life without care)*, and I would claim it is not a fully lived life at all.

III

Deciding on Deception

How We Decide on the Veracity of Various Claims

"We are never deceived, we deceive ourselves."
Johann Wolfgang von Goethe

INTRODUCTION

So far, we have discussed various case studies of deception and have examined some of the ways in which people process the information associated with deception. It has also been stated that sensory deceptions are mostly associated with bottom-up processing of sources of incoming environmental stimulation and the immediate perceptions they generate. In contrast, cognitive deceptions are mostly mediated by top-down processes that feature prominent access to long-term memories and are regulated by the active direction of attention. What needs to be explored now is exactly how individuals decide on whether the information they are offered is true or false. To do this, we have to understand more about how humans make decisions in general.

TWO FACES OF DECISION MAKING

To begin to understand how people make decisions, and particularly how decision making is linked to bottom-up and top-down processes, it is best to return to the model of human capacities presented earlier (see Figure III.1 over). On the outer ring we can see that there is one pathway that leads directly from the registration of information (the information flux, on the upper left of the diagram), directly through sensory registration to the decision process, and immediately on to the response selection and execution phase. This sort of sensory-mediated decision

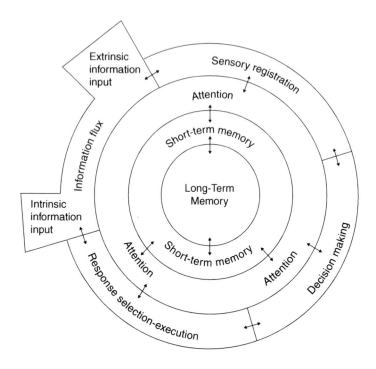

FIGURE III.1. The embedded spiral model of response capacities. Notice that some decisions can proceed with only implicit access to the inner loops of attention and memory while others require explicit access. In general, time is also a critical dimension that differentiates between these sorts of decision strategies.

making is dependent on the immediate pattern of information that the senses pick up. One of its characteristics is that the decision is made quickly. In fact, one popular characterization of this process has it happening in a "blink" [1].

Actually, however, such decisions are a little more complicated than this. In fact, the "blink" label really refers to the seminal work of Gary Klein, a research scientist, and his concept of recognition-primed decision making [2]. This latter label is itself quite a mouthful and, as we will need to understand this form of decision making rather more thoroughly, the following discussion is a more detailed exploration of this concept. The full panoply of work in this area is available in the specific scientific literature [3].

NATURALISTIC DECISION MAKING

It is often suggested that Klein's work actually began in response to another form of decision making theory generally called rational decision making theory, which we will also explore later [4]. This is not strictly true, but Klein himself was very concerned with how experts make real-world decisions, especially in stressful circumstances in which time is a very limited commodity. Perhaps his best-known work concerns the activities of expert firefighters [5]. He recounts one situation featuring such important, time-limited responses. One expert firefighter found himself trapped by a fire that was rapidly advancing up the side of a steep canyon. *Rapidly* in this context means the fire was moving faster than a person could run. What would you do? The fire is coming toward you at a tremendous pace and there is literally nowhere to hide. The answer the expert came up with was – start a fire! Yes, that's right: to avoid being burned up he decided to set his own small fire. Now that the answer is in front of you, it rather makes sense. By creating a small, controlled "burn," the expert created a bare patch of land that represented a safe "island" in the coming tide of the wildfire. With all of its fuel now gone, the wildfire circled around the controlled-burn area and passed him by. Of course, a significant part of the firefighter's expertise was knowing the fire was coming at him and exactly how much time he had to respond. It was these forms of critical insight that intrigued Klein and led to his theorizing about experts out there, "in the wild" as it were.

How did the expert know the fire is about to turn lethal and move in his direction? How do such practical experts know, for example, that a burning roof is about to collapse, when the rest of us just see a large and chaotic conflagration? Understanding this form of expertise was the task Klein set himself to achieve and his insights have been so intriguing that whole cadres of researchers are now following his lead. One of the central notions of the "naturalistic decision making" group is the theory Klein developed: Recognition-Primed Decision Making (RPD) [6]. This form of decision making depends directly on the pattern of stimulation the person experiences and the way in which these, sometimes subtle cues, serve to trigger a rapid, learned, expert response. In many ways we all prove to be "experts" at certain everyday tasks. The problem is that we often take such "expertise" for granted and therefore don't see it as such.

Consider what might be thought of as the simple task of crossing the street. Down the road we see an approaching car. Now we have to judge whether that car will get near enough to threaten us, whether it will cross our path, and how fast we must now walk, or run, so that we can reach the other side of the street before it poses the threat of immediate impact. These are actually quite complicated calculations, especially if the car is speeding up or slowing down. Yet such judgments and consequent actions are frequently accomplished with little or no reference to stored mathematics in long-term memory and often with only minimal use of attention. Indeed, most humans are very well attuned to this particular decision-making task; we readily spot the sensory cues that allow us to come up with the right answer almost instantly [7]. This is the essence of Recognition-Primed Decision Making. Through repeated exposure to the critical array of subtle cues we can "see" the answer without having to write everything down on paper and weigh each respective option before actually deciding what to do. And this capacity is essential, of course, because it allows us to save time and energy in crucial, sometimes life-threatening circumstances. The capacity is one founded in the imperatives of evolution and derives from our ancestors who had to be highly skilled at hunting in complex environments where the prey they pursued would never stop and kindly wait for well-measured and considered decisions to be taken. As we know from today's military, the time for careful and considered planning is before the mission, not in the mayhem of the actual engagement. Thus, these are not simply "residual" skills, but ones that still very much come to the fore in today's busy and demanding technological world.

Now, what can we make of deception in relation to this form of decision making? Since generally such decisions are arrived at very quickly, they are contingent upon specific patterns of sensory input. In fact, professional illusionists exploit precisely this form of decision making in their routines, particularly the ones involving familiar objects, such as playing cards, for example. Here, many of the illusions rely on the fact that you readily recognize cards and take their patterns as consistent and unvarying. As an audience member you are making the "expert" assumption that these cards are standard ones, familiar to you through years of playing card games or watching others play. The illusionist explicitly relies on this "expert" recognition and then uses it to implement deception. Many other sensory-dominated deceptions look to "fool" this form of long-assimilated expertise. For general "magic shows," the illusionist has to use items that are familiar to everyone, such as playing cards. However, when fooling experts in certain particular professional areas, *the deceiver must use their particular domain-specific skills to lead them into error* [8]. Although all such general formulations are dangerous if overstated, we might conclude here that because Recognition-Primed Decision Making involves distilling and reacting to specific patterns of sensory input, these

FIGURE III.2. Those deceptive playing cards are purpose-made to rely on the inherent "expertise" of the observing individual. Cards in possession of the Author, photograph by Szuhui Wu. The full effect with color can be seen at: www.peterhancock.ucf.edu. © Peter Hancock.

processes are most vulnerable to sensory-based, or bottom-up forms of deception.

As with all such general statements, we should recognize the associated cautions since all decision making to some degree involves both sensory inputs and access to long-term memory. It is to the more measured and time-consuming forms of "rational" decision making, and the deceptions associated with these capacities, that I now turn.

RATIONAL OR COMPUTATIONAL DECISION MAKING

Often considered the more traditional model of decision making and set in contrast to naturalistic and recognition-primed approaches, rational or computational decision making is based on econometric or rational approaches to the process. This approach relies heavily on mathematical models of risk and gain and looks to derive rational decisions that the individual *should* take, given a practical set of circumstances. Although this original form of decision theory is set in direct contrast to the naturalistic conception, there is no reason in principle or in practice why these two should not be complementary rather than mutually exclusive approaches [9]. Indeed, if we feature the dimension of time, we can see how the two can fit together rather nicely instead of clashing with each other.

The rational model suits certain domains well. For example, such an approach works reasonably well for decision making in business when an appropriate amount of time is available. Here, the rational model has been dominant, partly, of course, by virtue of being first on the scene. The more "bounded" the domain and the more the rules are fixed and known, the more the rational model has been applied. Problems of fixed gambles are particularly suited to this mathematical approach. However, as shown by the Nobel Prize–winning scientists Daniel Kahneman and Amos Tversky, even when the optimal solution can be known, there is no guarantee that the decision maker will choose the "right" solution. This is because of certain inherent biases that all humans possess [10]. In these sorts of decision, the deception is largely top-down and dominated by memory processes. These can be truly seen as "sleights of mind" [11]. However, the problem with these rational models emerges when the world becomes more complex and ambiguous and the range of possible responses cannot be completely known, much less calculated. Limits to such rational assessment are particularly exposed when there is very little time to make the decision.

There are a number of well-known heuristics and biases that people adopt in the rational calculation models, and it is these characteristics that play a crucial role in understanding decision making in cognitive deception [12]. This is because, unlike the time-limited "sleight of hand" deceptions involved in professional "magic shows," cognitive deceptions, especially of the sort presented in the current case studies, can be perused at length and contemplated for extended periods of time. Making decisions in time-limited situations proves to be of relatively "low cost" in terms of cognitive energy used. However, while the decision itself might not be very costly, the result of a wrong decision can be fatal. This is why we are highly skilled at tasks like spatial navigation and threat detection. In contrast, relatively slow rational decisions with extended time horizons cost quite large amounts in terms of cognitive effort. Whether the fabricator of a deception knows it or not, he/she must exploit these natural human biases to the extent possible in order to "sell" the deception. So, for example, for anyone who invests significant cognitive effort into a decision, they will want to see a positive return on their "mental" investment. The deceiver must exploit this tendency to its fullest extent. But this is by no means the only one of these inherent human characteristics. So, let us now look at some of the most relevant of these biases.

The majority of these biases have various modern labels attached to them. However, many derive directly from the original observations of Francis Bacon. Here, I have provided some specific illustrations with respect to cognitive deception. Subsequently, I relate them to their foundational principles in both the modern world and historical precedent. One of the most influential of all such biases bears the modern name of "confirmation bias." The modern research on this effect is quite extensive [13]. In general, this tendency shows up as a propensity to search out information and cues that support a previously adopted position. This concept has its origins in one of Bacon's propositions:

> Human understanding, once it has adopted opinions, either because they were already accepted and believed, or because it likes them, draws everything to support and agree with them. And though it may meet a greater number and weight of contrary instances, it will, with great and harmful prejudice, ignore or condemn or exclude them. [14]

This particular bias is very much related to an allied construct of wishful thinking [15]. Like a number of other intrinsic biases, these psychological dimensions act to lead the individual away from the purported "rational" choice. These particular biases are of great advantage to deceivers, but they require them to know much about who is to be deceived. On a statistical basis, if one throws a deception out into the world, a proportion of people will be seduced by biases such as wishful thinking and confirmation bias to support what is offered, but a truly inspired deception works on more than statistical chance [16].

Another form of bias to which people are particularly vulnerable is "hindsight bias" [17]. Here, we suppose ourselves to be very wise after an event and thus convince ourselves that we personally would not have fallen for some particular "scam" or deception. The forthcoming case of the Piltdown Man in this book illustrates this propensity well. This is not an exhaustive listing of all the various biases, since indeed there are many and varied examples. However, the fundamental bottom line with respect to the rational decision making is that people, for a number of intrinsic and extrinsic reasons, do not always make the rational or optimal decision. It is within the cracks of these nominal "irrationalities" that the deceiver can seek to exploit our human foibles.

DECISIONS ON DECEPTION AND SIGNAL DETECTION THEORY

Although there are some who adopt an ambiguous stance and many other people who are either apathetic or unaware of a particular issue, it is the case with respect to cognitive deceptions that the choice for the actively involved individual is largely a binary one. That is, you either believe or not believe, and so you either accept or reject the deception (or the truth). Fortunately, it turns out that there is a formal, mathematical approach to understanding this particular type of "yes or no" decision. It is termed Signal Detection Theory (SDT) [18]. Formal SDT starts by breaking the world into two states. These two states are called "signal" and "noise," but with respect to deception we can think of this as the claim being either "true" or "false." Next, you must make a decision about the situation that itself can be correct or incorrect. So, we create a simple matrix of four outcomes. If the claim is true and you accept this as correct, you are right about the state of the world. In SDT parlance this is known as a hit. Similarly, if the claim is false and you think it is incorrect, you are right again and in SDT parlance this is called a correct rejection. However, the claim may be true even though you think it is false, and this incorrect outcome SDT terms a miss. Finally, the last combination has the claim as being false but you actually believe it to be true, and this combination is known in SDT as a false alarm. It is the latter condition in which the hoax is successful, and so we are most interested in it here. The goal of the deceiver is to maximize the number of false alarms while minimizing other forms of response.

The advantage of SDT is that it provides a strong, quantitative basis on which to assess certain characteristics of the individual making the decision [19]. In particular, it allows insights into two decision capacities, namely their sensitivity (traditionally labeled d') and their decision bias (labeled B). *Sensitivity* refers to how one is able to distinguish hoax from authenticity, truth from untruth. If the hoax is an obvious one, then the distinction between truth and untruth is a large one and therefore the less sensitivity one needs to resolve the issue. For example, if someone tries to sell you a bridge in New York, you ought to suspect that he/she is not the true owner and hence you would not be fooled (although it should be remembered that someone once did successfully sell the Eiffel Tower!). If, however, the true state of the world and the hoax are very similar, then one would need great sensitivity (perhaps augmented with data from scientific measuring instruments) to tell the difference. *Decision bias* refers to how likely you are to say "yes" versus "no." Some people are very liberal in this regard and are willing to say yes to most things. Thus, they will make a large number of false alarms (saying true when the case is actually false) but will only have a limited number of misses (saying false when it is actually true). Other people are very conservative and will reject most claims. These individuals have the opposite propensity. They fall for very few false claims (saying true when the case is false) but similarly they will have a large number of misses (saying false when it is actually true). As is clear, these two approaches to bias form a trade-off and often depend on what the cost is of a false alarm and a miss, respectively.

By evaluating the combination of the measures (B and d') one can tell what sort of decision maker one is dealing with. This knowledge allows you to determine how to make bias and sensitivity more or less useful, depending on whether you are trying to train good detectors or produce people who are vulnerable to deception. Thus, our explorations so far have shown us that recognition-primed decisions are often time-limited and rely on specific sensory patterns on which people employ their situation-specific expertise. In these cases, SDT tells us that we need to work primarily on their sensitivity and we can do this by altering the evidence intrinsic to the deception. Further, we might think about times when the sensitivity of that individual decreases for some reason. For example, sensitivity varies with time of day, so that individuals trying to make detections in the early hours of the morning are less efficient than they are in the middle of the day. Also, fatigue affects sensitivity. So, if a person has been doing the task for a very long period of time and it is the middle of the night, they are more likely to accept a deception than if they are just starting a working shift. These facts are well known to smugglers and other criminals who have to get past law enforcement officers. As I have said now several times, since deception is an interactive process, you can increase the fidelity of the deception itself or you can reduce the capacity of the individual to detect it. In effect, these two different influences end up having the same end effect.

With respect to cognitive deception, we are more liable to encounter the use of time-consuming rational decision-making processes. Therefore, these sorts of decisions are more likely to be influenced by an individual's intrinsic bias. As a result, successful cognitive deceptions must play more on people's intrinsic biases, which are stored in their long-term memory. Inherently biased individuals will tend to ignore even quite strong evidence of deception if the proposition strongly agrees with their own established perspective on the world. While all forms of deception partake of both sensory and cognitive components to some degree, deceivers intent on deception can play on the relative domination of either sensitivity (d') or bias (B) to achieve their deceptive intent.

AN INTERIM CONCLUSION

Whether one spends a lifetime studying a particular artifact or makes a snap decision to believe or disbelieve, eventually one has to render a final deliberation on the respective information presented concerning each item or entity. This is a critical point in time, because the fact of rendering a decision often commits an individual to a particular stance. Having now adopted that stance, it is hard for the person to change because they will have become personally vested in their decision. So before you render your own decision on any of the present examples, please suspend judgment until we reach the final chapter.

REFERENCE NOTES

[1] Gladwell, M. (2005). *Blink: The power of thinking without thinking.* New York: Little, Brown & Co.

[2] Klein, G. (1998). *Sources of power: How people make decisions.* Cambridge, MA: MIT Press.

[3] See, for example, Hoffman, R. R. (Ed.) (2007). *Expertise out of context: Proceedings of the Sixth International Conference on Naturalistic Decision Making.* Boca Raton, FL: Taylor & Francis. We are also seeing this notion percolate more into the popular literature. Consider, for example, the following quote from Foer, J. (2011). *Moonwalking with Einstein.* New York: Penguin. "Experts see the world differently. They notice things that non-experts don't see. They home in on the information that matters most, and have an almost automatic sense of what to do with it. And most important, experts process the enormous amounts of information flowing through their senses in more sophisticated ways" (p. 55).

[4] Simon, H. A. (1979). Rational decision making in business organizations. *The American Economic Review*, 69(4), 493–513.

[5] http://www.fs.fed.us/t-d/pubs/htmlpubs/htm95512855/page13.htm

[6] http://www.au.af.mil/au/awc/awcgate/milreview/ross.pdf

[7] Hancock, P. A., & Manser, M. P. (1998). Time-to-contact. In A. M. Feyer & A. M. Williamson (Eds.), *Occupational injury: Risk, prevention, and intervention* (pp. 44–58). London: Taylor & Francis.

[8] See Grazioli, S., Jamal, K., & Johnson, P. E. (2006). A cognitive approach to fraud detection. *Journal of Forensic Accounting*, 7, 65–88, and Johnson, P. E., Grazoli, S., Karim, J., & Berryman, R. G. (2001). Detecting deception: Adversarial problem solving in a low base-rate world. *Cognitive Science*, 25, 355–392. Also see Kahneman, D., Slovic, P., & Tversky, A. (1982), *Judgment under uncertainty: Heuristics and biases.* Cambridge: Cambridge University Press. Most recently, see Kahneman, D. (2011). *Thinking fast and slow.* New York: Farrar, Strauss, and Giroux.

[9] Kahneman, D., & Klein, G. (2009). Conditions for intuitive expertise: A failure to disagree. *American Psychologist*, 64(6), 515–526.

[10] See Tversky, A., & Kahneman, D. (1974). Judgment under uncertainty: Heuristics and biases. *Science*, 185(4157), 1124–1131.

[11] Macknik, S. L., & Martinez-Conde, S. (2010). *Sleights of mind*. New York: Holt & Co.

[12] Kahneman, D., Slovic, P., & Tversky, A. (1982). *Judgment under uncertainty: Heuristics and biases*. Cambridge: Cambridge University Press.

[13] See Nickerson, R. (1998). Confirmation bias: A ubiquitous phenomenon in many guises. *Review of General Psychology*, 2(2), 175–220, and Oswald, M. E., & Grosjean, S. (2004). Confirmation bias. In R. F. Pohl (Ed.), *Cognitive illusions: A handbook on fallacies and biases in thinking, judgment and memory* (pp. 79–96). Hove, UK: Psychology Press.

[14] Bacon, F. (1620). Novum organum (*Idols of the tribe*, Aphorism, 46). Taken from Spedding, J., Ellis, R. L., & Heath, D. D. (1863). *The Works* (Vol. VIII). Boston: Taggard and Thompson.

[15] Baron, J. (1994), *Thinking and deciding* (2nd ed.). Cambridge: Cambridge University Press.

[16] There are a number of films (e.g., "The Sting") and television shows (e.g., BBC TV "Hustle") in which there is a particular "target," and much time is spent on understanding the individual characteristics of this "mark." As deception becomes more endemic in various social/electronic media, this necessity for greater individual focus will be the source of demand for greater computational power and greater degrees of data mining. Computers are particularly facile at each of these particular tasks, and so deception will become ever harder to combat in these realms.

[17] Fischoff, B., & Beyth, R. (1975). "I knew it would happen": Remembered probabilities of once-future things. *Organizational Behaviour and Human Performance*, 13, 1–16.

[18] Green, D. M., & Swets, J. A. (1966). *Signal detection theory and psychophysics*. New York: Wiley.

[19] Hancock, P. A., Masalonis, A. J., & Parasuraman, R. (2000). On the theory of fuzzy signal detection: Theoretical and practical considerations and extensions. *Theoretical Issues in Ergonomic Science*, 1(3), 207–230.

Piltdown Man

The Desire That the First Human Being Be an Englishman

INTRODUCTION

An account of Piltdown Man is unlike any of the other stories of cognitive deception discussed in this book. This is because we now know categorically that the Piltdown remains are, in fact, a hoax. Therefore, we naturally approach this story with a strong propensity toward a level of hindsight bias that encourages us to be wise after the event [1]. Our first thought, therefore, should be to appreciate that many of the individuals involved with the Piltdown finds were as certain of its authenticity in their time as we are now of its fraudulence. The real story of the Piltdown hoax, however, does not begin with the findings of the bones themselves. Rather, it is framed by the context of the times and especially the continuing aftershocks of Charles Darwin's pivotal proposition concerning the evolution of life on our planet [2]. If what Darwin had said concerning evolution were true, then the theory predicted that there ought to be recognizable fossils of the ancestors of modern human beings connecting us to our nonhuman forebears. For a number of decades, the race was on to find the definitive evidence of this "missing link."

To the great chagrin of the British scientific community, intriguing evidence of earlier hominids had been found in Belgium as well as in both Germany and France, the great European rivals of the British Empire [3]. However, after the turn of the century, with the Edwardian era replacing the venerable Victorian age, no such prestigious fossils had been found in "England's green and pleasant land." That Britain may not have actually been an island at the time that some of these European ancestors existed mattered not one whit to the members of the British establishment; the implied insult persisted. The geopolitical rivals had their "early man" while England did not. The French even had a derogatory term for their English colleagues; they called them "pebble hunters." It was in this receptive and fertile soil of

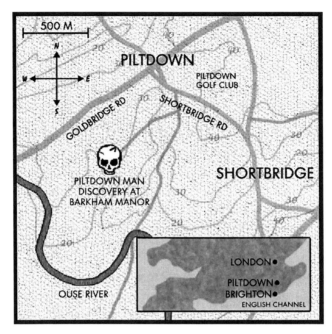

FIGURE 5.1. A map of the Piltdown area showing the find at Barkham Manor in relation to the village and the golf course. Drawing by Richard Kessler; © Peter Hancock.

fervent British patriotism that the Piltdown remains, produced by the amateur scientist Charles Dawson, so quickly took root. His discoveries were evidently a manifest "rival to the German's Ape Man." Eventually, the Piltdown fossils were to become much more than this and ended up being, arguably, the most explosive case of scientific fraud that has ever been uncovered [4].

A PERSONAL PERUSAL

As a result of this fame, or perhaps infamy, you might suspect that the site of the Piltdown finds would be well known locally and indeed would be a popular spot to visit. So strongly had I believed that this would be the case that, on a personal visit to the village, I had even neglected to secure a map of the area such as the one shown in Figure 5.1 [5]. Surely everyone in the village of Piltdown would be aware of their worldwide claim to fame. Apparently this was not so. Interested investigators will find themselves outside the town of Uckfield in East Sussex in England looking hopefully for local directions to the parish of Fletching and the famed Piltdown site. My own first stop on such an expedition was the Piltdown Golf Club, on the assumption that prominent members of the local "enthusiasts of the white ball" would immediately be able to guide me to my destination. I was sadly mistaken. No one present on that day could provide me with any explicit information at all, and I was instead advised to try the local public house appropriately entitled Piltdown Man – Family Tavern. [6] Here, I was confident, I would be able to find solid directions to the discovery site. Unfortunately, the regular landlord was away on his annual holiday, and his replacement – one of his relatives – was new to the area. He had no idea as to the whereabouts of the Piltdown Man excavations. In reality, I think he had absolutely no idea what this stranger at his back door was talking about.

By now I was getting rather frustrated. I had flown more than a quarter of the way around the world to find this location and now, within what must have been only a mile or two at most, I found myself stymied. My next stop was a local petrol station. The proprietor, originally from Pakistan, was a very pleasant and helpful individual. He apologized profusely that he was unable to help me with my quest but he simply did not know where the site was. With this declaration I seemed to have reached a complete impasse. As I was at the petrol station, I decided to refuel and try to think of other potential sources of enlightenment. There I fell into conversation with a lady at the adjacent pump, and here at last was my salvation. Yes, she knew where the site was, and apparently – and luckily – it was very near. Although she gave me precise directions, they were predicated on her local understanding, and so I still managed to get lost twice within the half-mile or so that it took me to get there. Eventually, after several twists and turns, I found myself facing the entry gates of Barkham Manor (see Figure 5.2). However, like William Blake at the entrance to the "Garden of Love," the gates of Barkham Manor were firmly shut. Annoyingly, there was no immediate way to contact anyone who might have been able to help, and my crowded travel schedule did not allow me to pursue the issue any further that day. Ultimately stymied, I left the area determined one day to return to see whether I could eventually look directly at the small gravel pit the contents of which had instigated such a furor. It remains one of my goals to the present day. An even greater sadness was that I was unable to inspect the actual remains themselves. Despite a number of requests to the Natural History Museum in London, apparently such an inspection was just "not possible."

FIGURE 5.2. The closed gates to Barkham Manor. The tree-lined road leads (presumably) to the site of the discovery. Photograph by the Author.

THE ORIGINAL DISCOVERY

According to the accepted story, had I stood at the same spot at the entrance to Barkham Manor almost a century earlier, I might well have met with the Sussex solicitor Charles Dawson on his way to talk with one of the local workmen. For it was one such anonymous workman who, reputedly, had found the original cranium in a small open dig at the far end of the avenue of trees that led so tantalizingly away from me on that cold November morning (and see Figure 5.3). On the other hand, I might not have met with Dawson at all! For one of the most curious and, in retrospect, more suspicious aspects of the tale of Piltdown Man is the lack of clear information as to precisely when and where the original find was made.

The story as represented in a recent television documentary, "The Boldest Hoax," has Dawson present virtually at the moment of the workman's discovery of the first fossil [7]. This character was portrayed as digging at the famous site at Barkham Manor of which Dawson, as a professional lawyer, had been the steward for thirteen years. Unfortunately, we do not have the precise date of this first discovery, although some accounts put it as early as

FIGURE 5.3. The gravel pit, in which Mr. Venus Hargreaves wields the spade to the left alongside Arthur Smith Woodward and Charles Dawson (at right). The attendant goose, Chipper, looks on. Image courtesy of The Natural History Museum, London.

1908 and some even before that. Suspicious as this may now seem, Costello suggests that the delay between any original finding and Dawson's subsequent communications concerning the find might be owing to the fact that Dawson was still searching for the rest of the skull [8]. Even when other parts had been found, the full import of the find might perhaps not have been evident because it added up only to the cranial case alone. Indeed, Costello concluded that it was only later, with Dawson and Smith-Woodward's mutual finding of the supposedly associated jawbone, that the hoax itself really began. We must also remember that this was a different era, and in such times it would be considered insulting and bad form not to take a gentleman's word for it. However, more modern perusal of the existing records suggests potential substance to Dawson's original story. This information indicates that the original find had been made by one Alfred Thorpe, a workman in the employ of the Kenward family that were, at that time, leasing Barkham Manor from a Mr. Maryon-Wilson [9]. Later testing suggested that what Thorpe actually found were the remains of an individual who may have died during the Black Death. The noticeable "thickening" of the skull might have been attributable to some disease state or even to natural variation [10].

Costello has reported that Dawson did indeed take the bones to a local colleague, Samuel Woodhead, and it was Woodhead who suggested hardening the pieces in potassium dichromate as a protective and preservation agent. It was the thickened cranial bones and the coloring of the fossils that encouraged the interpretation that these were prehistoric remains.

We do not have a definitive account of the earliest finds. The recent text by Russell gives a most insightful and detailed account, but even with his information we cannot say for certain exactly where the finds were originally made, who made them, or precisely how they came into Dawson's possession [11]. What we do know is that Dawson seems to have mentioned his discovery to some local colleagues, but it was only early in 1912 that he communicated the substance of his "find" to a friend and colleague. This colleague was Arthur Smith Woodward (hereafter Woodward), who was then Keeper of the Natural History Department at the British Museum [12]. Dawson had known Woodward, who was by specialty a paleo-ichthyologist, for some time. The original letter is intriguing but very strange, especially in respect of the hominid findings. Dawson says:

> I have come across a very old Pleistocene (?) bed overlying the Hastings bed between Uckfield and Crowborough which I think is going to be interesting. It has a lot of iron-stained flints in it, so I suppose it is the oldest known flint gravel in the Weald. I portion [sic] of a human skull which will rival H. Heidelbergensis in solidity.

How Dawson had only just "come across" this bed in 1912, when he had been associated with Barkham Manor for some decades and had also been asking local workmen to save interesting items, for which he paid them, is not explained. Despite retrospective attempts at justification, it is the mysterious origin of the first Piltdown fossils that is never satisfactorily explained. Indeed, Dawson and Woodward eventually produced somewhat differing accounts of both the first finds as well as the first formal explorations of the site. Woodward, for example, emphasizes that what the original workman(men) found was thought to be a "coconut" that they then inexplicably dashed into pieces, retaining only a small portion to subsequently show Dawson [13]. Why they should have destroyed this artifact when Dawson was reported to be paying them handsomely for such relics is also never explained. Coconuts do not seem to come into any account that Dawson renders of the original discovery.

Following on the original communication between the two men, efforts were set in motion to explore the site more thoroughly. The first organized expedition to Barkham Manor, which also included the subsequently famous French priest and philosopher Teilhard de Chardin, took place on June 2, 1912 [14]. The following excavations on the site were not continuous; indeed, the regular work duties of the major participants obstructed any consistent effort, which was thus confined to weekends and holidays. The amateur, the professional, and the priest were helped in their endeavors by one workman, a Mr. Venus Hargreaves, as well as one animal, the guardian goose Chipper (see Figure 5.3). The first efforts were given over to the examination of spoil heaps produced by the regular use of the gravel pits by workmen digging out material for road construction. Searching these heaps proved slow and painstaking since each spade-full had to be carefully sifted. It appears that Mr. Hargreaves was employed in the pit excavation doing the heavy digging while the others inspected what had previously come from the pit and what Hargreaves then shifted. Much of this material was spread out so that any rain would help the investigators by exposing the fossils. Unfortunately, this had the side effect of dissociating the finds from their original location and led to further confusion as to later accounts of each specific find.

What was certain was that the group was finding something interesting. Sporadic exploration went on throughout the summer of 1912, with the later accounts reporting finds of the teeth of elephant, mastodon, beaver, horse, and hippopotamus, as well as, of course, the critical hominid remains [15]. Dawson played down the excitement of the finds by suggesting that several days of digging revealed nothing at all of interest, but this is belied by de Chardin's account of just the first day on which Dawson apparently discovered new portions of the skull, which had triggered the work in the first place.

One can argue over precisely when the Piltdown hoax reached a critical stage at which it could not be dismissed as either some understandable mistake or misdirected high jinks. That moment was most probably the discovery of the jawbone that was associated with the cranial remains. It is true that the cranium and the fabricated context of the associated animal fossils in which its parts were found did generate much enthusiasm. However, the cranium alone – although it would have been a startling discovery – would not by itself have triggered the worldwide response that Piltdown engendered. It is worthwhile to examine when and how this crucial piece of evidence was uncovered. The critical fragment of a mandible, illustrated in Figure 5.4, was reportedly "found" by Dawson sometime in June 1912 or possibly September 23, as Walsh notes in his text [16]. The context of the find is really important. To set the scene, it is important to note first that Dawson himself did not find all of the skull fragments. Indeed, as we shall

Despite the need for a degree of secrecy in order to allow for a time of mature reflection, the story of the discovery seems to have been leaked to the press. As early as November 1912, the papers were already printing stories of the discovery of the "earliest man" [20]. Of course, we do not know who leaked these stories, but they served to whet the appetite of the media to the forthcoming announcement and thus the explosive coverage only a short time later. We might well ask who had the knowledge of the find and who would most benefit from its national exposure. However, as in much of Piltdown's story, we have fertile grounds for speculation but little definitive evidence. Regardless of who leaked the information, it was observed that the meeting rooms at which the formal announcement was scheduled had "never been so crowded." The formal introduction of Piltdown was certain to be an "event."

ANNOUNCING THE FIND

It was into this fervor of both scientific and public interest that Dawson and Woodward's collaborative reconstruction of Piltdown Man was announced to the world. He was revealed in the middle of winter, on December 18, 1912, at Burlington House, the home of the Geological Society in London – just in time for Christmas [21]. Naturally, the proceedings were headed by Woodward himself, then Keeper of Geology at the British Museum, and by Dawson, after whom the fossils were named *Eoanthropus Dawsoni* – Dawson's Dawn Man. At the meeting, the eminent professor of anatomy, Grafton Elliot Smith, talked at length on the implications of the endo-cranial markings of the skull fragments. Not so long divorced from the expositions of phrenology (the study of human capacities as supposedly represented on the morphology of the skull), Elliot Smith's discourse speculated on the functional capacities of such an individual and rendered a favorable assessment as to authenticity.

Although there was general acclaim for the find, acceptance was not universal. Concern naturally revolved around the issue of dating by association – that is, trying to establish the age of the fossils through reference to the strata they were supposedly found in. As we have seen, this association was weak at best, and had those evaluating the claim that evening been in possession of fuller knowledge of the actual course of discovery, their objections might have been voiced even more vehemently. Some cautions were also expressed even in the earliest days about the general nature of the finds themselves. Frustratingly, the collected remains did not show how the fossil jaw interconnected with the skull itself, a vital joint that would have been most informative. Also, the dentition that remained in the jaw was limited and a cause for concern. At this stage, however, the concerns expressed were not so much with respect to authenticity of the remains as with interpreting what the remains meant in the story of the evolution of man.

The most evident public criticism of the claims associated with Piltdown came from abroad. French, German, and American authorities each expressed doubts, but in some respects these could be ignored, and not without a degree of disdain. After all, this was just seen as jealousy on behalf of "Johnny Foreigner." Most English critics seem to have expressed only muted skepticism, with perhaps their natural patriotism in conflict with any deeper scientific concerns. Criticisms, such as they were, revolved mostly around Woodward's recreation of the skull, especially its contentious cranial capacity and most particularly the issue of the canine tooth. It is reasonable to assert that this concern was perhaps the major point of contention between advocates and critics. Of course, the canine tooth was missing, and what appeared at the public announcement was essentially a best-guess approximation. Paleoanthropologists would naturally be concerned about such hypothetical speculation. Here comes perhaps the strangest and in retrospect most suspicious event of all in the Piltdown story. Like a mythical fencing match, the critics cited concerns about the missing canine tooth and then, almost magically, in the following summer of 1913, that very tooth was found by the young Catholic priest, Pierre Teilhard de Chardin, who was helping with the dig [22]. Equally problematic in retrospect, it turned out that the recovered tooth fulfilled all of Woodward's speculations. His recreation of the skull was vindicated and the critics temporarily routed.

POINT, COUNTER-HOAX

Despite the wonderful and opportune find of the missing tooth, concerns about Piltdown continued to persist. The implications of the specific combination of an advanced cranium and primitive jaw were further questioned. Perhaps an ancient ape jaw had by chance been deposited alongside a genuine fossil human cranium. It was only the American scientist, William Gregory, who suggested in a contemporary report of 1914 that the finds could be a hoax [23]. However, he himself dismissed the idea. Some questions then arose in relation to the unique nature of the fossils. Although there had been finds of animal remains within the same diggings, as far as anyone knew, Piltdown Man was a unique individual. He could, therefore, conceivably have been some singular aberration rather than a general representative of early man. The critics again gained a foothold, and the value of the Piltdown finds was questioned once more. Just as the fossils were facing this important criticism, the hand of fate again seemed to exert its fateful influence. What at the time appeared to be so helpful, now in retrospect appears ultimately suspicious. For just as questions were expressed about the singular nature of the Piltdown Man, the remains of a second individual were uncovered. Piltdown II was announced and concerns about aberrant and unrepresentative individuals promptly quashed [24]. The story of Piltdown II and indeed Piltdown III is almost as convoluted as the tale we have heard so far. Most accounts of the Piltdown hoax give little consideration to these latter finds. This is unfortunate since they are also pivotal in understanding the hoax and perhaps a potential cover-up following Dawson's death. However, this treatment is somewhat understandable, given the primacy of Piltdown I. We are fortunate in that Russell's recent text reports in detail on these latter finds and thus a summarizing précis can be given here and the interested reader directed to the former, more comprehensive source [25].

What if Piltdown Man had been a one-off? If this had been so, the implications for hominid evolution might have been minimal. This was a serious objection and one that had to be met if Dawson's discovery were not to be consigned merely to the miscellaneous discovery cupboard of anthropological science. The evidence that scotched such dismissal came in the form of two subsequent discoveries, one attributed to the Barcombe Mills area and another to a location in Sheffield Park. They are referred to as Piltdown III and Piltdown II, respectively, even though chronologically the Barcombe Mills (Piltdown III) find preceded the Sheffield Park (Piltdown II) find. Their stories are intriguingly similar.

If you look at a map of the general area of the finds, Dawson seems to have been exploring deposits in the Ouse valley, lying between the North and the South Downs of England. At the southerly site, toward his home in Lewes, he claimed to make the next great find. In the summer of 1913, Dawson wrote to Woodward that he had found a further skull fragment, but not at Piltdown. His new discovery had occurred at a location that is now labeled as Barcombe Mills [26]. Like so much of the Piltdown episode, the precise location of this find is now also uncertain. Because the find consisted only of a small piece of cranium, Dawson again played it down and, importantly, did not share the precise location. Although Dawson seems to have shown the general area to de Chardin, its disputable whether Woodward himself was ever brought to the precise site of this find [27]. This is, of course, quite remarkable. In fact, almost everything about the Barcombe Mills find appears to be surrounded with a phenomenal degree of vagueness. It is, indeed, this selfsame vagueness that persists with the later find at the subsequent, but out of sequence, Piltdown II site at Sheffield Park. This location, to the north and west of Fletching, was purportedly the location from which Dawson reported his third triumph. As he wrote to Woodward in January 1915, "I believe we are in luck again." What followed was a description of the finding of a fragment of a cranium, to be followed some six months later by a report of the finding of another molar tooth, supposedly from the same new site. Why these claims superseded the Barcombe Mills finds is difficult to say. Perhaps they were more important and apparently diagnostic as individual pieces but as refutations to the objection about the unique nature of the Barkham Manor find. It is hard to explain why the Barcombe Mills finds were not published soon after their discovery.

Like Barcombe Mills, the Sheffield Park pieces were also kept under wraps. The possible situation here was that Woodward might have been unconvinced that the Barcombe Mills fragments were actually representative of *Eoanthropus* and reticent to publish this as confirmatory evidence. Naturally, this reticence would have disappointed Dawson, and the response seems to have been Dawson's subsequent production of the Sheffield Park finds. These were clearly much more aligned with the original Piltdown finds, but again, for inexplicable reasons, they did not immediately find their way into print. It was just after this time that Dawson began to show signs of the illness to which he eventually succumbed [28]. While it is understandable that excavations were not pursued during Dawson's home confinement, it is extremely strange that at no time from the beginning of 1915 until the summer of 1916 was Woodward shown the later discovery site. Indeed, Woodward later admitted that in respect of the Piltdown II remains, Dawson had told him that "he found them on the Sheffield Park Estate but he would not tell me the exact place – I can only infer from the information that I have," a phenomenal admission indeed. Sadly, Dawson died in August 1916 and amid the carnage of the First World War, Woodward's public announcement of the subsequent finds had much less public impact than did the initial unveiling in 1912. Scientifically, however, the discovery of confirmatory evidence was critical to the acceptance of Piltdown Man. As Russell has commented, "Anyone who had previously doubted the cranium and mandible recovered from Barkham Manor (Piltdown I) were in any way connected, must, it was now abundantly clear, eat humble pie" [29]. Having served his purpose, Sheffield Park Man (Piltdown II) left the stage for the further examination of his more famous cousin.

Here, at last, the sequence was complete. The original discovery had matched the theoretical model of a 'missing link' showing a large cranium and a primitive jaw. The objections over the jaw reconstruction and the canine tooth had been silenced by de Chardin's discovery of the critical tooth itself in 1913. Arguments as to the unique nature of the first Piltdown Man remains were addressed by Barcombe Mills Man (Piltdown III). Interestingly, Woodward does not seem to have been convinced, and Piltdown III stayed under wraps. Perhaps not certain that these remains were the same as *Eoanthropus Dawsoni*, Woodward appeared to require further concrete evidence, and lo and behold, in 1915 such evidence appeared in the form of Sheffield Park Man (Piltdown II). Now the critics were finally deprived of their last possible objection. Piltdown reigned supreme and *Eoanthropus Dawsoni* had truly arrived.

In retrospect, if we reexamine the events of those earliest years, the sequence of fortuitous appearances looks very diagnostic of a hoax. Like the finding of the *Speculum Historale* that tied the Vinland Map to the *Tartar Relation*, the finding of the canine tooth seems indicative of a hoaxer reacting to certain critical objections that were raised. Piltdown III looks like an attempt at corroborative support that failed, while Piltdown II appears to be the fraudster "over-egging" the pudding. On each occasion the forger apparently saw the balance of credibility tipping against their creation and so used subsequent fabricated evidence to help readjust the odds in favor of authentication. Indeed, perhaps this process itself is one dimension of a hoax, although, as we saw in previous stories, it cannot be a ubiquitous one.

EXPOSING THE HOAX

It has been stated that the hoax continued until its formal denouncement in 1953 [30]. However, this is a rather black-and-white interpretation of a much more fluid situation. It is more accurate to suggest that as a precursor to modern man, Piltdown became progressively more marginalized over the years, and by the time of the eventual dénouement, Piltdown played little if any role in the theorizing over the picture of the evolution of early man [31]. Thus, when the official announcement was made, the furor was over the cheating that had occurred some four decades earlier, not the fundamental role of Piltdown in the accepted picture of hominid evolution. It was not the case that the essential foundation of hominid anthropology had been upset; rather it was the community of scientists that was most disturbed.

To the credit of the British establishment, it was three of its own scientists who exposed the fraud. The anthropologist Joseph Wiener and the anatomist Wilfrid Le Gros Clark of Oxford University joined together with Kenneth Oakley of the British Museum of Natural History to reveal undisputed evidence that the jaw and the teeth of the Piltdown remains had been physically altered, chemically treated, and stained and subsequently planted in order to actively deceive [32]. They later showed that the cranium was also fraudulent, although the staining evidence is somewhat contentious since it has been claimed to result from attempts at preservation early in the sequence of discovery. The persistence of the Piltdown story had also been facilitated by the seclusion of the original finds in that many researchers referenced casts of the artifacts, not the remains themselves. The actual exposure itself was contingent on advances in testing, which allowed the reevaluation of evidence that science relies on to permit the crucial process of self-correction. It is evident that in this case the self-correction worked as it should. Perhaps one of the most interesting facets of the revelation is Weiner's own account of his suspicions, and it is here that Piltdown II proved so pivotal. He asserts that it had been the second (Piltdown II) group of finds that had convinced the majority in favor of authenticity. Thus, it stunned him that the site of these finds could not be identified so that subsequent excavations could be conducted. As he concluded, "This small puzzle turned my thoughts to the larger Piltdown conundrum." It was because of such suspicions that the whole edifice eventually came tumbling down.

WELL, WHO DUNNIT?

Perhaps the greatest sport among writers and commentators on the Piltdown hoax is the inevitable gravitation to the question of "who dunnit" [33]. Like the proliferation of candidates for the role of Jack the Ripper, the number of individuals who have been identified as either being the hoaxer or a member of a conspiracy has blossomed over the years. There are now well above twenty such candidates. However, in this case at least one part of the answer seems simple and straightforward. Dawson had the means, the motive, and the opportunity. In the same way the Piltdown remains themselves have been shown to be fraudulent, we also know that Dawson was himself implicated in multiple frauds and hoaxes [34]. Indeed, more recently, it has been suggested that Piltdown was not a singular example but the "culmination" of Dawson's life work as a serial deceiver [35]. Normally, if we have a hoax

FIGURE 5.5. The academic circle surrounding the Piltdown Hoax. Back row: Mr. F. O. Barlow, maker of the casts; Prof. G. Elliot Smith, anatomist; Mr. C. Dawson, and Dr. A. S. Woodward, zoologist. Front row: Dr. A. S. Underwood, Prof. Arthur Keith, W. P. Pycraft, and Sir Ray Lankester. From the painting by John Cooke, R. A., exhibited at the Royal Academy in 1915. Image courtesy of BEI Images.

and the initial discoverer of the hoax was associated with a number of previous hoaxes, most people would look no further. However, in the present case, perhaps from a general sense of fairness, we do need to explore possibilities beyond Dawson alone. Inevitably, this line of enquiry leads first to Arthur Woodward. As Dawson's initial contact and the individual who gave the patina of professionalism to the discoveries, Woodward must inevitably be considered [36].

Following Harrison's observation that the evidentiary basis for evaluation is the nature of the collective finds made at Piltdown and the tracing of those who would have had access to such material, Drawhorn identifies Woodward's association with the provenance of the specific pattern of fossils that were planted in the Barkham gravel pit [37]. This appears to implicate Woodward in an intentional fashion. However, Woodward is by no means the only individual accused; and see Figure 5.5. Philip Tobias leaves little doubt that he suspects Dawson's accomplice to be none other than Arthur Keith [38]. Similarly, others have accused Grafton-Eliot as well as members of the British Museum staff such as Marvin Hinton [39]. Piltdown casts its net even further afield, involving accusations against Teilhard de Chardin, a relatively unknown priest at the time of Piltdown but subsequently an internationally known scholar [40]. In regard to writers, the most famous name in the Piltdown dock is the creator of Sherlock Holmes himself – Arthur Conan Doyle [41]. A local resident and enthusiast for such pursuits, Conan Doyle is not beyond the bounds of possibility, although I would suspect that even Holmes would have been hard-pressed to provide a reasonable motive for Conan Doyle to partake in such a hoax. In the end, we must conclude that, delightful though such far-ranging speculation is, we have no definitive proof to implicate anyone, Charles Dawson included. Those who would look to an approach based primarily on investigation rather than seductive speculation should see Nickell [42].

WAS DAWSON MURDERED?

There seems however, to be relatively little doubt that Charles Dawson was intimately related to some aspects of the fabrication of the hoax at Piltdown [43]. He has been accused of creating numerous fraudulent artifacts that preceded the Piltdown discovery and was, of course, at the very epicenter of the original finds. Piltdown Man is officially named after him because he was the scientific discoverer. What remains at issue for most commentators is whether Dawson had any accomplices. A number of those commentators have suggested that he had. They point, for example, to the relative rarity of many of the associated Piltdown finds, as well as the way in which the hominid finds fit in with the latest anthropological theories. This being so, it implies that any co-conspirator was potentially a high-placed scientist or member of the establishment elite. In consequence, this individual would have had considerably more to lose than did the amateur Dawson had the hoax been exposed. Russell's recent book on Piltdown Man casts Dawson as a highly ambitious individual who, as a country solicitor, aspired to the position of Fellow of the Royal Society (FRS). This distinction is reserved for only the most accomplished academic achievements. At the time of his death, despite his success in being named Fellow of both the Geological Society and the Society of Antiquaries, he had yet to attain this pinnacle of scientific honors. Perhaps some of the continuing suspicion about Piltdown rendered the now famous amateur suspect. Perhaps Dawson was getting impatient and, as a consequence, more dangerous to his co-conspirators.

The cause of Charles Dawson's death remains uncertain to this day. What we do know is that he died fairly young, at the age of 52. This is especially true in relation to the social cohort to which he belonged. At the peak of his fame, when apparently he was about to announce even further discoveries, he became gravely ill. Spencer has suggested that he was suffering from pernicious anemia [44]. Despite being put on a course of serum injections, Dawson became progressively worse throughout the late summer of 1916. Around the time that Britain lost 60,000 men on the first day of the Battle of the Somme, Dawson was confined to bed. It was a confinement from which he was never to recover. He was to stay confined throughout July of that year and he died on August 10 and was buried in Lewes two days later.

Had Dawson been antagonizing his "silent" co-conspirator(s) by agitating for ever-higher scientific honors? Was he about to make even more exciting and dangerous revelations by which the whole skein of the hoax would become unraveled? If we examine Russell's account of Dawson's "career," it seems to be a litany of ever-more startling claims. Given that Piltdown had regaled the front pages of newspapers around the world, one can only speculate as to what Dawson's next announcement might have been. In simple terms, had Dawson become just too dangerous? Lurid and intriguing as this postulation might be, it simply piles speculation on top of speculation, and while it is by no means an impossibility, we have no factual or physical evidence to turn it into anything like a probability.

THE VERDICT ON PILTDOWN

Regarding Piltdown Man, our question is not so much whether the remains are a hoax – it is now clear that they are. Rather, the question revolves around who created this hoax and what was the purpose. The easiest conclusion to reach is that the hoax was created by Charles Dawson and was part of a continuing pattern of behavior in which he sought the approbation of the scientific community and their acceptance of him into their highest circles. In mitigation of this, we must also observe that Dawson has not been around to defend himself from such charges and that his early and unexpected death cheated him of the highest of these honors, if that was his goal. As there is no confession, and the evidence we have is not definitively conclusive of Dawson's guilt, we cannot say for certain that he was guilty. However, the fact that the remains that he produced for Piltdown II appear to come from exactly the same cranium as was originally discovered as Piltdown I is more than just suggestive that Dawson was the guilty party.

Some have argued that Dawson was the unsuspecting dupe of some other shadowy figure or mastermind. Yet if there was such an individual, they never exposed the hoax in their lifetime, and other than professional jealousy and the embarrassment of professional colleagues, it is hard to see what any of the establishment scientist or scientists would have gained from such a fraud. Indeed, in many ways, fraud is completely antagonistic to true science, and this perspective has also served to cast further suspicion on the principal amateur involved, namely Dawson, who after all was paying for "finds." If we are to use Occam's Razor (the principle of explanatory parsimony) [45] anywhere in this exposition, it may well cut here into the idea of anyone but Dawson himself as the perpetrator of Piltdown.

REFERENCE NOTES

[1] See, for example, Bernstein, D. M., Atance, C., Meltzoff, A. N., & Loftus, G. R. (2007). Hindsight bias and developing theories of mind. *Child Development*, 78(4), 1374–1394.

[2] Darwin, C. (1859). *On the origin of species by means of natural selection, or the preservation of favoured races in the struggle for life.* London: John Murray.

[3] Perhaps the most irksome were the discoveries at Neanderthal in 1856. Despite continued efforts, England has (with the exception of Piltdown) never had anything to match the German discoveries, which have recently reentered the news with explorations of Neanderthal DNA; see Green, R. E. et al. (2010). A draft sequence of the Neanderthal Genome. *Science, 328*(5979), 710–722. Lest you might think this issue does not persist into the present day, consider this from the story "From 44,000BC, its Fawlty Man!" from England's *Daily Mail* of November 3, 2011 (p. 31): "A fossilised jaw bone, complete with three teeth, unearthed in a cave on the outskirts of the Devon resort (Torquay) has been dated to between 41,000 and 44,000 years old. … The bone has been confirmed as human making it the oldest evidence of homo sapiens, or modern human life, in northern Europe." Take that, you continentals! (The reference to Fawlty is to Fawlty Towers, the classic English comedy set in a Torquay hotel.)

[4] Chaline, E. (2010). *History's greatest deceptions: And the people who planned them.* New York: Quid Publishing.

[5] See http://www.talkorigins.org/faqs/piltdown/piltmap2.gif

[6] Piltdown Man – Family Tavern [Freehouse] (undated). History of the area and menu (www.piltdownman.co.uk.).

[7] See NOVA (2006). The Boldest Hoax. WGBH/BBC television program. http://www.pbs.org/wgbh/nova/hoax/.

[8] For this work, see: Costello, P. (1981). Teilhard and the Piltdown hoax. *Antiquity*, 55, 58–59; Costello, P. (1985). The Piltdown hoax reconsidered. *Antiquity*, 59, 167–171; and Costello, P. (1986). The Piltdown hoax: Beyond the Hewitt connexion. *Antiquity*, 60, 145–147.

[9] http://www.clarku.edu/~piltdown/map_intro/science_enthus.html

[10] Montagu, A. (1960). Artificial thickening of bone and the Piltdown Skull. *Nature*, July 9.

[11] Russell, M. (2003). *Piltdown Man: The secret life of Charles Dawson and the world's greatest archaeological hoax*. Stroud: Tempus.

[12] See "Arthur Smith Woodward." *Encyclopaedia Britannica*, 2011 edition, and alsohttp://www.mnsu.edu/emuseum/information/biography/uvwxyz/woodward_arthur.html

[13] And see Woodward, A. S. (1948). *The earliest Englishman*. London: Watts & Co.

[14] See Aczel, A. D. (2007). *The Jesuit and the Skull*. New York: Penguin. (Although this text primarily deals with DeChardin and his work and life concerning the discovery known as Peking Man.)

[15] One of the most readable texts on this whole episode remains Weiner, J. S. (1955). *The Piltdown forgery*. London: Oxford University Press.

[16] Walsh, J. E. (1996). *Unraveling Piltdown*. New York: Random House.

[17] Russell, M. (2004). *Piltdown Man: The Secret Life of Charles Dawson*. Stroud: Tempus.

[18] And see Dawkins, W. B. (1915). The geological evidence in Britain as to the antiquity of man. *Geological Magazine*, 2, 464–466. Also Dawson, C., & Woodward, A. S. (1913). On the discovery of a Paleolithic human skull and mandible in a flint-bearing gravel overlying the Wealden (Hastings Beds) at Piltdown, Fletching (Sussex). *Quarterly Journal of the Geological Society of London*, 69, 117–151; Dawson, C., & Woodward, A. S. (1914). Supplementary note on the discovery of a Paleolithic human skull and mandible at Piltdown (Sussex). *Quarterly Journal of the Geological Society of London*, 70, 82–90; Dawson, C., & Woodward, A. S. (1915). On a bone implement from Piltdown (Sussex). *Quarterly Journal of the Geological Society of London*, 71, 144–149.

[19] And see accounts in: Dawson, C. (1913). The Piltdown skull. *Hastings & East Sussex Naturalist*, 2, 73–83; Dawson, C. (1915). The Piltdown skull. *Hastings & East Sussex Naturalist*, 4, 144–149.

[20] The story first broke in the *Manchester Guardian* of November 21, 1912, about one month before the formal announcement at the Geological Society Meeting; see Walsh, J. E. (1996). *Unraveling Piltdown*. New York: Random House.

[21] See Weiner, *The Piltdown forgery*, p. 1.

[22] See Walsh, *Unraveling Piltdown*, p. 39.

[23] Gregory, W. K. (1914). The dawn-man of Piltdown, England. *American Museum Journal*, 14, 189–200.

[24] http://www.talkorigins.org/faqs/piltdown/drawhorn.html

[25] See Russell, *Piltdown Man*. op cit.

[26] See Russell, *Piltdown Man*, pp. 231–249.

[27] One account suggests that one of the finds had actually been at Netherhall Farm, and that Woodward was aware that Dawson was the steward at both

Barkham Manor and Netherhall Farm. The fact that each find took place on land where Dawson was effectively in control of the property would have perhaps pushed coincidence over the edge, and thus Woodward never emphasized the Netherhall Farm location but allowed the Sheffield Park as an alternate designation for the find.

[28] Dawson died on August 10, 1916, merely a month past his 52nd birthday (July 11).

[29] Russell, *Piltdown Man*, p. 243.

[30] See *Time* magazine, November 30, 1953. See also: Oakley, K. P. (1955). *Piltdown Man*. Indianapolis, IN: Bobbs-Merrill; Burkitt, M. (1955). Obituaries of the Piltdown remains. *Nature*, 175, 569.

[31] See, for example, Hammond, M. (1979). A framework of plausibility for an anthropological forgery: The Piltdown case. *Anthropology*, 3, 47–58.

[32] See Gould, S. J. (1979). Piltdown revisited. *Natural History* (March); Oakley, K. (1949). Fluorine tests on the Piltdown skull. *Proceedings of the Geological Society of London*, 29–31. And subsequently: Weiner, J. S. (1955). *The Piltdown forgery*. London: Oxford University Press; Clark, W. Le Gros. (1955). Exposure of the Piltdown forgery. *Proceedings of the Royal Institute*, 20, 138–151.

[33] The number of candidates is really quite amazing. These vary from the obvious and favored view of Dawson as the culprit (see Dempster, W. [1996]. Something up Dawson's sleeve. *Nature*, 382, 202), to a consideration of Teilhard de Chardin (Costello, P. [1981]. Teilhard and the Piltdown hoax. *Antiquity*, 55, 58–59), to more exotic persons and candidates (Clermont, N. [1992]. On the Piltdown joker and accomplice: A French connection? *Current Anthropology*, 33, 587). Others ask if we should even care anymore (Chippindale, C. [1990]. Piltdown: Who dunnit? Who cares? *Science*, 250, 162–163).

[34] See Russell, *Piltdown Man*. For an earlier set of observations, see Nickell, J. (1992). The Piltdown perpetrator. In J. Nickell (with J. F. Fischer), *Mysterious realms: Probing paranormal, historical and forensic enigmas* (pp. 131–143). Buffalo, NY: Prometheus Books.

[35] In his text, Russell concludes that "Piltdown was not a 'one-off' hoax, more the culmination of a (Dawson's) life's work. See Russell, M. (2004). *Piltdown Man: The secret life of Charles Dawson*. Tempus: Stroud.

[36] See discussion in papers such as Halstead, L. B. (1979). The Piltdown hoax: Cui bono? *Nature*, 277, 596.

[37] Drawhorn, G. M. (1994). *Piltdown: Evidence of Smith-Woodward's complicity*. Paper presented at the American Association of Physical Anthropologists on April 1, 1994. Also at http://www.talkorigins.org/faqs/piltdown/drawhorn. html

[38] Tobias, P. (1992). An appraisal of the case against Sir Arthur Keith. *Current Anthropology*, 33, 243–293.

[39] See NOVA (2006). The Boldest Hoax. WGBH/BBC television program. http://www.pbs.org/wgbh/nova/hoax/

[40] De Chardin, an interesting and complex figure, was to have much to do with the subsequent work on Peking Man; see Aczel, A. D. (2007). *The Jesuit and the skull*. London: Penguin.

[41] Langham, I. (1984). Sherlock Holmes, circumstantial evidence and Piltdown man. *Physical Anthropology News*, 3(1), 1–5.

[42] Nickell, J. (1992). The Piltdown perpetrator. In J. Nickell (with J. F. Fischer), *Mysterious realms* (pp. 131–144). Buffalo, NY: Prometheus Books.

[43] See Russell, *Piltdown Man*.

[44] See: Spencer, F. (1990). *Piltdown: A scientific forgery*. London: British Museum; Spencer, F. (1990). *The Piltdown papers*. New York: Oxford University Press.

[45] Occam's Razor is a principle named after the philosopher William of Ockham. Frequently, this is given as a general statement that, all other things being equal, the simplest explanation is the one to be preferred. In fact, this itself is a simplification of Occam's own persuasion: *entia non sunt mulitplicanda* (roughly, "things should not be multiplied"), which is a Latin tag that comes from a theological position that emphasizes the perfection of God. At its heart, Occam's Razor is itself a statement of belief and is often misused and abused. See Thorburn, W. M. (1918). The myth of Occam's Razor. *Mind, 27,* 345–353. Also at http://en.wikipedia.org/wiki/Occam%27s_razor

CASE 6

The Shroud of Turin

"Blessed are the pure in heart – for they shall see God." [1]

THE SHROUD AND ITS CLAIM

The most seductive lies are those we wish to be true and in reading the Bible, it is clear that some of those who contributed to the New Testament were convinced that the second coming of the Lord would occur within their own lifetime. This would mean that many who had looked Jesus in the face while he was alive would again be witness to the risen Christ. Alas, like many other spiritual hopes and aspirations, this Biblical prophecy was not fulfilled. Indeed, there have been many generations of Christian believers since who have sought in vain to look upon the countenance of their personal God. We have no contemporary portrait of Jesus, still less any photograph of Christ. Thus, the reverend hope of Christians down the ages since, as expressed in the Biblical Beatitudes – to see their God in the face – has been thwarted across the span of history. Into this ineffable longing and iconic vacuum comes the Shroud of Turin, with its intrinsic promise to believers that they can themselves now see Christ's image and even potentially lay their hands on his very burial cloth. In light of this longing, it is little wonder that the photographer, Secondo Pia, upon staring at his momentous 1898 photographic negative, could, after nineteen empty centuries, exclaim, "It is the Lord!" [2] (see Figure 6.1). This is the intrigue and the mystery of the Shroud. Are we indeed looking at the face of Christ, and was this the cloth in which he was buried?

A QUESTION OF BELIEF

For many this is not even a question to ask. There are legions of devout, religious people who take the Shroud literally at face value. They wrap

FIGURE 6.1. Contrast enhanced Shroud of Turin facial image as it appears on a photographic negative. © 1978 Barrie M. Schwortz Collection, STERA, Inc.

their unquestioned view of its authenticity into the very fabric of their belief system. For such people, the question has already been answered, and answered purely on the grounds of faith alone. To some extent we must respect this right to express such a personal conviction. However, we ourselves need not necessarily accept such a claim, especially if it is one that concerns scientific authenticity as compared to one of subjective, personal belief. For the Shroud itself is very much a material object, and in its material form it allows for extensive scientific evaluation [3]. Such evaluations are directed to determine whether the Shroud is indeed the burial cloth of Christ himself or whether it is an artifact related to some other individual or perhaps even a medieval creation that might represent either fervent homage or malevolent hoax [4]. One of the most interesting characteristics of the Shroud is that even today it continues to generate a degree of legitimate scientific debate. Whether any final conclusion has been reached or even can be reached also remains a source of contemporary contention [5].

We know, with a reasonable degree of certainty, that the Shroud must be close to 600 years old, at least [6]. This assumes, of course, there has been no substitution or replacement of this artifact in the interim period. However, despite strong suspicions based on numerous quantitative tests, we cannot presently say with absolute certainty that the Shroud is not what it purports to be. While it is true that the persistence of possible authenticity may well be largely a function of the emotion and faith the object generates, there still remains a legitimate degree of doubt. In this sense, the Shroud is the quintessential example of the dimension of belief central to the present exploration of cognitive deception. Given its physical existence through several centuries, the most appropriate point of departure for any discussion is the known history of the Shroud [7]. However, as we shall see, the further back we go into its supposedly "known" history, the greater the uncertainty we encounter [8]. This is a natural propensity for any ancient artifact, but the Shroud is an especially good example.

THE KNOWN HISTORY OF THE SHROUD

Prior to its first appearance in the mid-1300s, we have no reliable evidence of either the Shroud's history or indeed its very existence. However, since this first recorded appearance, the Shroud of Turin has a relatively well-documented provenance [9]. For example, if we were to know as much about the precise history of the Vinland Map as we do about the Shroud of Turin, then there would be no controversy about the map's authenticity. We know, for example, that the Shroud arrived in Turin, Italy, on September 14, 1578, and has been located primarily in the Cathedral of San Giovanni Battista since that time. This is a period of residence of some 430 years, which is impressive in and of itself. However, the known history of the Shroud significantly predates its arrival and sojourn in Turin.

The Shroud's first established appearance occurs in the middle of the 14th century in north-central France. There it was reported as being owned by a knight, one Geoffroi de Charny. It has been suggested that the de Charny family had connections with the Knights Templar, an organization famous for the collection of and sale of religious relics. Indeed, one modern explanation of the Shroud's appearance very much relates it to the downfall of the Templars in France in 1307, some 45 years before we know of Geoffroi's possession. However, this may be due to a simple confusion over very similar names between two individuals both variously known as Geoffroi de Charny (Charney). The original location at which we first find the Shroud was the small town of Lirey, just outside of Troyes, the latter being a small city southeast of Paris.

Today, Lirey itself is a just small village. However, in 1356, Lirey saw the completion of its own church, which may possibly even have been built in order to house the Shroud. This, however, is uncertain, as is the history of the Shroud preceding this period. Some have dated the ownership of the Shroud to 1353; however, its original owner, Geoffroi de Charny, died at the Battle of Poitiers in 1356, never having divulged the way in which he had come to own it [10]. The first record of a pilgrimage to view the Shroud is said to have occurred in 1357. Evidence for this comes in the form of medallions struck, presumably as keepsakes, for enthusiastic pilgrims. One of these medallions was recovered from the River Seine in the mid-1800s.

Approximately 35 years after this first documented date of ownership, the de Charnay family began to display the Shroud publicly in the city square. Its exhibition inspired awe and rejoicing among the general public who revered it as a symbol of their faith. However, although noting its popularity among the masses, a local French bishop, Pierre D'Arcis, dismissed the Shroud as a painted fraud, indicating it was the work of a confessed artist: "the truth," he said "being attested by the artist who painted it" [11]. D'Arcis cited a precedent for his conclusion, noting that Archbishop Henri de Poitiers reached the same opinion some 34 years earlier, in 1355. It has also been suggested that D'Arcis's conclusion was subject to a conflict of interest as he may have hoped to gain control of the Shroud himself in order to recoup the losses he and his church had incurred with the collapse of the roof of Troyes Cathedral in 1389 [12]. He subsequently required the de Charnay family to desist in its exhibition. Clement VII, the antipope in Avignon, subsequently ordered that the Shroud could only be shown if it were announced loudly that it was only a copy or representation.

In 1453, the de Charnay family had fallen into severe financial difficulties, and the Shroud passed into the hands of the House of Savoy at Chambéry. Even with this transition of ownership, the public showings continued. As might be expected, the canons of Lirey were much perturbed by the possibility of the permanent loss of their relic, and in 1464, Duke Louis of Savoy agreed to pay them compensation for their loss in the form of an annual revenue. On December 4, 1532, the church in which the Shroud was housed caught fire [13]. The silver casket in which the Shroud was housed was engulfed in flames. Due to the extreme heat, the silver of the casket itself began to melt. Molten silver fell onto the Shroud, resulting in several holes being burned into the linen. The Shroud was rescued and subsequently repaired, but it still bears the marks of this damage today. Fortunately, much of the image itself escaped damage, most probably as a result of the way it was folded inside the casket.

Decades after the fire, in 1578, Cardinal Charles Borromeo of Milan embarked on a pilgrimage to see the Shroud. To alleviate the hazards and reduce the stress of such an arduous journey over the Alps, the Shroud's trustee, Emmanuel Philiberto, Duke of Savoy, sent the relic to meet the cardinal in Turin. Although this was presumably meant as a temporary change of venue, the Shroud was never to return to France and found its permanent home in Turin. More than 400 years after it was sent to meet Borromeo, the Shroud is still housed in Turin's Cathedral of San Giovanni Battista. On selected occasions, the Shroud is still exhibited to the public today [14].

In 1978, on the occasion of the 400th anniversary of the Shroud's arrival in Turin, the Shroud of Turin Research Project (STURP) aspired to provide a science-based examination of the relic. This project was charged with identifying the authenticity of the Shroud by determining whether or not it had the characteristics of a painting. This scientific effort was comprised of a series of tests conducted by experts in a variety of fields, including, among others, photographic and spectral analysis and X-ray evaluations. After 120 hours of continuous testing, researchers concluded that the image on the Shroud was not a painting. However, this consensus was achieved only by ignoring the evidence from the single art expert on the team. The question as to whether the Shroud is a painting is considered in more detail later in this chapter.

With the advent of viable radiocarbon dating technology (and the Catholic Church's permission to extract a sample of the Shroud in 1987), researchers were able to produce a scientifically based date of the Shroud's origin [15]. Three laboratories at Oxford in England, Zurich in Switzerland, and Tucson in Arizona in the United States each received samples of the Shroud for independent testing. In October 1987, the results of all three laboratories concurred that the sample they received from the Shroud was produced in the Middle Ages, sometime between 1260 and 1390 [16]. There were, however, inevitably those who expressed reservations regarding this conclusion. As we shall see, there almost certainly will always be those for whom belief supersedes science. Whether doubts about the scientific dating of the Shroud are valid is the issue to which I now turn.

THE SCIENTIFIC DATING OF THE SHROUD

Arguments over the nature of physical evidence presented by the Shroud have been present ever since its known origins. The primary concern has always centered on its date of creation. This appeared to have been resolved by the process of radiocarbon dating. Indeed, the 1987 results appeared to have put an end to the debate as to the Shroud's origins. As noted, three independent sources had each concluded that the Shroud was produced more than 1,000 years after Christ's death. This seems to establish that the Shroud of Turin was a later creation and therefore not the burial cloth of Jesus Christ. Proponents of the Shroud's divine origins, however, subsequently argued that the dating itself was incorrect. These advocates highlighted several events and conditions in the Shroud's past that may have acted as contaminating factors to distort the radiocarbon results. One of the most frequently cited examples of source contamination is that possibly caused by the catastrophic fire of 1532, which left the systematic pattern of damage we see on the Shroud today (see Figure 6.2). Unfortunately for those apologists who cite such contamination, there would have to be almost twice as much contamination by weight as there is actual cloth itself in order to alter the date of origin by some 13 centuries [17]. The most recent variation on this theme is the claim that the area of the Shroud from which the sample was taken is actually not representative of the area of the image [18]. Thus, the present claim by advocates is that the image area itself has not been dated at all. This issue of shifting emphasis points to one of the critical dimensions of the science of testing. This necessity involves the careful establishment of a prearranged agreement on behalf of all involved parties as to the conditions of the test. However, as noted earlier, for some true believers no test, however definitive, can ever serve to disabuse them of their devoutly held opinion. Such individuals are certainly lost to science and some would even say to reality itself [19].

One issue that clearly comes to the fore in current discussion is that new and innovative, nondestructive techniques are constantly in development. Eventually any destructive technique will not be acceptable and nondestructive approaches will be pervasive. However, the point here is that when the radiocarbon dating evidence was produced, it did not have the definitive – and perhaps hoped-for – effect on resolving the debate. Believers who were committed to the defense of the Shroud dismissed the evidence as flawed. Those who were skeptical had their doubts confirmed. In the case of an item such as the Shroud, the old observation – "For those who believe, no explanation is necessary; for those who do not believe, no explanation is possible" – seems to be particularly relevant. It poses the question: Can *any* evidence definitively end the argument as to the Shroud's authenticity? As

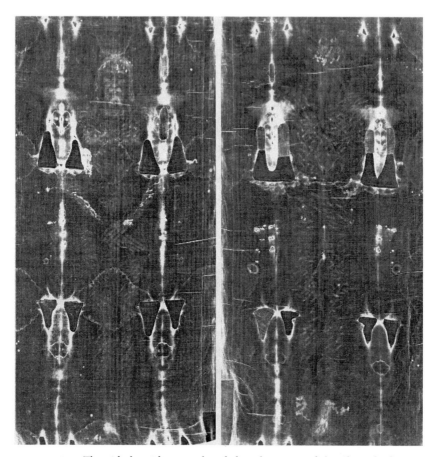

FIGURE 6.2. The side-by-side ventral and dorsal images of the Shroud of Turin as they appear on a photographic negative. © 1978 Barrie M. Schwortz Collection, STERA, Inc.

one skeptic has noted, there remains a small percentage of people who still believe in a flat earth. Such individuals appear to be with us in all matters of the human enterprise. This is an observation that itself begs the question regarding some of the fundamental aspects of basic human nature.

COULD THE SHROUD BE A PAINTING?

Another crucial piece of information that could potentially provide evidence-based clarification of the argument concerns the material that actually composes the image itself. In 1978, Dr. Walter McCrone, a respected research scientist we have met previously in relation to the Vinland Map, identified pigment particles on the Shroud's surface, and reported that there was no evidence of actual blood on the cloth. He demonstrated that the "blood" on the Shroud was red ocher and vermillion tempera paint. The scientific community considered this as confirmation that the Shroud was a painting and thus, in effect, a hoax. McCrone was neither the first nor the only scientist to come to this conclusion. Five years earlier, Dr. Giorgio Frache, an expert on blood, tested threads from the Shroud that were taken from the purported "blood" areas. He concluded, based on benzidine testing, that the "blood" on the Shroud was in fact not blood at all. However, in 1978, as part of the STURP project, Dr. Alan Adler, who, unlike Frache, is not a forensic serologist, found what he determined to be blood proteins. This latter discovery appeared to add credibility to the argument for authenticity. However, forensic expert John Fischer observed that not a single test that was conducted in this process was specific for blood, and results similar to those McCrone had observed could be obtained for tempera paint [20]. Those who argue for the Shroud's authenticity have offered an alternative explanation for the pigments McCrone has found [21]. They assert that copies of the Shroud were made in the Middle Ages so they could be displayed throughout Europe. These copies were subsequently pressed onto the original Shroud shortly after being painted in order to ensure them being an accurate copy. Paint, that was still wet from the copy, could then, it was argued, have found its way onto the original Shroud when the original and its copy were pressed together. Ultraviolet (UV) radiation analysis conducted during the STURP project provided further indications that the Shroud was a genuine relic. STURP concluded that the Shroud had not been painted, since the image appears exclusively on the surface of the linen, instead of soaking through to the deeper layers, as it was suggested paint would [22].

Additional modern evidence that declared the Shroud not to be a painting emerged from a computer analysis reported by Stevenson and Habermas, who observed that their investigation of the cloth

> found no directionality in image areas other than the vertical and horizontal patterns of the threads themselves. That meant there was no sign of brush strokes, finger strokes or other methods of artificial application. Even when the computer removed the vertical and horizontal patterns of the fabric weave from the photograph, the image was in essence untouched. In short, there is no evidence of a forger's methods, mediums, or pigments. [23]

The fire of 1532, thought to have been so detrimental to any conclusive verification of the Shroud's authenticity, has been suggested to actually provide a piece of evidence in its favor. Here, Stevenson and Habermas point out that the fire "would have discolored a painting by burning the pigment in some places. The water which extinguished the fire would have caused the image to 'run.' Neither happened." However, recent experiments on simulated forms of the Shroud have shown this reasoning to be largely specious [24].

THE SHROUD REPLICATED

There have been numerous efforts to replicate the Shroud, including numerous attempts using a camera obscura technique [25]. The postulated claim here is that the Shroud somehow represents the world's first photograph. A much more recent and realistic recreation has been undertaken by Professor Luigi Garlaschelli, an organic chemist from the University of Pavia [26], using techniques and hypotheses developed by Nickell. Laudably, Garlaschelli was not seeking to prove or disprove the authenticity of the Shroud, but rather was searching for the plausible mechanism of its creation. To accomplish this, he covered a volunteer with a purpose-created linen sheet and rubbed it over with a pigment containing traces of acid. The face was created using a bass relief to avoid the distortion that derives from a wraparound effect. Heating the cloth and washing it served to remove much of the pigment from the surface, and after recreating burn holes, water stains, and some scorching, Garlaschelli produced a viable simulacrum of the Shroud. The process produced a negative image derived from the chemical etching of the cellulose of the linen fibers. Of course, this represents a possible, and logically feasible, method of creation, but as Garlaschelli is quick to point out, it is unlikely to convince true believers. As he noted, "If they don't want to believe carbon dating done by some of the world's best laboratories, they certainly won't believe me." However, what this work has done is to demonstrate a plausible method through which the Shroud we see today may have come into being. The problem of belief versus evidence, however, still persists.

On the more outré front, some have suggested that the artist responsible for the Shroud's creation was Leonardo da Vinci, and that the Shroud may be another of his self-portraits [27]. This speculation requires some sleight of hand, however, since da Vinci was not born until 1452, many decades after the first recorded appearance of the Shroud. Side-by-side image analysis, performed by Todd Fenton, a forensic anthropologist at Michigan State University, has shown consistent proportionality between the image of the man on the Shroud and Leonardo da Vinci's self-portraits [28]. This may represent a necessary level of equivalence, but such evidence certainly does not rise to the level of exclusivity. The Da Vinci link remains a postulation, but support for it derives from post hoc confirmation bias rather than from any veridical linkage.

PHYSICAL AND FORENSIC ANALYSES

It is thought that the oldest surviving document written in Hungarian is the Pray Manuscript, created in 1190 [29]. It is a text that contains a graphical depiction of the death of Jesus Christ. The manuscript illustrates events surrounding Christ's burial and provides details about a burial cloth, as shown in Figure 6.3. We can see some markings on the forehead and the evident absence of thumbs on the corpse. However, a series of four holes in a corner of the ostensible wrapping cloth shown at the bottom of the illustration are of particular interest. These perforations appear in a roughly L-shaped pattern. An apparently equivalent pattern of holes, known as the Poker holes, also appears on the Shroud of Turin. It is suggested by advocates of the Shroud's authenticity that the similarity in the pattern of the two sets of holes is not merely coincidental. Accepting this explanation would push the date of the Shroud's creation back some two centuries before the start of our present timeline of provenance. Those who think the Shroud a hoax, however, point to this temporal disparity as an interval in which some hoaxer or copyist could have seen and studied such texts to ensure that the subsequent creation was as accurate and consistent as possible with the existing records. These Janus-type arguments haunt many efforts concerning authentication [30].

Forensic scientists have considered the various markings that appear on the Shroud for consistency with the manner in which Christ died as reported in the Gospels. The wounds of the man on the Shroud are indicative of death from torture and crucifixion. For instance, his back and shoulders display signs of abrasions. The hands and feet appear to have been run through with nails, and the torso is covered with what appear to be marks from extensive whipping. The figure on the Shroud also appears to have bled extensively from the scalp as well as other parts of the body. The head injuries are, of course, indicative of the potential results of having worn

FIGURE 6.3. Illustration of the "Pray Manuscript." © National Szechenyi Library, Budapest, Hungary.

the famous Crown of Thorns. However, herein again lies the trap of confirmation bias. Shroud advocates see these as untrammeled evidence of authenticity, but it would be asinine to suggest that knowledge concerning the manner of Christ's death was not known to many members of the religious and artistic communities of the fourteenth century. Indeed, the Bible itself would have been even more important then than it is in the present day because of the relative rarity of other texts. Someone wishing to create a visual veneration of Christ's suffering would have been very aware of these facts and would have adhered very carefully to them in as much detail as possible. The Shroud may well have been the culmination of a lifetime's work and study for some individual. It is the very level of detail and the knowledge that appears to underlie it that form much of the source of contention.

The blood rivulets especially have raised a number of questions. Proponents of the Shroud's legitimacy cite their presence as strong evidence for the Shroud's case. However, a number of scientists, specifically forensic anthropologists, declare the rivulets to be confirmation of a hoax. In his detailed text, Nickell [31] refers to eminent pathologist Dr. Michael M. Baden's doubts concerning the validity of the Shroud's "blood," saying that "in reality... [it] would mat the hair" instead of flowing down it. However, believers shoot back with the question as to "how the cloth was removed without smearing and dislodging the edges of the clotted blood?" That is, if it is indeed blood.

Another argument advanced in favor of the authenticity of the Shroud is that it is thought to conform to the Jewish burial practices that were recorded to occur at the time of Christ's death. Discussions of this issue center primarily on the act of using a burial shroud and the process of washing the body [32]. The Shroud's very existence attests to at least a possibility that it might at some time have covered a body. However, how exactly that body would have been covered by the Shroud without forming wraparound distortions remains an issue of concern. Distortions aside, whether or not the body in question was that of Christ is another step along the road of speculation. The funerary practices of washing appear to provide support for those who believe the image on the Shroud to be a hoax. Indeed, this act is critical since, according to the historian Ian Wilson, "only on the view that Jesus was not washed can the authenticity of the Turin Shroud be upheld" [33]. It is unlikely that the image as it currently appears could have been fixed on the linen sheet had the body been recently washed.

Also providing indications that the Shroud is a hoax is the Code of Jewish Law, which decrees that the corpse's hair and beard are to be completely shaved off prior to entombment. To rebut this evidence, Stevenson and Habermas have pointed out, on the behalf of proponents, that "the gospels tell us that Jesus' burial was incomplete. Because the Sabbath was about to begin, he was removed from the cross and laid in the tomb rather hurriedly. This is why the women returned to the tomb on Sunday morning.... The gospels [however] do not say to what extent the burial had been left unfinished" [34]. Despite possible evidence of the incomplete conformance with contemporary Jewish burial practices, there is further evidence that several rituals may not have been performed. The Code of Jewish Law states that "while washing and cutting of the hair and fingernails was the normal procedure in Jewish burial practice, these acts were not performed on persons executed by the government or the state, or those who died a violent death. Since both these exceptions applied to Jesus, the washing of his body would have been prohibited on two counts" [35].

Evidence for and against the authenticity of the Shroud based on the Jewish burial customs, which may or may not have been performed on Jesus, remain problematic, as there seems to be no consensus on which customs were in fact performed and to what extent they could or would have been adhered to. Indeed, this issue of ritual is a microcosm of the whole argument with those ranged on the respective sides emphasizing the elements most evidently in their favor. Since the whole issue is chronically underspecified, meaning that extant evidence is insufficient for an unequivocal resolution, debate continues to dominate. Indeed, a further aspect of the argument occurs in relation to another holy relic of Christ. In the Greek language, the word *sudarium* means handkerchief or sweat cloth. The famous relic labeled the Sudarium is a small blood-soaked piece of linen, similar to the Shroud of Turin, which is housed in the Cathedral of San Salvador in Oviedo, Spain [36], but see also Figure 6.4. Supporters of its authenticity claim that it was placed over the face of Christ after his death. According to the Gospel of John, Jesus was buried with spices and a handkerchief, as dictated by Jewish custom [37].

In his gospel, John mentions seeing the burial linens of Jesus on the floor of the tomb. He specifically mentions the Sudarium lying rolled up and separate from the other linens (see Figure 6.4). Thus, we read in John 20:6–7: "Then Simon Peter, who was behind him [John] arrived and went into the tomb. He saw the strips of linen lying there as well as the burial cloth that had been around His head. The cloth was folded up by itself separate from

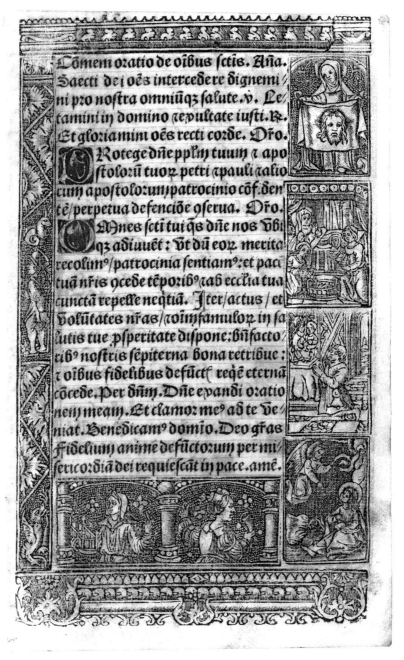

FIGURE 6.4. This is the illustration of the "Veil of Veronica" from a medieval *Book of Hours* [38]. Photograph by, and in possession of, the Author.

the linen." The presence of the Sudarium presents a fundamental problem for the Shroud. If indeed this small cloth were placed over the face of Jesus, then the famous image of Christ's face would be on it rather than on the Shroud. Those who claim it is genuine, however, rationalize that if it was rolled up (as John described), it may have been used to tie up Christ's chin. If this act of binding the chin with a rolled up cloth did occur, it may be consistent with John's gospel as well as the Mishnah, which is a holy text instructing Jews to bind the deceased's chin shut [39].

There are those who believe the blood patterns on the Sudarium are indicative of the face of Jesus [40]. The amount of blood on the cloth suggests numerous head wounds, perhaps from the Crown of Thorns. Also, the way in which the blood has soaked in points to a potentiality that whoever's head it covered was sunken downward and to the side. This is traditionally supposed to be the posture of Christ while still on the cross. These aforementioned patterns should, however, be treated with a fair degree of skepticism. This caution derives from the concern that stems from an understanding that pattern search is an intrinsic propensity of the human perceptual system [41]. For example, humans have a natural propensity to perceive human facial patterns where, in fact, they may not exist [42]. Research has even demonstrated that day-old infants pay more attention to facial features arranged in a typical human facial pattern than to those same facial features arranged randomly [43]. Thus, arranging a relatively flexible pattern to conform to recognized facial features is fraught with hindsight bias [44].

In addition to the potential pattern presented, the blood on the Sudarium is itself worthy of mention. When blood proteins were supposedly found on the Shroud of Turin, they were reported to be type-matched. The result was blood type AB, the same type of blood found on the Sudarium. These results have been highlighted, as this blood type was fairly common in the first-century Middle East but quite rare (composing a mere 3% of the population) in Medieval Europe. This typing, as well as claims to be able to extract DNA, must be taken with extreme caution [45]. This type of purported support is typical of where so-called Shroud Science departs from the mainstream of accepted science, especially since the assertion contradicts the current findings of professional forensic serologists [46]. It may be that future techniques might be able to elicit this information, assuming such information is there to find. We cannot, however, dismiss expansive and speculative claims merely because they are speculative. Rather, it is on those who make these sorts of claims that the burden of proof is placed. It has often been said that extraordinary claims require extraordinary proof.

However, I think that extraordinary claims actually require ordinary proof but to an extraordinary degree.

Claims regarding authenticity were further cast into doubt by the three-dimensional representations of the Shroud's image. Once rendered in 3-D, the body proportions are not consistent with those of normal individuals. They are instead stretched; the arms and legs are too long in relation to the torso. To counter this argument, those who believe the Shroud to be genuine explain the discrepancy by claiming that the head would have been tilted according to the Jewish burial custom of placing the head on a form of stone pillow [47]. The reliability of basing arguments on the use of supposed burial customs has already been discussed; the reliability of three-dimensional imaging, on the other hand, remains limited as not only the burns and water marks on the linen prove significant barriers to successful reconstruction, but there is also no information on the side elevations of the individual represented. Nevertheless, there have been, as we have seen, several modern claims of being able to replicate the Shroud using only materials available in the early fourteenth century [48].

The stitching on the cloth of the Shroud is in a three-to-one herringbone pattern; a "kind of weave [which] was special in antiquity because it denoted an extraordinary quality," according to Mechthild Flury-Lemberg, a German textile conservationist responsible for some of the recent preservative repair of the Shroud [49]. According to her, not only was this pattern very rarely seen in medieval Europe, but it is apparently so unique that Flury-Lemberg has seen it previously only in other examples of first-century textile work from the Dead Sea fortress of Masada, close to where the Dead Sea scrolls were found [50]. Therefore, in her opinion, the Shroud is liable to be authentic, dating from the time of Christ and certainly no later than 70 years after his birth. In contrast, a recently opened tomb in Jerusalem has provided evidence that apparently contradicts this assertion, and has added to the weight of evidence against the Shroud's authenticity. This evidence comes in the form of a shroud dated to between AD 1 and 50 [51]. One of only two known textiles associated with Jewish burials of this era, the recently discovered tomb shroud appears to represent a composition that is in contrast to the Turin Shroud. This again attests to how hard it is to find reliable evidence of this era to make comparisons. The tenor of the new evidence, however, appears to add further weight to the skeptics' case in this particular instance.

BACTERIAL ANALYSIS OF THE SHROUD

Over the centuries, the Shroud has been exposed to significant amounts of handling and thus potential pollution. There is no doubt that bacteria, at one time, existed in great numbers in the linen of the Shroud. Some Shroud advocates believe that these microorganisms hold the key to explaining the radiocarbon dating as well as the method by which the image was created [52]. However, this precise process has yet to be articulated. The most common bacteria on human skin is *staphylococcus epidermidis*. In its process of consuming oxygen, it is known to leave a yellowish stain on any cloth with which it comes into contact [53]. The greater the contact with the linen surface, the greater number of bacteria, and thus the darker the resulting image. *Staphylococcus epidermidis* grows most effectively at body temperature that would have been maintained until Christ's death. Due to the torture and exertion involved in carrying and subsequently being nailed to the cross, Christ was almost undoubtedly sweating profusely. He would have been bleeding freely and continuously from his head, torso, and limbs, providing abundant nutrients to these microorganisms. The image on the Shroud could, therefore, have been the result of the completely natural processes of bacterial growth and oxygen uptake.

An alternative explanation for the image's inception would be that, upon his virtually unprecedented resurrection, Christ's body would have experienced a burst of gamma radiation that would have affected the linen Shroud [54]. Proponents of this theory suggest that the image is thus akin to a modern X-ray image, so much so that the man's bone structure is clearly visible, even in parts of the body that did not come in contact with linen, such as the thumbs. These body parts are thus depicted on the Shroud due to Jesus' miraculous ascension into Heaven through the Shroud. Since there is no known way of testing whether resurrection is accompanied by gamma radiation, there is no present way (aside from faith alone) of ascertaining the potential truth of such a claim.

A HISTORICAL ALTERNATIVE EXPLANATION

Some have proposed that the Shroud is not authentic, but rather a result of a misunderstanding. While agreeing with the official radiocarbon date, they still believe that the Shroud does indeed contain the image and blood of a man with the injuries that were supposed to have been inflicted upon Christ. However, they deny that the Shroud is that of Jesus himself. Instead, they propose a compromise case and state that this particular cloth was used to cover Jacques de Molay, the last Grand Master of the Knights Templar, after an ordeal of torture and inquisition visited upon him by the French king, Philip IV [55].

In the early fourteenth century, King Philip IV had grown anxious and concerned over the power and wealth the Knights Templar possessed; in fact, he would know quite well the extent of their influence since he himself was in great financial debt to them [56]. Thus, in his quest to overthrow the Templars and capture their wealth, he requested (and indeed used threats to secure) the blessing of Pope Clement V. He accused the Templars of a variety of sins and blasphemies emphasizing their corruption and heresy. A document called the Chinon Chart, only recently discovered in the archives of the Vatican, provides a record of the trial of the Knights Templar [57]. Clement V eventually sided with the French king and colluded in the dissolution of the Order by proclaiming the Knights guilty of various acts of crime and immorality. Philip acted quickly and eradicated the Knights as swiftly as possible using a variety of harsh methods such as torture and fire.

Jacques de Molay, as the Templars' Grand Master, experienced torture at the hands of France's Chief Inquisitor William Imbert [58]. After his ordeal, he was purportedly placed on a linen shroud, which was subsequently wrapped over him, and then lay waiting, injured and exhausted, to be burned at the stake. This scenario is consistent with radiocarbon dating results that claim the Shroud is of 13th- or 14th-century origin. It does not contradict any of the forensic evidence regarding the placement and extent of the wounds that de Molay may have received, as his torture may have been purposively designed to mirror Christ's suffering. Nor does it necessarily disagree with the fragile and tenuous declarations concerning the presence of blood proteins or even paint, as the relic was considered a Templar icon and perhaps periodically "touched up" by its venerators. This is very much the sort of compromise explanation that develops when the primary item of concern, in this case the Shroud, represents an under-specification. In essence, into the vacuum of ignorance comes any number of speculative explanations. Like others that have been offered, this very fanciful one is seductively attractive, but its viability as a realistic account is liable to be very limited. In particular, there is an extremely large step between what is, on the surface, an apparently plausible hypothesis and its subsequent evidence-based confirmation. At present, perhaps the best that can be said of this proposal is that it remains another in the sequence of Shroud-based speculations.

THE VERDICT ON THE SHROUD

Like all of the artifacts discussed in this book, the crucial issue concerning the Shroud devolves to one single question: Is it real? This is certainly not as easy to resolve as it might initially appear. The Shroud itself is rather like a document that tells us its story, albeit only indirectly. This story purports to say that this is the burial cloth of one specific, indeed unique, individual whose life on Earth changed the course of human history [59]. Such was the magnitude of this change that this individual still stirs our deepest emotions to the present day [60]. This impact is especially true for committed believers. Naturally, the story the Shroud offers is appealing, for some perhaps overwhelmingly so; indeed, the Shroud remains an almost endless source of material for inventive conspiracy theorists [61]. But is the Shroud that we possess part of the original story of Jesus, or is it simply a reflection of later believers in that narrative? One Shroud researcher, John Walsh, has asserted: "*The Shroud of Turin is either the most awesome and instructive relic of Jesus Christ in existence ... or it is one of the most ingenious, most unbelievably clever products of the human mind and hand. It is one or the other, there is no middle ground*" [62]. However, reality need not necessarily descend to the stark choice between these two simple extremes, especially as each of these views necessarily invokes the need for a putative "miracle." Reality is rather more complex than such black-and-white assertions. The truth, however, is that the story of the Shroud has yet to be fully resolved.

At the present, the vast preponderance of scientific evidence supports a position that the Shroud is more likely to be a creation of the 14th century and of European origin than it is the Shroud of Jesus Christ – if indeed such a garment ever existed. The burden of proof remains incumbent upon those who argue most vehemently for its authenticity. Rather than Hume's aphorism that "extraordinary claims require extraordinary proof," I reiterate that it may well be that this extraordinary claim requires simply extra (that is further) ordinary proof. Such proof has yet to emerge, and, in general, one could say that it is unlikely ever to do so. Indeed, in some ways, the Shroud image that has come to us appears essentially too perfect. In the indirect story that the Shroud presents, we see almost exactly that which we wish to see. This is a very seductive quality, especially for true believers. In and of itself, this seductive capacity cannot address the factual issue of authenticity. Indeed, that any 14th-century fabricator could create such a simulacrum is itself startling enough. However, as an artifact at the very interface of science and religious belief, the Shroud is surely unique in almost all of human experience [63]. One of the greatest wonders of the Shroud then is that almost everyone sees in it what they want to see. At this time, although it is tempting to render the Scottish verdict of "not proven," the preponderance of reliable scientific evidence is strongly against authenticity. This should not be taken as a prima facie case of intentional hoax, however [64]. While there remain true believers, the court of general opinion will always, to some degree, remain sitting in judgment. Advances in forensic science, however, may generate new and innovative methods that could provide definitive tests. Thus, although the eventual verdict will most probably find this is a medieval creation, the Shroud still remains a wonderful and contentious relic.

REFERENCE NOTES

[1] Holy Bible, *Matthew*, Chapter 5, Verse 8.

[2] A lawyer and amateur photographer, Secondo Pia was born in 1855. His pivotal photograph, featuring the face on the Shroud, was taken on May 28, 1898. Pia died in 1941. See also "It is the Lord" (undated booklet) Editrice elle di ci, 10096, Leumann (Torino).

[3] Gove, H. E. (1996). *Relic, icon or hoax: Carbon dating the Shroud of Turin*. Bristol, UK: Institute of Physics Publishing. See also Bruce, R., & Wilson, I. (1982). *Jesus and the Shroud: A reserve book for religious studies*. Eastbourne, UK: Holt, Rinehart, & Winston.

[4] Nickell, J. (1987). *Inquest on the Shroud of Turin*. Buffalo, NY: Prometheus Books.

[5] Compare http://www.freeinquiry.com/skeptic/shroud/ and http://www.shroud.com/menu.htm

[6] Wilson, I. (1998). *The blood and the Shroud*. New York: Simon & Schuster.

[7] Wilson, I. (1978). *The Shroud of Turin: The burial cloth of Jesus Christ?* Garden City, NY: Doubleday & Company.

[8] Scavone, D. (2005). Geoffroy I de Charny did not obtain the present Turin Shroud on the Smyrna campaign of 1346. The issue was revisited, with a new assessment of primary documents at http://www.shroud.com/pdfs/scavone2.pdf

[9] See, for example, Scavone, D. C. (1989). *The Shroud of Turin: Opposing viewpoints*. San Diego, CA: Greenhaven Press. Also see http://www.shroud.com/scavone3.pdf

[10] Gove, H. E. (1996). *Relic, icon or hoax? Carbon dating the Turin Shroud*. Bristol, UK: Institute of Physics Publishing.

[11] See Thurston, H. (1903). The Holy Shroud and the verdict of history. *The Month, 51*, 17–29.

[12] Nickell, *Inquest on the Shroud of Turin*.

[13] Humber, T. (1978). *The sacred shroud*. New York: Pocket Books.

[14] Rinaldi, P. M. (1979). *When millions saw the Shroud*. New Rochelle, NY: Don Bosco Publications.

[15] For the foundation of this effort, see also *Proceedings of the 1977 United States Conference of Research on the Shroud of Turin*. Albuquerque, NM.

[16] Damon, P. E. et al. (1989). Radiocarbon dating of the Shroud of Turin. *Nature*, 337, 611–615, and see also Nickell, *Inquest on the Shroud of Turin*.

[17] See Pickett, T. J. (1996). Can contamination save the Shroud of Turin? *Skeptical Briefs*, June 3. Also cited in Nickell, *Inquest on the Shroud of Turin*, p. 151. See further Gove, *Relic, Icon or Hoax?* Also see some recent, purported "revelations" in Is the Turin Shroud genuine after all? *Daily Mail*, April 11, 2009, p. 37, concerning the reservations of Dr. Raymond Rogers who died in 2005.

[18] Nickell, *Inquest on the Shroud of Turin*.

[19] As Nickell has recently commented in an article on the Shakespeare authorship controversy, "those who have stepped through the looking glass will not be dissuaded." See Nickell, J. (2011). Did Shakespeare write Shakespeare? *Skeptical Inquirer*, 35(6), 38–43.

[20] See Nickell, *Inquest on the Shroud of Turin*, pp. 155–158.

[21] See, for example, Killmon, J. (1997–1998). The Shroud of Turin: Genuine artifact or manufactured relic? *The Glyph: The Journal of the Archaeological Institute of America, San Diego*, 1, No. 10 (Sept 1997); No. 11 (Dec 1977); No. 12 (March 1998). Retrieved from http://www.historian.net/shroud.htm

[22] Nickell, *Inquest on the Shroud of Turin*. See also Decoding the Past: Unraveling the Shroud. *The History Channel*, 2005.

[23] Stevenson, K. E., & Habermas, G. R. (1981). *Verdict on the Shroud*. Wayne, PA: Banbury Books.

[24] For an example of Shroud simulation experiments, see Vincent, J. B. (1999). Simulating the Shroud of Turin: A laboratory experiment. *The Chemical Educator*, 4 (3), 102–104.

[25] Allen, N. P. L. (1993) *The methods and techniques employed in the manufacture of the Shroud of Turin*. Unpublished DPhil thesis, University of Durban-Westville. See also Allen, N. P. L. (1993). Is the Shroud of Turin the first recorded photograph? *The South African Journal of Art History*, November 11, 23–32, and for a disputational argument, see Schwortz, B. M. (2000). *Is the Shroud of Turin a Medieval Photogrpah? A Critical Examination of the Theory*. Retrieved from http://www.shroud.com/pdfs/orvieto.pdf

[26] See Polidoro, M. (2010). The Shroud of Turin duplicated. *Skeptical Inquirer*, 34(1), 18.

[27] Is the Turin Shroud really a self-portrait by Renaissance man Leonardo da Vinci? See http://www.dailymail.co.uk/news/article-1196520/Is-Turin-Shroud-really-self-portrait-Renaissance-man-Leonardo-da-Vinci.html#ixzzoYBEWBkxA

[28] http://www.tqnyc.org/2006/NYC063363/turin/leon1.htm

[29] See http://www.shroudstory.com/faq-pray-manuscript.htm. The Pray Codex (named after the scholar who first made a systematic study of it) is held in the Budapest National Library. And see http://www.skepticalspectacle.com/history06.htm

[30] Nickell, J. (2001). Scandals and follies of the "Holy Shroud." *Skeptical Inquirer,* September/October, 17–20, especially page 18–19.

[31] Nickell, J. (1998). *Looking for a miracle.* (PP. 19–22), Amherst, N.Y.: Prometheus Books.

[32] Zugibe, F. T. (1989). The man of the Shroud was washed. *Sindon N.S., 1.*

[33] Wilson, *The blood and the Shroud.*

[34] See Stevenson & Habermas, *Verdict on the Shroud.*

[35] See also Stevenson & Habermas, *Verdict on the Shroud.*

[36] Bennett, J. (2001). *Sacred blood, sacred image: The Sudarium of Oviedo, new evidence for the authenticity of the Shroud of Turin.* San Francisco: Ignatius Press. See also Nickell, J. (2007). *Relics of Christ.* Lexington: The University Press of Kentucky, especially pp. 154–166.

[37] It is in the Gospel of John: Chapter 19: Verses 39–40 that we read: "Nicodemus, who had come to Jesus earlier at night, went with Joseph too, carrying a mixture of myrrh and aloes weighing seventy-five pounds. So they took Jesus' body and wrapped it, with the aromatic spices, in strips of linen cloth according to Jewish burial customs."

[38] See also: "New skeptiseum feature exhibit: Miraculous portrait of Jesus? *Skeptical Briefs* (2004), *14*(2), 7.

[39] http://www.archive.org/stream/MN40161ucmf_8/MN40161ucmf_8_djvu.txt

[40] Monreno, G.H., Villalaín Blanco, J.D., & Rodríguez Almenar, J. M. R. (1998). *Comparative study of the Sudarium of Oviedo and the Shroud of Turin.* III Congresso Internazionale di Studi Sulla Sindone Turin. Such conclusions must be approached with extreme care since the actual evidence on the cloth is capable of many differing forms of interpretation.

[41] This issue is also relevant to the recent suggestion with respect to the recognition of writing on the Shroud. See Barbara Frale's contention concerning "Faint writing seen on the Shroud of Turin," http://news.yahoo.com/s/ap/eu_italy_shroud_of_turin

[42] Chen, C.C., Kao, K.L.C., & Tyler, C.W. (2007). Face configuration processing in the human brain: The role of symmetry. *Cerebral Cortex, 17*(6), 1423–1432.

[43] Slater, A. (2002). Visual perception in the newborn infant: Issues and debates. *Intellectica, 34,* 57–76.

[44] For a discussion of the specific issues of hindsight bias, see, for example, Dekker, S. (2004). Hindsight bias is not a bias and not about history. *Human Factors and Aerospace Safety, 4*(2), 87–100; Fischhoff, B. (2003). Hindsight does not equal foresight: The effect of outcome knowledge and adaptive learning. *Quality Safety and Health Care,* 12(Suppl. 2), ii46–ii50; and Fischhoff, B. (1975) Hindsight is not foresight: The effect of outcome knowledge on judgment under uncertainty. *Journal of Experiment Psychology: Human Perception and Performance,* 1(3), 288–299.

[45] Much care must be taken over the typing of blood from the Shroud. Not only has there been extended controversy over the presence of blood, but recent observations suggest that typing may be beyond current technology. See http://www.factsplusfacts.com/shroud-of-turin-blood.htm. See also PBS, Secrets of the Dead: Shroud of Christ?; Nickell, J. (2001). Scandals and follies of the "Holy Shroud." *Skeptical Inquirer,* September/October, 17–20.

[46] The aspiration to blood type and DNA analyze the Shroud is appealing but has been dismissed by Dr. Andrew Merriwether; see http://en.wikipedia.org/wiki/ Shroud_of_Turin, note 76.

[47] See http://www.world-mysteries.com/sar_2.htm

[48] http://news.yahoo.com/s/nm/20091005/sc_nm/us_italy_shroud

[49] http://www.pbs.org/wnet/secrets/previous_seasons/case_shroudchrist/inter-view.html and http://de.wikipedia.org/wiki/Mechthild_Flury-Lemberg

[50] VonderKam, J. C. (1994). *The Dead Sea Scrolls today*. Grand Rapids, MI: Eerdmans Publishing Co.

[51] Milstein, M. (2009). *Shroud of Turin not Jesus' Tomb discovery suggests*. Retrieved from http://news.nationalgeographic.com/news/2009

[52] See, for example, the discussion on sites such as http://www.uthscsa.edu/mis-sion/spring96/shroud.htm

[53] http://en.wikipedia.org/wiki/Staphylococcus_epidermidis

[54] For more on this issue, see Rogers, R. N. (2005). *The Shroud of Turin: Radiation effects, aging and image formation*. Accessible at http://www.shroud.com/pdfs/ rogers8.pdf

[55] Knight, C., & Lomas, R. (2001). *The Second Messiah: Templars, the Turin Shroud and the great secret of Freemasonry*. Gloucester, MA: Fairwinds Press.

[56] Frale, B. (2004). *The Templars: The secret history revealed*. New York: Arcade Publishing.

[57] Frale, B. (2004). The Chinon chart. Papal absolution to the last Templar, Master Jacques de Molay. *Journal of Medieval History*, 30(2), 109–134. See also Frale, *The Templars*. Among the more interesting notes in the latter text is the follow-ing: "Upon hearing the verdict of life imprisonment, Grand Master Jacques de Molay and his most trusted comrade, Preceptor of Normandy Geoffrey de Charny, refused to accept the sentence, proclaiming the Temple's abso-lute innocence of all the charges brought against them" (p. 196). Of course, the inevitable, and indeed reasonable temptation is to link this companion of the last Grand Master of the Temple with Geoffroi de Charnay in whose possession we find the Shroud first recorded some few decades later. See also the comments on p. 200 of the same text concerning the link between the Templars and the Shroud.

[58] See, for example, the discourse at http://www.bbc.co.uk/dna/h2g2/A462458

[59] See Hoffmann, R. J., & Larue, G. A. (Eds.). (1986). *Jesus in history and myth*. Amherst, NY: Prometheus Books.

[60] See Wuenschel, E. (1953). *The Holy Shroud of Turin*. Bronx, NY: Redemptionist Fathers; Favaro, O. (1978). *The Holy Shroud in the light of the gospels and of modern science: The way of the cross*. (Translation: P. Rinaldi). Sac. Valentino Scarasso.

[61] See the involving text by Kersten, H., & Grober, E. R. (1995). *The Jesus conspir-acy: The Turin Shroud and the truth about the resurrection*. New York: Barnes and Noble Books. See also Brooks, II, E. H., Miller, V. D., & Schwortz, B. M. (1978–1981). *The Turin Shroud: Worldwide exhibition*. Northbrook, IL: Shroud of Turin Presentation Inc.

[62] Walsh, J. (1963). *The Shroud*. New York: Random House.

[63] The use of the word "unique" must be qualified a little here since Humber (Humber, T. [1978]. *The sacred shroud*. New York: Pocket Books, p. 78) has reported that there are at least 43 "True Shrouds" in existence.

[64] See also http://www.skepticalspectacle.com/PapalCustodianvsVatican.htm as well as other information from this and similar sites. But see also Nickell, J. (2009). *Real or fake: Studies in authentication*. Lexington: The University Press of Kentucky.

IV

DECEPTION REDUX

Assumption Is the Mother of Deception

"The mark of a really good fraud seems to be that it lives on even after all reasonable evidence has shown it up" [1]

INTRODUCTION

To this point I have explored various aspects of the psychology of deception through the examination of a number of specific examples concerning the way people have taken advantage of others' ardent wish to believe. Indeed, it was Jean-Jacques Rousseau himself who pointed out that "it is hard to prevent oneself from believing what one so keenly desires" [2]. I presented some examples of deception, but they are only a limited selection from a vast universe of possible instances [3]. There are any number of others that I could have focused on, including certain personal favorites [4]. I hope that, having read to this point, you might now recall and explore your own personal examples using some of the principles outlined here. What is important as we consider each respective story is, of course, a set of general principles that emerge, and it is on these I focus next.

THE CONSTITUENTS OF A SUCCESSFUL HOAX

It is evident that the main characteristics of a successful hoax are fairly consistent. Above all things, the deceiver must *identify a constituency*. That is, for a deception to be successful there must be either an individual or a group of people who are ready to be deceived. If no one cares about the explicit or implied issue, then the hoax or deception fails. There are, of course, some basic concerns that we all share. Thus, some deceptions can be universal and compulsive, but in the case of cognitive deception, it is the specific hopes and beliefs of the deceived that come prominently to the fore. The hoax must always concern something that the constituency cares about passionately. If one tries to perpetrate some sort of intellectual hoax, it may be enjoyed as a cerebral "rag" but it will almost never be the subject of wide-scale passionate dispute. These intellectual cases may provide amusement, but they never rise to the great popular debates that surround the examples contained in this book, although some examples do attain notoriety in the academic world [5].

The classic way of creating a successful deception is to ask: What are the dreams of the people it is to be perpetrated upon? What is it they most greatly desire? Typically, a hoax will play upon widespread human fail-ures, such as greed. The most ubiquitous form of deception in the modern Western society can be characterized as "get rich quick" schemes. They are so widespread, in general, as to be mundane and are therefore not really the cases of deception I am particularly concerned with. Commonplace decep-tions such as these are founded on criminal activity [6], and while poten-tially informative, they do not engage in the fashion the present stories do. So let us raise ourselves, for just a moment, from the shibboleth of finan-cial greed and focus our attention on some purportedly "higher" levels of aspiration.

Having once identified this dream, be it glory, fame, or pride, the ques-tion for the deceiver is what sort of artifact, item, entity, information, or person can be convincingly fabricated to support that aspiration. In the pre-sent examples I have mostly looked at physical artifacts, since these prove of greatest interest. All but one of the items I have discussed can still be readily viewed, and, with the exception of King Arthur's Cross, we can conduct contemporary, empirical evaluations of these items. As investigative tech-niques increase in diagnostic capacity and sophistication, it is feasible that an eventual definitive answer may be had to the inherent questions posed by each of these items. Physical artifacts render the tangible possibility of closure in a way myth and legend never can. In the same way, advances in DNA techniques now permit a much more definitive answer about indi-viduals posing as someone else. However, having created an artifact or even having passed oneself off as another individual, most of the work to com-plete a successful hoax is still ahead for the hoaxer.

Now the challenge is either to manufacture an "accidental" discovery or to find a way in which the initial discovery can be obscured to a suffi-cient degree so that origins themselves cannot be unequivocally fixed. In the world of antique artifacts, provenance is crucial, and much time in all of the cases discussed here has been given over to the effort to establish provenance back to the point of what would have been a potentially true origin. Like much of history, this part of the story requires a sequence of different leaps of faith and is very much subject to a phenomenon termed confirmation bias. That is, *people often search out information that supports their case, but are not equally as diligent in searching out facts that contradict their hopes.* This human foible was commented on by Francis Bacon in his original advocacy for experimental evaluation of the natural world [7].

Having found the realm of the deception and the physical incarnation of that deception, the next thing needed is an *unsuspecting champion*. If the hoaxer is this "champion" or main advocate, and especially if obvious monetary gain is involved, even those naturally accepting of fairly outlandish claims may eventually become suspicious. Rather, the champion is often the target of the hoaxer, for whom the hoax represents not just one part of a panoply of dreams; it is *the* dream. These are the people who carry the torch. If they have the imprimatur of authority, so much the better, for their opinions will carry all the more weight. Ardent amateurs are fine, but deluded professionals are even better, since they bring their credentials to the subject

The next qualification is strange but true: the hoax must not be *too* perfect. If the hoax is to raise contention, it must possess characteristics that are open to some degree of interpretation and contention by both sides involved in the associated argument. This factor actually works in favor of the deceiver, because components of the actual artifact itself that are not evident giveaways actually serve to foment greater interest, discussion, and debate. These are always advantages in selling the deception and, in essence, foster incorrect decision making. The most effective way of providing such ambiguity is to leave crucial aspects under-specified. That is, do not over-elaborate the hoax itself, leave room for the participation and contribution of others. Hoaxes that provide complete, closed-end explanations are not generative and fail to allow involved individuals to actively participate in the discovery, elaboration, and elucidation. Evidence that is discovered by an individual who is not the primary deceiver is particularly persuasive.

THE PROCESS OF DECEPTION

When all the parts of a deception are set in place, the trigger must be pulled and the deception set in motion. Often this takes the form of a "discovery";

a successful deceiver is often peripheral to this initial announcement. This is where the "champion" steps forward and reaps the plaudits that tie them wholeheartedly to the cause of authenticity. This champion is now publicly invested in the deception, although most probably still ignorant of its deceptive nature. The next stage of the elaborate process acts something like an outbreak of psychogenic illness. Indeed, it may well be considered in those very terms [8]. The initial discovery causes a flurry of activities and comment. The item has its supporters *and* its detractors, but often the supporters who assert the positive case have the easier task; after all, if it is a good hoax, the general public already wants to believe. A good hoax allows room for this belief to expand and blossom. Following on the initial positive episode, there occurs a wave of general but more diffuse support. At this stage great advantage can be taken of the hoax by various constituencies. A superb hoax looks to attract more than one of these constituencies, and if it can cause argument in both then it has scaled the heights of some of the examples I have given. During this stage of development, the critics and detractors summon up their objections. But for the master deceiver, they also co-opt and even "manage" this criticism. Criticism is not to be shunned and avoided, but rather it should be embraced. This is what turns a merely effective deception into a legendary hoax. It is apathy and neglect, not criticism, that kills a viable hoax.

An additional characteristic of a good hoax is longevity. The secret to longevity is twofold. First, one can create a perfectly ambiguous item in which any element can be used either for support or detraction. Such an artifact is rare and difficult to fabricate. It is especially difficult to sustain because it requires a good degree of foresight. In this respect, having the item itself disappear is always an advantage. The second key to longevity resides in the continuing need for people to believe. The life of a hoax is only extinguished when people no longer care about what it represents. Thus, the good hoaxer must look to what is perennial and persistent and not to what is temporary, faddish, and of the moment. Having established some of these points, let us see how they play specifically into the stories I have presented previously.

The Definition of a Constituency

In the case of the cross of King Arthur, there are several constituencies. The proximal constituency, of course, is the visitors who were attracted to the abbey to see the tomb of the legendary king. They would bring money and trade, and the religious house of Glastonbury would then be reborn and flourish as desired. A great advantage here is the secular nature of King Arthur. He appeals not only to the pious but also to the patriotic. Even better, he appealed to the patriotism of a number of cultures. Arthur was claimed by both the English and the Welsh (or more precisely Celts) who were the proximal geographical populations. In the years since, Arthur has been claimed by almost everybody (including Hollywood)! A second constituency here was the ruling house of England. The establishment of a fixed memorial for Arthur and the subsequent public link with this legendary monarch was a good strategy for the ruling dynasty. Establishing a memorial removed the possibility of his promised return, which might have actually been in the guise of an enemy leader. Thus, Arthur's tomb at Glastonbury was good business for the Norman Kings, so no wonder they supported this. Arthur works very well for those in power and because he addressed multiple constituencies, which made his appeal even stronger. We might also conclude that it is tragically anachronistic to believe that there were no smart people in the twelfth century.

The Vinland Map and the Kensington Runestone appeal directly to those of the Norse origin and descent. Each of these two artifacts plays on the understandable pride of that diaspora toward their forebears who faced extreme dangers during early voyages into the unknown. Each one of these items is a subtle creation since they are founded on the limited history of such early explorations. We know that groups of Norse explorers did venture all the way across the north Atlantic. We know that these peoples were great seafarers; the map and the stone merely extend these established achievements a bit further in space and time. The map is clever in the way that it "doth not protest too much." The stone is clearly embedded in the transshipment of the Scandinavian culture to the northern states of the emerging United States. If each of these artifacts seems to depend on one collective constituency, each plays on the major strength of that constituency, which is their core values and pride in their nationality and heritage. A wise deceiver always seeks to turn their target population's greatest strength against them [9].

Piltdown played on almost exactly the same form of emotion – patriotic pride in one's country. How could it be that England was the most powerful country in the world and had the most active and esteemed scientific community, and yet no evidence of early human presence had been found? To rub salt in the wound, such remains had been found around the world: some in Africa, some in Asia, some in Germany and even some in France! This state of affairs was simply too humiliating. Expressed or not, the desire for early English remains of primitive man was very deeply entrenched.

Here the hoaxer knew his constituency well. After all, Piltdown was not primarily an appeal to the masses. No, this was a direct targeting of the scientific, paleoanthropological community. This hoax took subtlety and planning. It was not enough to appeal only to the English sense of pride; the deception also had to incorporate the aspirations of scientists with respect to the so-called evolutionary missing link. The community that was targeted consisted of many who were beginning to revel in Darwin's startling theory. Arguably the greatest scientific insight ever, the link between the human and the rest of the anthropoid family would prove to be the capstone discovery. It would validate Darwin and establish English supremacy in the origins of man all in one stroke. Whoever the perpetrator(s) was (were), the hoax was one of real genius. So, Piltdown had to have more than a jingoistic fanfare; it had to be intellectually satisfying as well as emotionally appealing. Thus, multiple levels of motivation also prove critical to the hoaxer's armory.

As with Piltdown Man, Drake's Plate also had to appeal primarily to a smaller, tighter-knit community. This respective constituency was largely composed of professional and amateur historians of the American West. The Plate had to satisfy the need created by the maddening and frustrating lack of detail in the reports on Drake's voyage. Involved in arcane arguments about the site of Drake's anchorage, the Plate also had a wider appeal for anglophiles who could now point to their legitimate claim on the west coast of the United States predating any Spanish occupation. It is of course strange how the indigenous peoples always seem to be left out of these considerations – perhaps, as non-Christians, they were seen as "non-persons" whereas the Spanish were considered the traditional enemy and, paradoxically, accorded the status of personhood. Whether and how such considerations played a role in the late 1930s is best left to historians of the west coast of the United States of that era. However, the specificity of the Plate and the way it addressed a targeted community argues strongly for an inside job. The subsequent identification of E Clampus Vitus members as the culprits is psychologically satisfying. However, whether or not this explanation accords with ground truth, or could itself be just another unintentional deception, remains to be resolved. This points toward the very thorny philosophical issue of what is reality and whether we can eventually be sure of anything. As may be remembered, the French philosopher Rene Descartes was only sure that he could think and doubt. Perhaps this is the way to cope with the potential infinite regress of uncertainty.

The constituent group can be composed of any membership, as long as membership can be classified as a specific set. Members of scientific communities have proved vulnerable; members of certain nationalities and specific cultures have also been frequent targets. Our final case of the Shroud of Turin focuses on just such a community knitted together by religious belief. Given that they are primarily composed of those of the Catholic denomination, we must be cognizant of the known history of the Shroud in predating the European Reformation. Part of that schism depended on the nature of the worship of icons and relics. After the split of the Church of England from Rome, veneration of these representations largely devolved to Roman Catholics as compared to their Protestant brethren. We must not forget that Jesus is also an important figure in other religions around the world, such as in the Muslim community. However, Muslims have invocations against the use of iconic representations and thus they have no specific investment in the Shroud as a relic. Further, we should not underestimate exactly how large a constituency the Catholic Church represents. It has adherents estimated in billions across the globe. Clearly, the church has the largest constituency of any of the entities recounted in the stories told here, and therefore, the Shroud of Turin will be the best known of any of the exemplar stories I have presented. Certainly, the constituencies for Arthur's Cross or Drake's Plate pale in comparison. They are obviously less well known, even by any knowledgeable reader on hoaxes who acquires this book. As people care about the veracity of these claims, it is probably the case that people who care about the Shroud outnumber all of the others combined. Of course, the respective constituencies need not be mutually exclusive either.

Identify the Dream

In reality, identifying the dream to be addressed is relatively easy. This is because people will readily tell you what their dream is. For the secular British of the twelfth century, it was the chance to touch Arthur. For the monks of Glastonbury, it was the rebuilding of their revered house. For the Pilgrims, it was a chance to stand in awe and wonder surrounded by the relics of mythical kings and saints. For the ruling house of England, it was a chance to secure their hold on their own lands while undermining their potential enemies as they, in their turn, sought to occupy the territory of other native peoples. Arthur in Avalon fulfilled the dreams of many; he and Guinevere still do!

Individuals of Scandinavian origin know that they come from great seafarers and explorers. They have the famous sagas describing those feats.

They also have solid, archeological evidence of their early occupation on the North American continent. The question that they ask is: Why isn't everyone else aware of this? Why do we still celebrate Columbus Day, but have no national holiday for Leif Eriksson? [10] Why is 1492 so feted? Can't people see our brave explorers were here so much earlier? Frustration is a powerful human motivator. Well, since the Scandinavians know this actual history, perhaps some have thought to provide some additional assistance that would finally convince everyone. Maybe a map, perhaps a stone; what's the harm? After all, it's only confirmation of what we already know [11]. The Kensington Runestone is especially meaningful to settlers moving into new lands whose character and climate are so similar to their original home. Surely, this just confirms their right of possession. As the Runestone Museum video proudly proclaims "Yup, them boys was here all right!" It is the dream becoming reality.

Piltdown drew many into its web. Famous figures, such as Arthur Conan Doyle and Pierre Teilhard de Chardin, among others, were drawn to the site to partake of the excitement of the "Earliest Englishman." And what an evocative phrase that is, considering that *Eoanthropus Dawsoni*, had he ever existed, must have lived well before the idea of England was ever conceived, along with the fact that England would still have been attached to mainland Europe during his supposed lifetime. Imagine calling him the "Earliest Frenchman" or even worse, the "Earliest European"; such a bizarre nomenclature was not even to be imagined in Victorian and Edwardian England. Since the English were the height of creation and evolution, they also naturally had to be first. When one dreams in absolutes, it is totalities that have to be erected. Piltdown served its constituency, arguably as well as any deception ever could. The only redeeming feature to the story is that it was English scientists who exposed the dream as an illusion. Let us not even mention that it was an American who first voiced such concerns so very shortly after Piltdown was purportedly dug from the earth! As Wittgenstein implied, some things are better passed over in silence.

Drake's original Plate of Brass as a physical object is presumably no dream. After all, *The World Encompassed* stated that the plate was actually erected. One would have no reason to believe this was not so and therefore no reason to believe the plate did not still physically exist somewhere and in some form or another [12]. As a metal plate, it would not have rotted away as perhaps the supporting post would have done. No, it was presumably there somewhere, perhaps lying close to the place where Drake spent his five weeks of recovery. Finding it was the dream and it would be the greatest event in California history. Heck, it would precede the history of the state itself and would establish the good old British influence in the American West. After all, it is not much more than two centuries ago that England ruled the world. Who would not want to be associated with these winners? It must be somewhere, if only we could find it! Some continue to dream of that day.

Identify a Champion

It is not as easy to specify a particular champion as it is to identify a list of potential candidates. It may well be that the desired champion is also the prime object of the hoax. In the case of Drake's Plate, we seem to have a ready-made champion as well as the target for the purported student joke in Professor Bolton. Expressing his innermost desire to many classes of rambunctious students was probably asking for some sort of spoof. However, we cannot ensure that the person we wish to be either the target or the champion is indeed the person who actually embraces it. Such eventualities depend on the circumstances of the find, which can only be managed to a certain degree. In general, the narrower the community to which a specific hoax appeals, the greater the certainty that the target person will be the eventual recipient. For the Piltdown hoax, we do not know whether Smith Woodward was the selected target, although evidence suggests that, like Bolton, he was. In the case of the Shroud, it seems fairly certain that the Catholic Church would end up the eventual custodian whoever its specific owners were through the ages.

One can always ensure that a hoax is accepted by creating some form of commitment. In both of the cases in which science and history were intimately involved, such commitment took the form of professional authentication, and in the case of the Plate the transfer of money. The Vinland Map presents a similar profile. The case of Arthur's Cross is somewhat different because of the antiquity of its first discovery and its subsequent physical loss. Certainly the writer of contemporary and subsequent texts reported favorably on the cross, and a local champion may well have been evident in the Abbey of Glastonbury itself. The ultimate champions of the cross turned out to be the monarchs, Henry II, Richard I, and Edward I, although whether they believed the cross and the tomb of Arthur were real may never be known. Any hoax may fulfill the dream of its champion and there again it may fulfill other purposes also. The case of Hjalmar Holand and the Kensington Runestone is probably the most interesting in this respect.

Did Holand really believe the Runestone to be a fake but changed his mind after seeing it? Or was he simply an individual with an eye for the main chance? Indeed, did such dissonance ever exist? And if it did, did it simply dissolve as his life with the Runestone went on? Whether culturally or financially driven, Holand was the Runestone's champion for more than 50 years, and one has to admire such persistence, misplaced or not.

If the Shroud has a champion, it is probably the reluctant Secundio Pia. In creating the first negative image of the Shroud, he unleashed a torrent of discourse that continues well into the present day. Unlike other champions, Pia's advocacy was embedded within a single, albeit unconscious, action. However, this is to take the modern view of it. Both before and after Pia's photograph, the Shroud had its share of champions, those who owned it and bought it for the church, those who rushed in to save it from the fire, and those modern-day advocates who still continue to seek ways to establish its authenticity. The map, the plate, and the stone are fundamentally all concerns of this immediate past century. They have not had time since their discovery to collect a whole lineage of heroes. However, as the history of each grows longer, the number of champions tends to proliferate, and the name of each individual champion is slowly diminished among their peers as each artifact garners supporters from each succeeding generation. Perhaps in this respect, the Kensington Runestone is currently the most "active" of the three [13]. As long as people care about a specific dream, there will always be champions.

Create Support for the Dream

The act of creation of these artifacts is paradoxical. This is because it is both the simplest and at once the most difficult element in generating a successful hoax. It is simple in that it is often easy to say exactly what would support the dream. In our present examples, these are the identified body of King Arthur, the true image of Christ, the evolutionary missing link, the lost map, evidence of cultural primacy, or the missing plate. Each of these are intrinsic to the specific dreams themselves, although some, such as the Runestone, take a little more imagination than do some others, such as Drake's Plate, which was already specified to an extensive degree in the written record. The problem now is twofold. What do these things look like and how does one create a representation that will pass muster? Again, the plate presents few difficulties. Its fundamental characteristics are given in the text of Drake's voyage, and it is a matter of following what is a reasonably well-specified blueprint. Similarly, the map has a number of predecessors that provide a fairly good idea of what is required, and again under-specification can help fill in the rest. When there is no precedent, then the forger can let their imagination run a little. For example, Arthur's Cross need only specify that it was Arthur buried there. No worries of a metallurgical sort concerned any such maker, nor could they have envisaged the sorts of modern techniques that could eventually test such creations. Nor need the maker of the cross have worried anyway, as we no longer have it for any modern testing to occur. The fabricator of the Piltdown hoax had to be a little more circumspect. To fulfill the scientific aspiration, the find had to match the conceptions of the times. In matching the jaw and the cranium to the expected configuration, it might seem that a significant chance was being taken but the fact that the articulation between the two was removed, and the very fortuitous fact that most scientists got to see only casts and not the real thing allowed the fraudster(s) to get away with what now seems an evident mismatch.

The Runestone is a little more complex. There are numerous "carvings" and "mooring holes" over the expanse of North America that have been suggested as remnants of Viking exploration, but none of them prove very compelling. The Runestone is different because it tells a story. A scratched inscription, even dated back to 1362, would be somewhat dry and uninspiring. There is no way some line carving is going to catch the general public's imagination. No, the stone had to provide a rip-roaring story in a very few lines – and how well it accomplished its task! Establishing both spatial and temporal parameters, it still manages to tell the tale of an intrepid group of Norse explorers surrounded by danger yet adherent to their faith. This was a small group of brave individuals far from home, still showing the fortitude and steadfastness so much appreciated by the "later" immigrants. At one level, the Runestone is indeed the immigrants' own story. The brilliance of the Runestone lies in this wonderful ability to pack the whole narrative into just a few lines. Although why anyone discovering one-third of their companions "red with blood and dead" would sit down to chip away noisily at a stone monument in evidently dangerous circumstances I personally cannot say.

The Shroud is the most difficult. Whatever one's view of the authenticity of the Shroud, we know its provenance since the mid-1300s. This being so, assuming that it has not been altered or replaced over that interval, the face itself is simply extraordinary. Some have argued that this is indeed the iconic "face of Christ", and it may well be that various subsequent representations of Christ have actually evolved from a small number or even a single visual representation of Jesus. As to whether the shroud is one of these, and as to whether the Shroud is *the* one, presently we cannot say. It is a complex issue that returns to the dating evidence. If the intention of the Shroud's creator (whomever we take that to be) was to represent a tortured and beaten man of singular visual characteristics, we cannot argue that this aim has not been achieved. In so doing, some would claim the process of fabrication is blasphemous (assuming that it is a medieval artifact). Of course, although it may appear blasphemous in modern eyes, it need not necessarily have been all that bad or unusual a thing to do in the Middle Ages. Thus, we know of many other shrouds and numerous relics of the saints. Concerning the Shroud, others adhere to the notion that it is the burial cloth of Christ. Either way, in itself, this is a fabulous article, and the craftsmanship as well as the initial conceptualization is simply superb, although crucially it is a production not without evident flaws. Whether it is the burial cloth of Jesus Christ remains very much a contentious and, sadly, a highly unlikely proposition.

Having dealt with the inspiration of each of these items and the thought behind their individual production, we have to go on a little to evaluate the craftsmanship that allows most of these enigmas to persist today. Obviously, one has to have materials of a contemporary form, and here again the creators of the Runestone exhibit a considerable degree of intelligence. There has never been an argument related to the Runestone that the stone itself is not old enough to have been around in 1362. Like all forms of hoax, this argues for adherence to a clear policy – keep it simple. By using such a stone, the creators did not face the problem of the makers of Drake's Plate who had to ensure at least a semblance of contemporary metal on which to engrave their inscription. Some near-contemporary accounts of Drake's voyage mention brass while one other mentions lead, and this under-specificity provides at least some degree of freedom. However, modern rejection of the plate has been based primarily on evidence concerning its physical constitution. Not so for the stone; objections and arguments have to be based on the characteristics of the inscription, although recent efforts to evaluate the age of the physical surfaces of the stone have been evident [14]. The map seeks to use a contemporary surface, which is clear from the age of the paper itself and its watermark. Thus, while here the primary medium is of authentic age, the next material question revolves around the ink, which has been suggested to be modern. Again, this seems to be a case of the fabricator not taking enough care with the age of the materials used.

No such issues bedevil the cross of King Arthur, or if they do, we cannot demonstrate that it is so. Fabricating an artifact and then effectively having it "disappear" is a great tactic. We must remember that few individuals were permitted to examine the Piltdown bones, and although replica casts were available, the original artifacts also did a bit of a disappearing act. Dating is at the very heart of the Piltdown issue, and, of course, we now know that the bones are far too modern. However, look here at the antithesis. Had the forger actually had hominid bones of the right age, the notion of any sort of hoax may well have been obviated, although the issue of the ancestor being an Englishman may still have remained. The Shroud again is a special case, since it is the physical composition of the artifact about which the furor circulates. Some claim it is a medieval painting, others see it as the burial cloth of Christ. The fact that there can still be unresolved arguments about this is certainly a credit to the craftsman who created it. As I have noted earlier, in the end, if the hoax is well enough conceived and grounded, the actual physical artifact can become almost secondary. Nowhere is this more evident than in discussion of the Shroud. It may well be that one day the Shroud is shown to be a medieval creation. This is a feasible eventuality and one that appears to be well supported by the existing carbon-dating evidence. However, this possibility never has and indeed never will stop many people from believing in Christ's divinity. Similarly, even if the Map and the Stone are each categorically shown to be fakes, it will not stop people of the Norse descent from believing in their early discovery of the American continent – nor should it, given that other evidence of a much more substantive nature supports them in doing so. (Although how far one can "discover" a continent proposed to be as populous and advanced as the one you are coming from is again finessed in most discussions [15]).

The filmmaker Alfred Hitchcock was very aware of the above human propensity, and in his films he realized that the story was the thing. This being so, the item of concern – what he called "The McGuffin" – could be almost of any sort. It only had to have a narrative-related "value" to the characters involved. In and of itself, it need not necessarily have any explicit meaning. Like all tales of specific artifacts portrayed here, the story itself is larger than the entity and can stand alone if it absolutely has to. Of all those dashed by hoaxes and fakery, perhaps the English have taken the greatest punishment. Piltdown Man no longer occupies his perch in our tree of descent, and King Arthur is less the mystic figure of the modern world than he is the star of a musical motion picture, although some seek to keep his shadow alive. Belief in these respective myths and stories has diminished and the intellectual and emotive energies associated with such controversies have waned considerably. The English seem also to have lost out over Drake. Never a high priority in England itself, it would be nice to believe that the Crown still owned the rights to California, having forfeited the rest of the country to a group of disgruntled Englishmen in a petty intramural squabble. However, today even that solace is denied the English nation.

Make Sure the Deception Is Under-Specified

Creation of any artifact that seeks to achieve deception must comprehend the importance of a characteristic I have called under-specification. By under-specification I mean that the item must present sufficient degrees of freedom so that others can "read" things into it, impose their own prejudices on it, and interpret the resident ambiguity without reaching a conclusion of absolute certainty. This is the essence of deception that allows the individual faced with the ambiguous artifact to fit it into their preconceived framework of understanding without excessive dissonance. Make the item *too* perfect, or make it match the dream exactly, and one arouses suspicion. In contrast, if it is made so that it countermands every preconceived notion of the judging individual, then you are courting immediate rejection. But by creating something that is suggestive, indicative, and open to interpretation, you have made an artifact that many people can use to support their view of the world, and rarely will they stop to ask an excessive number of awkward questions. Unlike the other elements of a hoax, the nature of under-specification is contingent upon what is created. There is no simple formulaic approach to such fabrication. This is where the inspiration and insight of the fraudster come into play. It depends on knowing both the artifact itself and the desires and persuasions of the constituency one is aiming at. If it were simple, anyone could do it. However, successful forgery on the scale presently discussed requires an inspired flight of imagination.

Arrange to Have It Accidentally Discovered

The last thing one wants is to go to all the trouble of creating a wonderful hoax, having read the dimensions of psychological desire expressed by one's target audience, fabricated an undetectable but persuasive artifact, and then have it all blow up in one's face at the first moment. Yet here again is the hand of fate. If one is to ensure appropriate discovery, then, like the monks of Glastonbury, one has to engineer the event itself. However, this can look very suspicious. One can leave the discovery to chance and, like the situation with Drake's Plate, have fate eventually bring the thing to life. Perhaps there are many Drake's Plates out there waiting to be discovered. Perhaps they were all collected after the one necessary example had come to the fore. Poor Olof Ohman found himself under suspicion for the rest of his life, being repeatedly accused of being the originator of the Runestone hoax. One wonders if by the end of his life Ohman, whether the fabricator or not, regretted having ever seen the stone.

The Piltdown hoaxer has yet to be unequivocally pinned down. Not quite as many candidates have emerged as we have seen for Jack the Ripper, but the number continues to grow. Pride of place must go to Charles Dawson, and even though he died prematurely, suspicion continues to linger that he must at least have been part of any group of conspirators if more than one individual was involved. The most successful case here is the Shroud. Its origins prior to our first recorded sighting are shrouded in mystery, if you will pardon the well-intended pun. Again, candidates have been brought forward, but this artifact achieves what all should aspire to: a mystery as to some critical elements of provenance [16]. Each of these facets plays on particular human frailties. They were first articulated in detail by Francis Bacon in his advocacy of the empirical method. Although we now realize we can never take the affective element of judgment and decision making from the human process, the degree to which one can disassociate vital decisions from emotional turmoil proves to be crucial in their subsequent effect. As Aristotle noted in *Politics*, "The law is reason unaffected by desire" (often rendered as "The law is reason free from passion"). While humans are never truly free from passion, the vulnerability to deception is most certainly increased when our passions are aroused. But hoax and deception are not a thing of history; they are interwoven with the very fabric of life.

SELF-WORTH AND DECEPTION

As a final consideration in this chapter, let us consider explicitly how people fool themselves. One central key to deception will always lie in the way the deceived individuals think of themselves. Powerful deceptions must focus on most cherished beliefs, and for most human beings such beliefs are founded in religion. At first, it may seem that of all of the artifacts discussed here, only the Shroud of Turin has any direct religious significance. However, this vastly underestimates the role religion plays in each case. It is worth at least a brief examination to articulate the underlying motivations in the other cases. As we have seen, the author of the Vinland Map might well have been a Jesuit priest and his assertions concerning the exploration of the North American coast by the Viking voyages includes a direct inclusion of Bishop Erik, whose purpose would very much have been pastoral and evangelical. Exploration was not their only purpose, of course; these individuals were bringing Christianity, and specifically the Catholic faith, along with them. So too were their nominal descendants some three and a half centuries later in central Minnesota; the inscription "AVM" on the Stone has always been interpreted as Ave Maria. This nomenclature again references the Catholic Church and its primacy as much as any other motivation for the purported exploration of the northern Great Lakes region [17].

If Catholicism has been championed with the Norse claims for the early occupation of and nominal rights to North America, then Drake's Plate is very much set in the same realm but cast in terms of the religious conflict of its own times. The father of Elizabeth I, Henry VIII, had broken with the Pope and the Catholic Church over the question of the annulment of his marriage to Katherine of Aragon. Primarily this was about the lack of a son to continue his line of succession. We must remember that prior to Henry VIII, no woman had ruled England solely in her own right, even if we include the Empress Maud and the contentious times of King Stephen. Henry VIII could not know that his two daughters would rule and that his daughter by Anne Boleyn would become "Gloriana." Thus, at the time of Drake's voyage, contention was not simply over land and wealth. There was direct antagonism between Catholic and Protestant forms of the Christian faith. Establishing the claim on the region surrounding the anchorage was not only an act on behalf of his monarch; it was a claim for the Protestant against the Catholic faith.

The Cross of King Arthur was truly a vehicle for religious expansion. The house of worship at Glastonbury had achieved a primacy among all places of worship in England. It had its church that had been blessed as perhaps built by the hands of the earliest Christians. Bound up in the legend of the visit of Joseph of Arimathea, Glastonbury was in the ascendancy, with Canterbury certainly lower in the hierarchy. The fire changed all that. With the death of St. Thomas in 1170 came the ascendancy of Canterbury, and what Glastonbury needed was not a more religious purpose, but rather an attraction by which also to expand Christianity, even if it was only in the form of benefit for this one house.

The Bible prohibits the creation of graven images, which is parenthetically a very astute tactic for a religion that seeks to imbue God with omnipresence. But who would not want to look their savior in the face? In fact, how many of the so-called faithful as well as the heathen would not be persuaded by a glimpse of God's son, even if it were only a representation? Graven images of Christ on the Cross are now ubiquitous. It is clearly the case that if one is going to see proliferation of a religion, one has to have an icon as well as the sound bites people can remember. The Shroud is an icon for Christians. But the Piltdown fossils were an icon for the British scientists who also wished to believe. *Just as religion makes poor science, so poor science can make a religion.* When the wish to believe overcomes the responsibility to doubt, individuals leave the lighted world of the rational and enter the shadow world where desire supersedes evidence. Showing icons to those on the border between these worlds encourages their brainstem to conquer their neocortex. To suggest that those who normally pursue the practice of science are not tempted by their hopes and aspirations is as facile as the dismissal of those who look for evidentiary foundations for their already cherished beliefs. No matter which part of the brain is, for the moment, in ascendancy, thinking is most often a good thing.

REFERENCE NOTES

[1] Whittaker, J. (1992). The curse of the Runestone: Deathless hoaxes. *Skeptical Inquirer*, 17, 59–63.

[2] Rousseau, J. J. (1776). Reveries of a solitary walker.

[3] See Chaline, E. (2010). *History's greatest deceptions*. New York: Metro Books. For some potential explanations, see also Shermer, M. (1997). *Why people believe weird things*. New York: W. H. Freeman.

[4] One of my favorite examples following those I have detailed here is the "holy blood" of Hailes Abbey (Coad, 1970; St. Clair Baddeley, 1960). Also, I have a strong affinity with the way the origins of the Coral Castle are now being turned into a myth and thus are slowly evolving into a hoax also.

[5] See Sokal, A. D. (1996). Transgressing the boundaries: Towards a transformative hermeneutics of quantum gravity. *Social Text*, 46/47, 217–252. See http://en.wikipedia.org/wiki/Sokal_affair

[6] The recent case of Bernard Madoff and the reincarnation of the ever-recurring Ponzi type scheme being one of the more recent examples. See http://en.wikipedia.org/wiki/Bernard_Madoff

[7] "Human understanding, once it has adopted opinions, either because they were already accepted and believed, or because it likes them, draws everything

to support and agree with them. And though it may meet a greater number and weight of contrary instances, it will, with great and harmful prejudice, ignore or condemn or exclude them" (Francis Bacon).

[8] See Waller, J. (2009). Looking back: Dancing plagues and mass hysteria. *The Psychologist*, 22(7), 644–647. See also Colligan, M. J., Pennebaker, J. W., & Murphy, L. R. (Eds.). (1982). *Mass psychogenic illness: A social psychological analysis*. Hillsdale, NJ: Lawrence Erlbaum Associates.

[9] Sun Tzu (1910 Trans.). *The Art of War by Sun Tzu – Special Edition* (L. Giles, Ed, 2005). El Paso, TX: El Paso Norte Press.

[10] http://www.mnc.net/norway/LeifErikson.htm

[11] It is relevant to note here that the sites like *l'Anse aux Meadows* were discovered around 1960, and thus well after the creation of the Runestone or even after the revelation of the Vinland Map.

[12] Interestingly, relatively few people have suggested that as valuable an object as the Plate would have been immediately removed by some of the indigenous Indian population, even though this would seem a very likely eventuality.

[13] The recent text – Nielsen, R., & Wolter, S. F. (2006). *The Kensington Rune Stone: Compelling new evidence*. Evanston, IL: Lake Superior Agate Publishing – has confirmed the contemporary presence of such champions.

[14] Nielsen & Wolter, *The Kensington Rune Stone op cit.*

[15] See Mann, C. C. (2005). *1491: New revelations of the Americas before Columbus*. New York: Knopf.

[16] I would be remiss if I did not explicitly state that hoax and deception continue to flourish in the modern day. Examples of intentional deception such as the Hitler diaries and perhaps inadvertent deceptions like the 'cold fusion' incident still grace our media almost on a daily basis.

[17] The most recent "theories" have now linked the expedition to the Knights Templar and the now (almost inevitable) discovery of a hidden code on the Stone itself. For a critique of such forms of confirmation bias in the "Bible code," see http://www.peterhancock.ucf.edu/Downloads/add_pubs/ Hancock_2003_4%20%28Elucidation%20of%20the%20Bible%20Code%29. pdf

Summary

Hoax Springs Eternal

"Human understanding ... is infused by desire and emotion, which give rise to 'wishful science.' For man prefers to believe what he wants to be true. He therefore rejects difficulties, being impatient of enquiry."

Francis Bacon

Through exploring the proposition that Hoax Springs Eternal, I have argued in this book that deception is a fundamental part of life. The various forms deceptions take, each adapt to the organism(s) that practice(s) them. Most animals practice deception in defense of their own continuing existence. In the ongoing battle between predator and prey, the primary expressions of deception are the sensory and perceptual adaptations that look to confuse and fool the senses. Human beings certainly continue to practice these sensory and perceptual deceptions in their various forms, which is perhaps most evident in modern military operations. However, I have argued that humans are different from other animals because they also create and practice cognitive deceptions. As our brains have evolved, and especially as our reliance on our resident cognitive capacities have increased, humans have created an ever-greater capacity for generating differing dimensions of deception. Thus, cognitive deceptions have become progressively more sophisticated and specialized as our social and cultural capabilities have expanded. Humans also practice deception at higher social and political levels, in which certain groups of individuals seek to persuade even larger groups of people about states of the world that are in reality not so. These forms of historical revisionism and propaganda are directed more toward social and political control than any individual profit per se. Although I have not focused on these latter dimensions of deception in this particular work, they certainly share many of the basic psychological dimensions that have been examined and discussed here.

The central focus in this work has been on establishing the identity and dimensions of cognitive deception. Each of the stories I have recounted here have illustrated different aspects of cognitive, social, and cultural specializations. As technology improves and our various cultures each become more dependent on these technological expressions, the capacity for individual as opposed to group-based deceptions increases. Elsewhere, this line of progress has been called "individuation" [1]. So, what has previously depended on persuading some group of people through rather limited and imperfect communication channels has, with modern interactive media, begun to change to deceptions customized for one specific individual; bespoke deception, if you will. In the future, it will not be mass e-mails from benevolent people addressed to "dearly beloved" [2]; it will be personal deceptions aimed at each specific individual by name. Beware; you have been warned [3]!

Although this book has explored some of the psychological dimensions of cognitive deception, it is equally possible to examine the neurological basis of these deceptions, and this form of effort is largely founded on the explosion of modern brain-imaging techniques [4]. However, such an exploration is beyond the present purview, and my goal now is to summarize the various observations I have made. To accomplish this, I want first to draw a parallel between the penetration of a hoax into the public mind and episodes of what have been termed "psychogenic illness."

"[L]iterary evidence supplies the words, archeological (evidence) supplies the objects. Connecting one with the other is often a matter of conjecture."

Rook (2002)

HOAX AND THE ETIOLOGY OF PSYCHOGENIC ILLNESS

Psychogenic illness is primarily a social phenomenon and is thus often referred to as mass psychogenic illness. Unlike certain related forms of mass hysteria, psychogenic illness produces actual and recognizable physical symptoms. However, although there are evident medical disturbances, there is no immediately identifiable organic cause. I have had professional experience with such an event and can attest to its very real effects. Typically, however, symptoms most often show themselves in the more subjective dimensions, such as headaches and light-headedness. In the case with which I am most familiar, a data-mining company had changed their offices to a new and expensive facility. This required a reorganization of the physical positions of the personnel involved. When the people were relocated to the new facility, they immediately began to suffer nonspecific symptoms that were attributed initially to the new air-handling system. There followed a very expensive survey and cleaning of that system, which in reality was in no way at fault. What had actually happened was that two socially very powerful members of the office in question had lost their prime position of "power" in terms of being able to oversee all of their junior colleagues. Indeed, it was these very individuals who first exhibited the symptoms, and the implication was that they had "suggested" the problem to their various colleagues. The solution engaged was to reestablish the old order of power by shuffling desks in the new, open-plan area. Apologies were made about the purported failure of the air-handling system, and just as quickly the medical issues evaporated. (As to whether this was the correct or even appropriate [moral] solution, I leave that discussion to another occasion). Such incidents of illness show a typical time profile. There is a sudden and abrupt rise of the problem followed by a growing number of related, if less pointed, complaints. The condition persists until the perceived source of disturbance is dealt with. Fundamentally, this is an "infection" of the mind, and I believe there are strong parallels (indeed, arguably, an exact parallel) between such conditions and the acceptance of deception.

In the case of a hoax, there is initially an influential "discovery" that proves to be the source of "infection." In some ways we can consider this infection akin to the invasion of a form of maladaptive "meme" [5]. Like the comparable condition of the penetration of technologies into society, we have enthusiastic "early adopters." Previously I have identified this role as a singular one, with one "champion" making the discovery and spreading the "infection." However, there is, of course, no reason why this champion role cannot be shared among many individuals. Excitement surrounding the "discovery" leads to much media attention, which in turn is often accompanied by rapid and relatively uncritical public acceptance. (To some degree this makes sense; after all, who in the busy modern world has time to check out all of these claims?) Enthusiasm and acceptance reach a peak as the object or entity becomes the "news event" of the day. This level of excitement is proportional to the size of the constituency at which the hoax is aimed. For example, some hoaxes are merely local affairs and attract little attention and following. However, some are of global significance and can attract the attention of billions of people [6]. Modern forms of communication facilitate this information distribution. What at one time were necessarily only local events can now go global in a very short time indeed. Following the early peak, there is a gradual decline; the object is superseded by newer "news", and then substantive and sometimes profound criticisms begin to exert their impact. Finally, there is the extinction phase in which there remains a "residual level" of acceptance or a ghostly reflection of the enthusiasm of the prior acceptance. We can see that this pattern holds for each of the case studies I have illustrated in this book, as well as for numerous other examples and is potentially a general principle. Thus, acceptance of information is indeed a part of a ubiquitous human pattern, but in the case of deception it is false information. It is indeed a maladaptive meme, or *malmeme*, as opposed to adaptive or *benememe* [7]. The central question that follows is how such problematic penetration can be excised. It is here that we come to the role of science and of the skeptic.

"The ill-informed are often swayed by a confidently asserted doubt and even those who should know better will jump on a skeptic's bandwagon."

Frederick. J. Pohl

EVALUATING UNUSUAL CLAIMS

If a deception can be thought of as a maladaptive meme, then we can ask how this is to be excised [8]. Like infections in the body itself, these influences have to be fought, and that battle is engaged by the skeptic. I suspect that many skeptics are romantics at heart. They often very much wish to believe what is being offered. However, they have one tragic character flaw: they have to "know" rather than simply take various tall stories at face value. To that end, they generally bring the methods and tools of science to bear on the topic at hand to help distinguish fact from fiction. However, the phenomena themselves also possess distinct characteristics, and it is clear that a formal taxonomy of these various and varied "extraordinary claims" is needed in advance in order to know what form or forms of "proof" is required [9]. Among the possible dimensions of this taxonomy is the temporal persistence of the observation itself. The act of observation can range from a single instance viewed by one single, unaccompanied observer for only the briefest of moments to multiple repetitions of events seen by multiple individuals [10].

With the exception of Arthur's Cross, all of the items in the present set of examples have (and still can) be seen by anyone with access to the place where they are located. A second dimension might refer to the nature of what it is that is actually observed. Is the claim related to a psychic event that is not open to external inspection? Or, in contrast, does the claim relate to some concrete object that is permanently on public view? For example, claims of "remote viewing" – the ability to perceive visual scenes beyond the normal range of sight – can be evaluated through different test procedures [11]. The actual internal "vision" itself, however, is a private experience and cannot be shared; it can only be probed by external questioning. It was these very issues concerning the validity of such forms of "introspection" that proved to be so problematic to the science of psychology itself at the turn of the 20th century [12]. The "introspectionist" approach failed for precisely this reason. What was claimed could not be externally measured. The pendulum of psychology then swung violently away from subjective experience to the extent that only observable phenomenon were considered valid topics of exploration [13]. The content of psychological research has oscillated between these extremes ever since [14]. Concrete evidence is often claimed in many exceptional claims, but unfortunately such evidence is virtually never forthcoming when critical public evaluation is invoked. Skeptics are skeptical, while adherents sometimes take the absence of evidence as confirmation of some conspiratorial activity designed to suppress the truth [15]. Finally, there are objects about which claims are made that can and are subject to experimental evaluation and are, in principle, open to any observer. It is why in this work I have focused almost exclusively on these particular and peculiar forms of hoax, and not explicitly examined any of the other, more ephemeral and polemic forms as a basis for introducing cognitive deception. But well beyond the form and features of the hoax itself, the key to deception will always lie in understanding human psychology.

"It should come as no surprise that fame – showbiz fame anyway – is so disorienting. After all, the theater, where it all begins, is founded on a conspiracy of mutual deception. The performer pretends to be someone he is not, and the audience willingly suspends its disbelief. It's a confidence game in which both partners risk the humiliation of being played for a sucker. The actor makes himself vulnerable to the embarrassment of failure by trusting that the audience will grant him the time and attention to craft his lie. In return, the audience depends upon the actor's gift to keep them from feeling like fools for believing. Artfully transacted, this is one con where the potential exists for everyone to win. The payoff is an hour or so of collective – and harmless – magical thinking."

Fox (2002)

LAST WORDS

At a Conference on Rational Thinking I attended, participants were asked to coin a phrase that would epitomize the resistance to psychological deception. My epithet "Know Doubt" was gratifyingly adopted. I readily admit it is a distant progeny of the Royal Society's original motto "*Nulla in Verba*" (which can be roughly translated as 'take no one's word for it.") Both of these observations point to one of the most potent observations in all of science, and one with which I would like to conclude this text. *It remains essential that we reserve our greatest doubt for our most cherished beliefs.* Where doubt is our companion, hoax will find it difficult to flourish. The purpose of this work has been to present some of what can be considered the "hallmarks of hoax." It was intended to show that many of these hallmarks are common to all deception and find their origin in the human brain and its extension from the lower levels of cognition. It may well be that life actually needs deception [16]. In expressing these central characteristics, it is of course inevitable that one brings to light avenues and methods by which deception can be perpetrated. I leave myself open to criticism that what I have created is a "Hoaxer's Handbook," but it is always possible to use knowledge in differing ways, contingent upon individual motivation. It has been said that for those who believe, no proof is necessary, and for those who disbelieve, no proof is possible, but for the rest of us, we should believe in proof of the possible and the possibility of proof. While one can hope to educate and to entertain at the same time, it is an even greater challenge to drive that education in a direction considered in support of the moral good. This is because, despite all of our best efforts, as long as there are human beings, hoax springs eternal.

VALE

In a 1978 song recorded by the Doobie Brothers, Kenny Loggins and Michael Mcdonald proposed that "what a fool believes he sees ... No wise man has the power to reason away." Let us hope that this is not so. But in so doing, the wise man must be careful that in seeking to explain he does not merely explain away.

REFERENCE NOTES

[1] See Hancock, P. A., Hancock, G. M., & Warm, J. S. (2009). Individuation: The N=1 revolution. *Theoretical Issues in Ergonomic Science*, 10(5), 481–488.

[2] Like all forms of expression in modern electronic media, this particular reference will be somewhat anachronistic before this work is even published. This
is just to note that this is/was a common form of e-mail scam in the form of a
"get quick rich" scheme designed to get the unsuspecting individuals to part
with their money. Hopefully, by the time you read this, that specific form of
fraud will be outdated. Sadly, as a whole, fraud or deception for gain most certainly will not.

[3] In fact, as I was revising this text, I was hit by a hoaxer who sent an e-mail,
seemingly from a friend, by hijacking that person's e-mail address book. The
message claimed my friend was stuck in a foreign country and needed money
desperately. This was no longer a general scam; it had a very personal appeal,
and I put in some effort to ensure my friend was not in peril. I was reminded
of this episode because one of the reviewers of a draft of the book had been
scammed in exactly the same fashion.

[4] Singer, E. (2007). Imaging deception in the brain: Can brain imaging truly
detect lies? *Technology Review*, February 7.

[5] The noted scientist and polemicist Richard Dawkins has argued, with more
than some degree of conviction, that certain forms of religious dogma can be
viewed in the same way: "God exists, if only in the form of a meme with high
survival value, or infective power, in the environment provided by human culture." For a more technically oriented understanding of specific memory failures, see Schacter, D. (2001). *The seven sins of memory*. New York: Houghton
Mifflin.

[6] A recent example that comes to mind is the purported "James Ossuary."
See   http://www.antiquities.org.il/article_Item_eng.asp?module_id=&sec_
id=17&subj_id=175&id=266 as well as Marcus, A. D. (2008). Ancient objects,
dubious claims: James, son of Joseph, brother of Jesus: The inscription caused
a sensation. It was also new. *The Wall Street Journal*, October, 20.

[7] Blackmore, S. J. (2010). Dangerous memes; or, what the Pandorans let loose.
In Ed. S. Dick & M. Lupisella (Eds.), *Cosmos and culture: Cultural evolution
in a cosmic context* (pp. 297–318). Washington, DC: NASA. From http://www.
susanblackmore.co.uk/index.htm. We can distinguish between the maladaptive meme (the *malmeme*) and its positive counterpart (the *benememe*)
through their respective concordance with objective reality and the concomi-
tant positive or negative value they render in practice. This distinction is considered in coming work.

[8] Inevitably, the distinctions between harmful and beneficial ideas involve
value judgments and the exercise of moral principles. The degree to which
certain notions accord with "ground truth" (to the degree that such truth can
be known) is certainly one dimension on which judgment can be exercised.
However, few socially contentious disputes revolve around statements in
mathematics or assertions about known laws of physics. In the former, more
contentious situations, disputations about judgment inevitably arise and cannot, on occasion, be rationally resolved. Life is, indeed, not a closed and deterministic system.

[9] In skeptical circles, a famous phrase has emerged in which "extraordinary claims
require extraordinary proof," which is often – and incorrectly – attributed to

Carl Sagan. The precise statement – "An extraordinary claim requires extraordinary proof" – is from the work of Marcello Truzzi (Truzzi, M. [1978]. On the extraordinary: An attempt at clarification. *Zetetic Scholar*, 1[1], 11). Truzzi would no doubt acknowledge a precedent in David Hume's 1748 Essay "Of Miracles" in which he notes: "[T]he evidence, resulting from the testimony, admits of a diminution, greater or less, in proportion as the fact is more unusual." Truzzi's observation is pithier but is contained in its essence by Hume. In contrast, I would argue that extraordinary claims do not require extraordinary proof, but rather require extra but ordinary sorts of proof. There is a small and, initially, apparently subtle difference. However, I would argue this difference is not merely semantic, but different in substance.

[10] The conundrum of individual, idiographic observation and its reliability is the centerpiece of Carl Sagan's lone novel, *Contact*. Sadly, the conundrum presented in the work was eminently resolvable by repetition, one of the central pillars of empirical science.

[11] Baker, R. (1996). Scientific remote viewing. *Skeptical Inquirer*, 6(June). See also http://www.csicop.org/sb/show/scientific_remote_viewing/

[12] See Editorial. (2006). Introspection in science. *Consciousness and Cognition*, 15, 629–633.

[13] Watson, J. B. (1913). Psychology as the behaviorist views it. *Psychological Review*, 20, 158–177.

[14] Hancock, P. A., Weaver, J. L., & Parasuraman, R. (2002). Sans subjectivity: Ergonomics is engineering. *Ergonomics*, 45(14), 991–994.

[15] This whole principle was one of the bedrock foundations for the extremely popular television series, "The X-Files."

[16] See Trivers, R. (2011). *The folly of fools*. New York: Basic Books.

GLOSSARY

Apophenia	Formally, apophenia is the experience of seeing patterns or connections in random or meaningless data. Of course, seeing such patterns may eventually provide great meaning.
Bottom-Up Processing	The processing and understanding of information derived from the sensory input of the moment. Of course, this rarely if ever happens in a pure and unamended form.
Confirmation Bias	People's natural tendency to favor data and information that confirms their prior beliefs or aspirations. This was one bias that Francis Bacon warned of at the very beginnings of modern science.
Cock a Snook	A derisive gesture accomplished by bringing your open hand up to your face and touching your thumb to your nose.
Jape	To mock or make fun of.
Occam's Razor	Among competing hypotheses, the hypothesis with the fewest assumptions should be adopted. However, what precisely represents simplicity of assumption and how it should be measured is rarely explained in the natural sciences, although it is somewhat clearer in mathematics.
Pareidolia	A component of apophenia that frequently involves seeing human faces (e.g., faces in clouds, the "face" on Mars, etc.). Its origins are in the fact that humans are especially sensitive

	to facial patterns, and this represents a very primitive but highly useful capacity. It is more adaptive to occasionally see a face that is not there than to miss a face that is.
Top-Down Processing	The companion to bottom-up processing in which experiencing reality is dominated by prior knowledge and expectation rather than by the immediate sensory input. Of course, this also rarely if ever happens in a pure and unamended form.

REFERENCES

1. THE TANGLED WEB

Source Materials

The literature on deception is both vast and highly diverse. There are many areas and disciplines that have sought to deal with various faces of deception. These range from early, formal studies at the birth of psychology and philosophy to more recent explorations in areas as different as economics, political science, forensics, criminology, and even studies of magic and illusion in entertainment. While my present study focuses most directly on experimental psychology, I have also looked to use knowledge and insight derived from a number of other areas in order to begin to set the scene for the present text.

References

Anderson, M. (1986). Cultural concatenation of deceit and secrecy. In R. W. Mitchell & N. S. Thompson (Eds.), *Deception: Perspectives on human and nonhuman deceit* (pp. 323–348), Albany: SUNY Press.

Anderson, R. (1980). Hunt and conceal: Information management in Newfoundland deep-sea trawler fishing. In S. K. Tefft (Ed.), *Secrecy: A cross-cultural perspective* (pp. 205–228). New York: Human Sciences Press.

Bartlett, F. C. (1932). *Remembering: A study in experimental and social psychology.* New York: Cambridge University Press.

Barzun, J., & Graf, H. F. (1969). A medley of mysteries: A number of dogs that didn't bark. In R. W. Winks (Ed.), *The historian as detective: Essays on evidence* (pp. 213–231). New York: Harper & Row.

Bennett, W. L., & Feldman, M. S. (1981). *Reconstructing reality in the courtroom: Justice and judgment in American culture.* New Brunswick, NJ: Rutgers University Press.

Blum, R. H. (1972). *Deceivers and deceived: Observations on confidence men and their victims, informants and their quarry, political and industrial spies and ordinary citizens.* Springfield, IL: Charles C. Thomas, Publisher.

Buller, D. B., Strzyzewski, K. D., & Comstock, J. (1991). Interpersonal deception: I. Deceivers reactions to receivers' suspicions and probing. *Communication Monographs, 58,* 1–4.

Ceci, S. J., Leichtman, M., & Putnick, M. (1992).*Cognitive and social factors in early deception*. Mahwah, NJ: Lawrence Erlbaum.

Chevalier-Skolnikoff, S. (1986). An exploration of the ontogeny of deception in human beings and nonhuman primates. In R. W. Mitchell & N. S. Thompson (Eds.), *Deception: Perspectives on human and nonhuman deceit* (pp. 205–220). Albany, NY: SUNY Press.

Dekker, S. (2004). Hindsight bias is not a bias and not about history. *Human Factors and Aerospace Safety*, 4(2), 87–100.

Ekman, P. (1985). *Telling lies*. New York: Norton.

Fischhoff, B. (1975). Hindsight is not foresight: The effect of outcome knowledge on judgment under uncertainty. *Journal of Experiment Psychology: Human Perception and Performance*, 1(3), 288–299.

   (2003). Hindsight does not equal foresight: The effect of outcome knowledge and adaptive learning. *Quality Safety and Health Care*, 12(Suppl. 2), ii46–ii50.

Fisher, D. (1983). *The war magician*. New York: Coward-McCann.

Gombos, V. A. (2006). The cognition of deception: The role of executive processes in producing lies. *Genetic, Social, and General Psychology Monographs*, 132(3), 197–214.

Hankiss, A. (1980). Games con men play: The semiosis of deceptive interaction. *Journal of Communication*, 30, 104–112.

Harrington, B. (Ed.). (2009). *Deception: From ancient empires to internet dating*. Stanford, CA: Stanford University Press.

Haywood, I. (1987). *Faking it: Arts and the politics of forgery*. New York: St. Martin's Press.

Hyman, R. (1977). Cold reading: How to convince strangers that you know all about them. *The Zetetic*, 1, 18–37.

Innes, B. (2005). *Fakes and forgeries*. Pleasantville, NY: Reader's Digest.

Jastrow, J. (1935). *Error and eccentricity in human belief*. New York: Dover.

Jeppson, L. (1970). *Fabulous frauds*. London, UK: Arlington Books.

Kintner, E. W. (1978). *A primer on the law of deceptive practices*. New York: Macmillan.

Kohn, A. (1988). *False prophets: Fraud and error in science and medicine*. New York: Basil Blackwell.

Krebs, D., Denton, K., & Higgins, N. C. (1988). On the evolution of self-knowledge and self-deception. In K. B. MacDonald (Ed.), *Sociobiological perspectives on human development* (pp. 103–139). New York: Springer-Verlag.

Lambert, D. R. (1987). *A cognitive model for exposition of human deception and counter-deception: Final report*. San Diego, CA: Naval Ocean Systems Center.

MacDougall, C. D. (1958). *Hoaxes*. New York: Dover Publications.

Macknik, S. L., Martinez-Conde, S., & Blakeslee, S. (2010). *Sleights of mind: What the neuroscience of magic reveals about our everyday deceptions*. New York: Henry Holt & Co.

McCornack, S. A., & Parks, M. R. (1990). What women know that men don't: Sex differences in determining the truth behind deceptive messages. *Journal of Social and Personal Relationships*, 7, 107–118.

Melton, K., & Wallace, R. (2009). *The official CIA manual of trickery and deception.* New York: Harper Collins Publishers.

Mitchell, R. W. (1988). Ontogeny, biography, and evidence for tactical deception. *Behavioral and Brain Sciences, 11,* 259–260.

(1996). The psychology of human deception: Truth-telling, lying and self-deception. *Social Research, 63*(3), 819–861.

Mitchell, R. W., & Thompson, N. S. (Eds.). *Deception: Perspectives on human and nonhuman deceit.* Albany: SUNY Press.

Moss, N. (1977). *The pleasures of deception.* New York: Crowell.

Nevins, A. (1969). The case of the cheating documents. In R. W. Winks (Ed.), *The historian as detective: Essays on evidence* (pp. 192–212). New York: Harper & Row.

Osman, M., Channon, S., & Fitzpatrick, S. (2009). Does the truth interfere with our ability to deceive? *Psychonomic Bulletin and Review, 16*(5), 901–906.

Phelan, J. (1982). *Scandals, scamps, and scoundrels.* New York: Random House.

Quiatt, D. (1988). Which are more easily deceived, friends or strangers? *Behavioral and Brain Sciences, 11,* 260–261.

Scheibe, K. E. (1979). *Mirrors, masks, lies and secrets: The limits of human predictability.* New York: Praeger.

Sexton, D. J. (1986). The theory and psychology of military deception. In R. W. Mitchell & N. S. Thompson (Eds.), *Deception: Perspectives on human and nonhuman deceit* (pp. 349–356). Albany: SUNY Press.

Shapiro, D. (1996). On the psychology of self-deception. *Social Research, 63*(3), 785–800.

Smith, W. J. (1986). An informational perspective on manipulation. In R. W. Mitchell & N. S. Thompson (Eds.), *Deception: Perspectives on human and nonhuman deceit* (pp. 71–86). Albany: SUNY Press.

Spence, S. A., Hunter, M. D., Farrow, T. F. D., Green, R. D., Leung, D. H., Hughes, C. J., & Ganesan, V. (2004). A cognitive neurobiological account of deception: Evidence from functional neuroimaging. *Philosophical Transactions of the Royal Society of London B: Biological Sciences, 359*(1451), 1755–1762.

Sporer, S. L., & Schwandt, B. (2007). Moderators of nonverbal indicators of deception: A meta-analytic synthesis. *Journal of Nonverbal Behavior, 20,* 65–80.

Vasek, M. E. (1986). Lying as a skill: The development of deception in children. In R. W. Mitchell & N. S. Thompson (Eds.), *Deception: Perspectives on human and nonhuman deceit* (pp. 271–292). Albany: SUNY Press.

Vrij, A., Fisher, R., Mann, S., & Leal, S. (2006). Detecting deception by manipulating cognitive load. *Trends in Cognitive Sciences, 10*(4), 141–142.

Werth, F., & Flaherty, J. (1986). A phenomenological approach to human deception. In R. W. Mitchell & N. S. Thompson (Eds.), *Deception: Perspectives on human and nonhuman deceit* (pp. 293–311). Albany: SUNY Press.

Website

http://www.museumofhoaxes.com/hoax/history/index

2. THE CROSS OF KING ARTHUR

Source Materials

The Cross of King Arthur is probably the least known of the examples I have chosen, especially for an international audience. Largely, I suspect this is also because we do not now possess the physical artifact itself. I have known of Arthur's burial and the Cross for some decades, but source materials in this area remain meager compared to other examples. Most readers will be able to get an outline of the story from some of the informative and popular texts on Glastonbury, and in this I think the book by Chambers is an outstanding example, with the earlier text by Robinson also very helpful. However, one can also pursue the observations of the technical, working historians. In this I found the articles by Wood – a highly under-rated historian as I know from other work – and Crick to be of the greatest value. They each rely to a certain degree on some earlier observations by Nitze, and I would also especially recommend a copy of his 1934 article. Reference is often made to original, contemporary accounts. These should be approached with humility because a full understanding requires considerable knowledge about their original formulation and purpose as well as the information they purport to contain. Such an effort is certainly a specialist study. What makes Arthur's cross so seductive is that there is a possibility the artifact may be rediscovered. If it ever is, look for this topic to rise to the very peak of popular interest.

References

Abbey Guide (undated). *A guide to Glastonbury and its Abbey*. Bristol: UK, Elworthy & Son.

Alexander, M. (1982). *British folklore, myths and legends*. London: Book Club Associates.

Ashe, G. (1966). *King Arthur's Avalon: The story of Glastonbury*. New York: Collins.

(1985). *The discovery of King Arthur*. New York: Henry Holt and Company.

Barber, C., & Pykitt, D. (1993). *Journey to Avalon: The final discovery of King Arthur*. Abergavenny, Wales: Blorenge Books.

Barber, R. (1961). *King Arthur: Hero and legend*. New York: St. Martin's Press.

(1973). *The figure of Arthur*. Totowa, NJ: Rowan and Littlefield.

Birley, R. (1932). The battle of Mount Badon. *Antiquity*, 6, 459–463.

Bulletin of the Enfield Archaeological Society (1982–1989). Volume (86) September 1982; Volume (87) December 1982; Volume (88) March 1983; Volume (89) June 1983; Volume (110) September 1988; Volume (111) December 1988; and Volume (113) June 1989.

Camden, W. (1607). *Brittania*. London, George Bishop, (1970 Georg Olms Verlag, Hildesheim).

Carley, J. P. (1988). *Glastonbury Abbey*. New York: St. Martin's Press.

(2001). *Glastonbury Abbey and the Arthurian tradition*. Cambridge: D. S. Brewer.

Castleden, R. (2000). *King Arthur: The truth behind the legend*. London: Routledge.

Chambers, E. K. (1964 [1927]). *Arthur of Britain:* Speculum Historiale. Cambridge: Cambridge University Press.

Crawford, O. G. S. (1931). King Arthur's last battle. *Antiquity,* 5, 236–239.

Crick, J. (1991). The marshalling of antiquity: Glastonbury's historical dossier. In L. Abrams & J. P. Carley (Eds.), *The archeology and history of Glastonbury Abbey* (pp. 217–243). Woodbridge: Boydell.

Domerham, Adam of. (1291 [1727]). *Historia de rebus gestis glastoniensibus.* Ed. T. Hearne. 2 vols. Oxford: Theatio Sheldoniano.

Franklin, A. (2009). *Relics of the dead.* London: Bantam Press.

Geoffrey of Monmouth (Bishop of St. Asaph) (1154 [1968]). *The history of the Kings of Britain.* Ed. G. M. Thorpe. Harmondsworth: Penguin.

Gidlow, C. (2004). *The reign of Arthur: From history to legend.* Sutton: Stroud.

Gillam, G. (undated). The King Arthur Cross rediscovered? Retrieved March 20, 2011 from http://www.britannia.com/history/cross.html.

Giraldus Cambrensis (c. 1191 [1978]). *The journey through Wales and the description of Wales.* Harmondsworth: Penguin.

   (c. 1193 [1964]). *De principis instructione liber.* Ed. G. F. Warner. London: HMSO.

Goodrich, N. L. (1986). *King Arthur.* New York: F. Watts.

Gransden, A. (1976). The growth of the Glastonbury traditions and legends in the twelfth century. *Journal of Ecclesiastical History,* 27, 337–358.

Hall, M. L. (1937). *Arthur of the Holy Grail. The myth as associated with Avalon and Glastonbury.* Cheltenham: F. C. Dodwell & Sons.

Hibbert, C. (1969). *The way of King Arthur.* New York: Simon & Schuster.

Jenkins, E. (1975). *The mystery of King Arthur.* New York: Coward, McCann & Geoghegan.

   (1990). *The mystery of King Arthur.* New York: Dorset Press.

Johnstone, P. K. (1950). The date of Camlann. *Antiquity,* 24, 44.

Jones, W.A. (1860). *On the reputed discovery of King Arthur's remains at Glastonbury.* Taunton: Printed by F. May.

Lacey, R. (2003). *Great tales from English history.* New York: Little, Brown, & Co.

Leland, J. (c. 1550 [1908]). *The itinerary of John Leland.* Ed. L. Toulmin Smith; George Bell & Sons, London.

Loomis, R. S. (1956). *Wales and the Arthurian legend.* Cardiff: University of Wales Press.

Mann, N. R. (1996). *Isle of Avalon: Sacred mysteries of Arthur and Glastonbury Tor.* St. Paul, MN: Llewellyn.

Newell, W. W. (1903). William of Malmesbury on the Antiquity of Glastonbury. *Transactions and Proceedings of the Modern Language Association of America,* *18*(4), 459–512.

Nitze, W. A. (1934). The exhumation of King Arthur at Glastonbury, *Speculum,* 9(4), 355–361.

Rahtz, P. (1993). *Glastonbury.* London: English Heritage.

Reno, F. D. (1996). *The historic King Arthur: Authenticating the Celtic hero of post-Roman Britain.* Jefferson, NC: McFarland & Co.

   (2011). *Arthurian figures of history and legend: A biographical dictionary.* Jefferson, NC: McFarland & Co.

Robinson, J. A. (1926). *Two Glastonbury legends: King Arthur and Joseph of Arimathea*. Cambridge: Cambridge University Press, UK.

Simpson, C. (1983). Double cross. *The Sunday Times*, April 3.

Thorpe, L. (Trans.). (1966). *Geoffrey of Monmouth: The History of the Kings of Britain*. London: Penguin Books.

(Trans.). (1978). *Gerald of Wales: The Journey through Wales and The Description of Wales*. London: Penguin Books.

Treharne, R. F. (1967). *The Glastonbury legends: Joseph of Arimathea, the Holy Grail and King Arthur*. London: Cresset Press.

White, T. H. (1958). *The once and future King*. New York: Putnam.

Williams, M. (1962). King Arthur in history and legend. *Folklore, 73*(2), 73–88.

Wood, C. T. (1991). Fraud and its consequences: Savaric of Bath and the reform of Glastonbury. In L. Abrams & J. P. Carley (Eds.), *The archeology and history of Glastonbury Abbey* (pp. 273–283). Suffolk, England: St. Edmundsbury Press.

Websites

http://www.glastonburyabbey.com
http://www.britannia.com/history/arthur/cross.html

3. DRAKE'S PLATE OF BRASS

Source Materials

Despite several decades of research study and discussion, there is no one single text that tells the whole story of Drake's Plate of Brass. There are a number of helpful and informative websites, and I have indicated which of these I found most helpful. However, study of Drake's Plate must necessarily begin with the California Historical Society and its various publications. Fortunately, the offices of the Society are located very conveniently in San Francisco, and the staff there were most helpful to me. Original materials are not hard to find, and a chronological reading gives a sense of the history and progression of this controversy. The recent publication by Von der Porten and colleagues in *California History*, which is the journal of the Society, concludes that the Plate is a hoax and proceeds to provide a detailed account of how such a hoax could come about and who perpetrated it. It is a very valuable source of information and a good point of departure because it also provides an excellent précis of the whole history. Again, I have drawn extensively from many publications of the Society for that chapter. The question of Drake's Plate is inevitably and irrevocably bound up in the controversy surrounding the site of Drake's Bay. Although I do not focus specifically on this here, I have referenced some source materials should the reader wish to follow this equally contentious and interesting dispute. I myself started with Oko's paper on this topic, although several websites can serve equally well as an initial entry. If one is interested in the Bay, one cannot ignore the Plate, and vice versa.

References

Allen, E. W., Dickinson, E. D., Farquhar, F. P., Grabhorn, E., Kent, A. H., et al. (n. d.). *Nova Albion*. San Francisco: The Silverado Squatters.

Bancroft Library. (1977). *The plate of brass reexamined: A report*. Berkeley, CA: Bancroft Library.

(1979). *The plate of brass reexamined, a supplementary report*. Berkeley, CA: Bancroft Library.

Bolton, H. E., Watson, D.S., & Bancroft, E. (1937). *Drake's plate of brass: Evidence of his visit to California in 1579*. Special Publication, No. 13. San Francisco: California Historical Society.

Bolton, H. E. (1937). Francis Drake's Plate of Brass. *California Historical Society Quarterly*, 16(1), 1–16.

California Historical Society. (1953). *The plate of brass: Evidence of the visit of Francis Drake to California in the year 1579*. San Francisco: California Historical Society.

(1961). *Francis Drake's visit to California, 1579, and his plate of brass*. San Francisco: California Historical Society.

Chickering, A. L. (1937). Some notes with regard to Drake's Plate of Brass. *California Historical Society Quarterly*, 16, 275–281.

(1939). Further notes on the Drake Plate. *California Historical Society Quarterly*, 18, 251–253.

Chickering, A. L., Farquhar, F. P., & Starr, W. A. (1957). Drake in California: A review of the evidence and the testimony of the Plate of Brass. *California Historical Society Quarterly*, 36(1), 21–34.

Chickering, A. L., & Heizer, R. F. (1953). *The Plate of Brass: Evidence of the visit of Francis Drake to California in the year 1579*. San Francisco, CA: California Historical Society.

Davidson, G. C. (1908). Francis Drake on the northwest coast of America in the year 1579. The Golden Hinde did not anchor in the bay of San Francisco. *Transactions and Proceedings of the Geographical Society of the Pacific*, V, Series II.

Dillingham, M. P., & Aker, R. (1960). *A review of the findings of Dr. Adan E. Treganza relative to the site of Drake's landing in California*. Point Reyes, CA: Drake Navigators Guild.

Doerr, A. E., & Dunn, O. (1977). Drake's California Harbor: Another look at William Caldeira's story. *Terrae Incognitae*, 949–959.

Drake, F. (1628). *The world encompassed*. (Being his next voyage to that to *Nombre do Dios* formerly imprinted); *Carefully collected out of the notes of Master Francis Fletcher, Preacher in this employment, and diverse others his followers in the same. (Offered now at last to public view both for the honor of the actor, but especially for the stirring of heroic spirits to benefit their Country, and eternize their names by like noble attempts.* London: Bourne, Royal Exchange.

Farquhar, F. P., & Starr, W. A. (1957). Drake in California: A review of the evidence and testimony of the Plate of Brass. *California Historical Society Quarterly, 36,* 21–34.

Fink, C. G., & Polushkin, E. P. (1938). *Drake's plate of brass authenticated.* Special Publication No. 14. San Francisco: California Historical Society.

Gale, I. (2003). Drake's 'plate of brasse' proven a hoax. *Point Reyes Light.* February 20.

Hanna, W. L. (1979). *Lost harbor: The controversy over Drake's California anchorage.* Berkeley: University of California Press.

Hart, J. D. (1977). *The plate of brass reexamined.* Berkeley: Bancroft Library, University of California.

(1979). *The plate of brass reexamined: A supplementary report.* Berkeley: Bancroft Library, University of California.

Haselden, R. B. (1937). Is the Drake Plate of Brass genuine? *California Historical Society Quarterly, 16*(3), 271–274.

Heizer, R. F. (1947). *Francis Drake and the California Indians, 1579.* Berkeley: University of California Press.

Holliday, J. S. (1974). The Francis Drake controversy: His California anchorage, June 17–July 23, 1579: An introductory perspective. *California Historical Quarterly, 53*(3), 197–202, 203–292.

Hume-Rotherby, W. (1939). Drake's Plate of Brass analyzed. *The Geographical Journal, 94*(1), 54–55.

Hyman, A. D. (1937). Drake's Plate claiming Bay area found. *San Francisco Examiner,* April, 7.

Kelsey, H. (1990). Did Francis Drake really visit California? *The Western Historical Quarterly, 21*(4), 444–462.

Maclay, K. (2003). Who made Drake's "plate of brass?" *UC Berkley News,* February 18.

Michel, H. V., & Asaro, F. (1979). Chemical study of the Plate of Brass. *Archaeometry, 21*(1), 3–19.

Miller, F. P., Vandome, A. F., McBrewster, J. (Eds.). (2010). *Drake's Plate of Brass.* Beau Bassin, Mauritius: VDM Publishing House.

Morison, S. E. (1978). *The great explorers: The European discovery of America.* New York: Oxford University Press.

Neasham, V. A., & Pritchard, W. E. (1974). *Drake's California landing: The evidence for Bolinas Lagoon.* Sacramento, CA: Western Heritage.

Oakland Tribune. (1932). How far did he sail? June 26.

Oko, A. S. (1964). Francis Drake and Nova Albion. *California Historical Society Quarterly, 43*(2), 1–24.

Power, R. H. (1973). Drake's landing in California: A case for San Francisco Bay. *California Historical Quarterly, 52*(2), 101–130.

(1974). *Francis Drake & San Francisco Bay: A Beginning of the British Empire.* Davis: University of California Press.

Power, R. H., & Pike, D. C. (1978). A Plate of Brass "By Me ... C. G. Francis Drake." *California History, 57*(2), 172–185.

Reck, A. P. (1937). Brass Plate left by Drake found by Oaklander, hints Briton discovered S.F. bay. *Oakland Tribune,* April 6.

Robertson, J. W. (1926). *The harbor of St. Francis: Francis Drake lands in a fair and good bay near north latitude 380, also a narrative of the arguments advanced by certain historians in their selection of the "harbor of Sir Francis" together with a relation of the Spanish discovery of the bay of San Francisco.* San Francisco.

  (1927). *Francis Drake and other early explorers along the Pacific coast.* San Francisco: The Grabhorn Press.

Sheehy, J. S. (1938). Experts rule Plate authentic relic of Francis Drake visit. *Berkeley Daily Gazette*, December 6.

Sommer, A. (1935). When California had a King. *San Francisco News*, December 19.

Starr, W. A. (1962). Drake landed in San Francisco bay in 1579: The testimony of the plate of brass. *California Historical Society Quarterly, 41* (3), 1–29.

Von der Porten, E. P. (1965). *Drake – Cermeno: An analysis of artifacts.* Point Reyes, CA: Drake Navigators Guild.

Von der Porten, E., Aker, R., Allen, R. W., & Spitze, J. M. (2002). *Who made Drake's plate of brass? Hint: It wasn't Francis Drake. California History: Magazine of the California Historical Society, 81*(2), 116–133.

Wagner, H. R. (1926). *Sir Francis Drake's voyages around the world: Its aims and achievements.* San Francisco: J. Howell.

Wallis, H. (1979). *The voyage of Sir Francis Drake mapped in silver and gold.* Friends of the Bancroft Library (No. 27). Berkeley: University of California Press.

Watson, D. S. (1937). Drake and California. *California Historical Society Quarterly, 16*(1), 18–24.

Watson, D. S., Kennedy, L., & Seeger, H. (1937). *Drake's plate of brass: Evidence of his visit to California in 1579.* San Francisco: California Historical Society.

Williamson, J. A. (1938). Drake's Plate of Brass. *The Geographical Journal, 91*(6), 543–545.

Ziebarth, M. (1974). The Francis Drake controversy: His California anchorage, June 17–July 23, 1579. *California Historical Quarterly, 53*(3), 196–292.

Text Notes

1. The modern translation of the text on the Plate reads:
"be it known unto all men by these presents. June 17, 1579. By the grace of God and the name of her majesty Queen Elizabeth of England and her successors forever, I take possession of this kingdom whose King and people freely resign their right and title in the whole land unto her majesty's keeping. Now named by me and to be known unto all me as Nova Albion. Francis Drake."

Websites

http://en.wikipedia.org/wiki/Ferdinand-Magellan.
http://www.answers.com/topic/drake_s_plate_of_brass
http://www.mcn.org/2/osecles/plate.htm

4. THE PSYCHOLOGY OF DECEPTION

Source Materials

The source literature on the psychology of deception is vast. Indeed, it spills well beyond the formal science of psychology into the most interesting of places. You can find relevant information in areas as diverse as accounting fraud, performing magic, military and civilian intelligence work, and even modern websites on dating. Where there are people, animals, or perhaps any living system, there is something concerning or related to deception. I have selected from a range of these materials, some of which are cited in this section. In no way do I deceive myself that I have more than scratched the surface of this literature, which actually goes back to the earliest formal foundations of psychology as practiced by some of its earliest pioneers. Just tracking this literature alone would be a life's work.

References

Abe, N., Suzuki, M., More, E., Itoh, M., & Fujii, T. (2007). Deceiving others: Distinct neural responses of the prefrontal cortex and amygdala in simple fabrication and deception with social interactions. *Journal of Cognitive Neuroscience, 19,* 287–295.

Ben-Shakar, G., & Elaad, E. (2003). The validity of psychophysiological detection of information with the guilty knowledge test: A meta-analytic review. *Journal Applied Psychology, 88,* 131–151.

Benz, J. J., Anderson, M. K., & Miller, R. L. (2005). Attributions of deception in dating situations. *The Psychological Record, 55,* 305–314.

Binet, A. (1894). Psychology of prestidigitation. In *Annual Report of the Board of Regents of the Smithsonian Institution* (pp. 555–571). Washington, DC: Government Printing Office

Bond, C. F., & De Paulo, B. (2008). Individual differences in judging perception: Accuracy and bias. *Psychological Bulletin, 4,* 477–492.

Buller, D. B., Strzyzewski, K. D., & Comstock, J. (1991) Interpersonal deception: Receivers' reactions to receivers' suspicions and probing. *Communication Monographs, 58,* 1–24.

Caspi, A., & Gorsky, P. (2006). Online deception: Prevalence, motivation, and emotion. *CyberPsychology, 9,* 54–59.

DePaulo, B. M., Lanier, K., & Davis, T. (1983). Detecting the deceit of the motivated liar. *Journal of Personality and Social Psychology, 45*(5), 1096–1103.

DePaulo, B. M., Lindsay, J. J., Malone, B. E., Muhlenbruck, L., Charlton, K., & Cooper, H. (2003). Cues to deception. *Psychological Bulletin, 129,* 74–118.

Dessoir, M. (1983). The psychology of legerdemain. *The Open Court, 7,* 3599–3602.

Ekman, P., & Friesen, W. V. (1974). Detecting deception from the body or face. *Journal of Personality and Social Psychology, 29*(3), 288–298.

Ekman, P., & O'Sullivan, M. (1991). Who can catch a liar? *American Psychologist, 46,* 913–920.

Fetzer, J. H. (2004). Disinformation: The use of false information. *Minds and Machines, 14,* 231–240.

Frank, M. G., & Ekman, P. (2004). Appearing truthful generalizes across different deception situations. *Journal of Personality and Social Psychology*, *3*, 486–495.

Gerwehr, S., & Glenn, R. W. (2000). *The art of darkness: Deception and urban operations*. Santa Monica, CA: Rand Corporation.

Gombos, V. A. (2006). The cognition of deception: The role of executive processes in producing lies. *Genetic, Social and General Psychology Monographs*, *132*, 197–214.

Gouzoules, H., & Gouzoules, S. (2002). Primate communication: By nature honest, or by experience wise? *International Journal of Primatology*, *23*, 821–848.

Hill, M. L., & Craig, K. D. (2004). Detecting deception in facial expressions of pain accuracy training. *Clinical Journal of Pain*, *20*, 415–452.

Hyman, R. (1989). The psychology of deception. *Annual Review of Psychology*, *40*, 133–154.

Jastrow, J. (1896). Psychological notes upon sleight of hand experts. *Science*, *3*(71), 685–689.

Johnson, P. E., Grazioli, S., & Jamal, K. (1993). Fraud detection: Intentionality and deception in cognition. *Accounting, Organizations and Society*, *18*(5), 467–488.

Johnson, P. E., Grazoli, S., Karim, J., & Berryman, R. G. (2001). Detecting deception: Adversarial problem solving in a low base-rate world. *Cognitive Science*, *25*, 355–392.

Leal, S., & Vrij, A. (2008). Blinking during and after lying. *Journal of Nonverbal Behavior*, *32*, 187–194.

Lewis, M. (1993). The development of deception. In M. Lewis & C. Saarni (Eds.), *Lying and deception in everyday life* (pp. 90–105). New York: Guilford Press.

Lewis, M., Stanger, C., & Sullivan, M. (1989). Deception in 3-year-olds. *Developmental Psychology*, *25*, 439–443.

Malcolm, S. R., & Keenan, J. P. (2005). Hemispheric asymmetry and deception detection. *Laterality*, *10*, 103–110.

Mann, S., Vriji, A., & Bull, R. (2004). Detecting true lies: Police Officers' ability to detect suspects' lies. *Journal of Applied Psychology*, *89*, 137–149.

Mann, S. A., Vrij, A., Fisher, R. P., & Robinson, M. (2008). See no lies, hear no lies: Differences in discrimination accuracy and response bias when watching or listening to police suspect interviews. *Applied Cognitive Psychology*, *22*, 1062–1071.

McHugh, L., Barnes-Holmes, Y., Barnes-Holmes, D., Stewart, I., & Dymond, S. (2007). Deictic relational complexity and the development of deception. *The Psychological Record*, *57*, 517–531.

Mertens, R., & Allen, J. J. B. (2008). The role of psychophysiology in forensic assessments: Deception detection, ERPs and virtual reality mock crime scenarios. *Psychophysiology*, *45*, 286–298.

Miller, G. R., & Stiff, J. B. (1993). *Deceptive communication*. London, UK: Sage.

Orne, M. T., Thackray, R. I., & Paskewitz, D. (1972). On the detection of deception: A model for the study of the physiological effects of psychological stimuli. In N. S. Greenfield & R. A. Sternbach (Eds.), *Handbook of psychophysiology* (pp. 743–785). New York: Holt, Rinehart & Winston.

Osman, M., Channon, S., & Fitzpatrick, S. (2009). Does the truth interfere with our ability to deceive? *Psychonomic Bulletin and Review, 16*(5), 901–906.

Park, H. S., Levine, T. R., & McCornack, S. A. (2002). How people really detect lies. *Communication Monographs, 69*, 144–157.

Pavlidis, I., Eberhardt, N., & Levine, J. A. (2002). Seeing through the face of deception. *Nature, 415*, 35–37.

Pavlidis, I., & Levine, J. (2002). Thermal facial screening for deception detection. *Proceedings of the Second Joint EMBS/BMES Conference*, 23–26.

Pearson, P. N., Ditchfield, P., & Shackelton, N. J. (2002). Male ants disguised by the Queen's Bouquet. *Nature, 419*, 897–988.

Porter, S., & Brinke, L (2010). The truth about lies: What works in detecting high-stakes deception? *Legal and Criminology, 15(1)*, 57–75.

Porter, S., Campbell, M. A., Stapelton, J., & Birt, A. R. (2002). Influence of judge, target and stimulus characteristics on the accuracy of detecting deceit. *Canadian Journal of Behavioral Science, 34*, 172–185.

Porter, S., Juodis, M., Brinke, L.M., Klein, R., & Wilson, K. (2009). Evaluation of the effectiveness of a brief deception detection training program. *The Journal of Forensic Psychiatry and Psychology, 26*, 1–11.

Rothwell, J., Zuhair B., O'Shea, J., & McLean, D. (2006). Silent talker: A new computer-based system for the analysis of facial cues to deception. *Applied Cognitive Psychology, 20*, 757–777.

Searcy, W. A., & Nowicki, S. (2005a). *The evolution of animal communication: Reliability and deception in signaling systems.* Princeton, NJ: Princeton University Press.

(2005b). The evolution of animal signals: Reliability and deception in signaling systems. *Ethology, 113*, 207–208.

Shakhar, G. B., & Elaad, E. (2003). The validity of psychological detection of information with the guilty knowledge test: A meta-analytic review. *Journal of Applied Psychology, 88*, 131–151.

Singer, B., & Benassi, V. A. (1980). Fooling some of the people all of the time. *Skeptical Inquirer, 5*(2), 17–24.

Spence, S. (2008). Playing the devil's advocate: The case against fMRI lie detection. *Legal and Criminology Psychology, 13*, 11–25.

Sporer, S. L. (1997). The less traveled road to truth: Verbal cues in deception detection in accounts of fabricated and self-experienced events. *Applied Cognitive Psychology, 11*, 373–397.

Sporer, S. L., & Schwandt, B. (2007). Moderators of nonverbal indicators of deception: A meta-analytic synthesis. *Psychology, Public Policy and Law, 13*, 1–34.

Stanley, J. T., & Blanchard-Fields, F. (2008). Challenges older adults face in detecting deceit: The role of emotion. *Psychology and Aging, 23*, 24–32.

Stieger, S., Eichinger, T., & Honeder, B. (2009). Can mate choice strategies explain sex differences? The deceived persons' feelings in reaction to revealed online deception of sex, age, and appearance. *Social Psychology, 40*, 16–25.

The Global Deception Research Team. (2006). A world of lies. *Journal of Cross-Cultural Psychology, 37*, 60–74.

Tripplett, N. (1900). The psychology of conjuring deceptions. *American Journal of Psychology, 11,* 439–510.

Vendemia, J. M. C., Buzan, R. F., & Simon-Dack, S. L. (2005). Reaction time of motor responses in two- stimulus paradigms involving deception and congruity with varying levels of difficulty. *Behavioral Neurology, 16,* 25–26.

Vrij, A., Akehurst, L., Brown, L., & Mann, S. (2006). Detecting lies in young children, adolescents and adults. *Applied Cognitive Psychology, 20,* 1225–1237.

Vrij, A., Akehurst, L., Soukara, S., & Bull, R. (2004). Let me inform you how to tell a convincing story: CBCA and reality monitoring scores as a function of age, coaching and deception. *Canadian Journal of Behavioral Science, 36,* 113–126.

Vrij, A., Fisher, F., Mann, S., & Leal, S. (2008). A cognitive load approach to lie detection. *Journal of Investigative Psychology and Offender Profiling, 5,* 39–43.

Vrij, A., & Mann, S. (2001). Who killed my relative? Police officers' ability to detect real- life high-stake lies. *Psychology, Crime & Law, 7,* 119–132.

Walczyk, J. J., Schwartz, J. P., Clifton, R., Adams, B., Wei, M., & Zha, P. (2005). Lying person-to-person about life events: A cognitive framework for lie detection. *Personnel Psychology, 58,* 141–170.

Whaley, B. (1982). Toward a general theory of deception. *Journal of Strategic Studies, 5,* 178–192.

Whiten, A., & Byrne, R. W. (1988). Tactical deception in primates. *Behavioural and Brain Sciences, 11,* 233–273.

Wiseman, R. (1997). *Deception and self-deception.* Amherst, NY: Prometheus.

Websites

http://www.youtube.com/watch?v=NAiUDzPcdOY
http://www.fraudwatchers.org/forums/showthread.php?p=17569

5. THE KENSINGTON RUNESTONE

Source Materials

If you are going to pursue the issue of the Runestone, there is only one place to start and that is the Runestone museum and the artifact itself. There you will find largely supportive materials, including several of the more recent commentaries. Although not the way I became involved, Kehoe's recent text is most readable and balanced and certainly would be a good point of departure. I first encountered the Runestone through Whittaker's critique, although my view is that the case is a little more equivocal then he concludes. A thorough effort at the Runestone must include a careful reading of Blegan who is a clear and erudite commentator. After that one is faced with Wahlgren and Holand and the various contentions they present. Much of the modern information concerns the runes themselves and their possible authenticity, and this is quickly evolving to be a specialist study. Finally, serious scholarship on the Runestone has to find its way to the Minnesota Historical Society located close to the capital building in St. Paul. Dedicated individuals will have to search through the same boxes, files, and folders that occupied my own evaluation, from which, no doubt, there is still much to be learned.

References

Aaberg, E. E. (1899). Further account of the discovery written by a local resident acquainted with its details. *Skandinaven*, March 1.

Anderson, R. B. (1910). The Kensington Runestone fake. *Wisconsin State Journal*, 8.

(1920). Another view of the Kensington Rune Stone. *Wisconsin Magazine of History*, 3, 413–419.

Armstrong, J. M. (1937). The numerals on the Kensington Rune Stone. *Minnesota History*, 18, 185–188.

Betten, F. S. (1934). The Kensington Stone. *St. Louis University Historical Bulletin*, 12(66), 72–73.

Blegen, T. (1925). The Kensington Rune Stone: Discussion and early settlement in western Minnesota. *Minnesota History*, 6, 370–374.

(1964). Frederick J. Turner and the Kensington puzzle. *Minnesota History*, 39, 133–140.

(1968). *The Kensington Rune Stone: New light on an old riddle*. St Paul: Minnesota Historical Society.

Breda, O. J. (1899). An interview giving an account of the discovery of the Rune Stone. *Minneapolis Journal*, February 22.

Christensen, T. P. (1954). Study of the Kensington stone. *Annals of Iowa*, 32, 297–301.

Davis, E. (1932). New chapters in American history: Studies indicate that the Kensington Stone of Minnesota is a record left by Goths and Norsemen in 1362. *Science News Letters*, November 12, 306–307.

Editorial (1954). A farmer's fun. *Time*, February 8, 69.

Flom, G. T. (1910). The Kensington Rune Stone. *Transactions of the Illinois State Historical Society*, 105–125.

Fridley, R. W. (1977a). Debate continues over the Kensington Rune Stone. *Minnesota History*, 45, 149–151.

(1977b). More on the Rune Stone. *Minnesota History*, 45, 195–199.

(1977c). The case of the Gran tapes: Further evidence on the Rune Stone riddle. *Minnesota History*, 45, 152–156.

Gathorne-Hardy, G. M. (1932). A comment on the Kensington Rune Stone. *American Scandinavian Review*, 20, 382–383.

Gilman, R. (1993). Vikings in Minnesota: A controversial legacy. *Roots*, 21(2), 3–35.

Hagen, S. N. (1950). The Kensington runic inscription. *Speculum*, 25, 321–356.

Hall, R. A. (1982). *The Kensington Rune-Stone is genuine*. Alexandria, MN: Hornbeam Press.

(1994). *The Kensington Rune-Stone: Authentic and important*. Lake Bluff, IL: Jupiter Press.

Hartig, H. (1948). Mystery of the Kensington Runestone. *Science Digest, 24,* 37–40.

Henry, T. R. (1950). The riddle of the Kensington stone. In J. Gehlmann (Ed.), *The challenge of ideas: An essay reader* (pp. 45–56). New York: Odyssey Press.

Herrmann, P. (1952). The rune stone of Kensington and the mystery of the Greenland Vikings. In P. Herrmann, *Conquest by man: The saga of early exploration and discovery* (pp. 217–266). London: Hamish Hamilton.

Holand, H. R. (1909a). An explorer's stone record which antedates Columbus: A tragic inscription unearthed in Minnesota, recording the fate of a band of Scandinavian adventurers. *Harper's Weekly, 53,* 15.

(1909b). Runestenen fra Kensington. *Skandinaven,* January 11.

(1910). Are there English words on the Kensington Runestone? *Records of the Past, 9,* 240–245.

(1919). The Kensington Rune Stone: Is it the oldest native document of American history? *Wisconsin Magazine of History, 3,* 153–183.

(1921). The "Goths" in the Kensington inscription. *Scandinavian Studies and Notes, 6,* 159–175.

(1923). Five objections against the Kensington Rune Stone. *Scandinavian Studies and Notes, 8,* 122–134.

(1935). The "myth" of the Kensington Stone. *New England Quarterly, 8,* 42–62.

(1936). Concerning the Kensington Runestone. *Minnesota History, 17,* 166–188.

(1947). The truth about the Kensington Stone. *Michigan History, 31,* 417–430.

(1951). The origin of the Kensington inscription. *Scandinavian Studies, 23,* 23–30.

(1953). A review of the Kensington Stone research. *Wisconsin Magazine of History, 36,* 235–239.

(1957a). Stones that speak: More evidence on the authenticity of the Kensington inscription. *Minnesota Archeologist, 21,* 12–18.

(1957b). Was there a Swedish-Norwegian expedition to America in the 1360's? *Swedish Pioneer Historical Quarterly, 8,* 93–96.

(1958). Nicholas of Lynn: A Pre-Columbian Traveler in North America. *American-Scandanavian Review, 46,* 19–32.

(1959a). *A holy mission to Minnesota 600 years ago.* Alexandria: Minnesota Park Region Publishing Company.

(1959b). An English scientist in America 130 years before Columbus. *Transactions of the Wisconsin Academy of Sciences, Arts, and Letters, 48,* 205–219.

(1962). *A pre-Columbian crusade to America.* New York: Twayne Publishers.

(1969 [1940]). *Westward from Vinland: An account of Norse discoveries and explorations in America (962–1362).* New York: Dover Publications.

Huber, R. M. (1947). Pre-Columbian devotion to Mary in America: The testimony of the Kensington Stone. *American Ecclesiastical Review, 117,* 7–21.

Ingestad, A. S. (1971). Norse sites at L'Anse aux Meadows. In G. Ashe (Ed.), *The quest for America* (pp. 175–196). New York: Praeger Press.

(1977). *The discovery of Norse settlement in America: Excavations at L'Anse aux Meadows, Newfoundland, 1961–1968.* Oslo: Universitetsforlaget.

Kehoe, A. B. (2005). *The Kensington Runestone: Approaching a research question holistically.* Long Grove, IL: Waveland Press.

Keillar, G. (1985). *Lake Woebegone days.* New York: Penguin.

Landsverk, O. G. (1961). *The Kensington Runestone: A reappraisal of the circumstances under which the stone was discovered*. Glendale, CA: Church Press.

   (1969). *Ancient Norse messages on American stones*. Glendale, CA: Norseman Press.

   (1974). *Runic records of the Norsemen in America*. New York: Twayne Publishers.

Landsverk, O. G., & Monge, A. (1967). *Norse medieval cryptography in runic carvings*. Glendale, CA: Norsemen's Press.

Larson, C. (1916). The Kensington Rune Stone: Ancient tragedy. In C. Larson, *History of Douglas and Grant counties Minnesota: Their people, industries and institutions*. Volume 1 (pp. 72–122). Indianapolis, IN: Bowen.

Larson, L. M. (1921). The Kensington Rune Stone. *Wisconsin Magazine of History, 4*, 382–387.

   (1936). The Kensington Rune Stone. *Minnesota History, 17*, 20–37.

Leuthner, M. (1962). *Mystery of the Runestone*. Alexandria, MN: Park Region Publishing.

Leuthner, M. B. (1982). *Crusade to Vinland: The Kensington Runestone*. Alexandria, MN: Explorer.

Mallery, A. H. (1951). The Kensington Runestone. In A. H. Mallery, *Lost America: The story of iron age civilization prior to Columbus* (pp. 176–181). Washington, DC: Overlook Co.

McCusick, M., & Wahlgren, E. (1980). Vikings in America: Fact and fiction. *Early Man, 2*(4), 7–11.

Minnesota Historical Society. (1910). The Kensington Runestone: Preliminary report of the Minnesota Historical Society by the Museum Committee. *Collection of the Minnesota Historical Society, 15*, 221–286.

Moltke, E. (1951). The Kensington stone. *Antiquity, 25*, 87–93.

   (1953). The ghost of the Kensington Stone. *Scandinavian Studies, 25*, 1–14.

Nielsen, R. (1986). The Arabic numbering on the Kensington Runestone. *Epigraphical Society Occasional Publications, 15*, 47–61.

   (1987). The aberrant letters on the Kensington Runestone. *Epigraphical Society Occasional Publications, 16*, 51–83.

   (1988). New evidence which supports that the Kensington Runestone is genuine. *Epigraphical Society Occasional Publications, 17*, 124–178.

   (1988/1989). New evidence which supports that the Kensington Runestone is genuine, *Epigraphic Society Occasional Publications, 18*, 110–132.

Nielsen, R., & Wolter, S. F. (2006). *The Kensington Rune Stone: Compelling new evidence*. Evanston, IL: Lake Superior Agate Publishing.

Nilsestuen, R. (1994). *The Kensington Runestone vindicated*. Lanham, MD: University Presses of America.

Nordling, C. O. (1957). The Kensington Stone – fiction or historical truth? *Norseman, 15*, 19–22.

Peterson, C. S. (1946). *America's Rune Stone of A.D. 1362 gains favor*. New York: Hobson Book Press.

Pohl, F. J. (1952). Kensington Runestone. In F. J. Pohl, *The Lost Discovery: Uncovering the Track of the Vikings in America* (pp. 200–204). New York: W. W. Norton.

   (1961). Kensington Runestone. In F. J. Pohl, *Atlantic crossings before Columbus* (pp. 208–226). New York: W. W. Norton.

(1966). Runes and artifacts in Minnesota. In F. J. Pohl, *The Viking explorers* (pp. 207–217). New York: Crowell.

Quaife, M. M. (1934). The myth of the Kensington Rune Stone: The Norse discovery of Minnesota, 1362. *New England Quarterly, 7*, 613–645.

(1947) The Kensington myth once more. *Michigan History, 31*, 129–161.

Pinckney, R. (1995). Minnesota's Vikings. *American History, 30*(6), 22–25, 64–65.

Reiersgord, T. E. (2001). *The Kensington Rune Stone: Its place in history.* St Paul, MN: Pogo Press.

Roddis, L. H. (1923). The Kensington Rune Stone. In L. H. Roddis, *The Norsemen in the New World* (pp. 7–20). Minneapolis, MN: Augsburg Publishing House.

Rogers, E. E. (1998). *Labyrinths of speculation: The Kensington Rune Stone 1989–1998.* Freeman, SD: Pine Hill Press.

Salverson, L. G. (1954). *Immortal rock: The saga of the Kensington Stone.* Toronto: Ryerson Press.

Schaefer, F. J. (1910). The Kensington Rune Stone. *Acta et Dicta, 2*, 206–210.

(1920). The Kensington Rune Stone. *Catholic Historical Review, 6*, 330–334, 387–391.

Skog, C. E. (1928). *The Kensington Runestone: Illustrated.* Evansville, MN: Enterprise Printery.

Skordalsvold, J. J. (1913). The Kensington Stone and "the Learned Ones." In N. H. Winchell Papers (147.D.6.5 (B), Folder B16.M56b), Minnesota Historical Society, St. Paul, MN.

Sprunger, D. A. (2000). J. A. Holvik and the Kensington Runestone. *Minnesota History* (Fall), 141–154.

Steefel, L. D. (1965). The Kensington Rune Stone. *Minnesota Archeologist, 27*, 97–115.

Struik, D. J. (1964). The Kensington Stone mystery. *Mathematics Teacher, 57*, 166–168.

Thalbitzer, W. (1951). Two runic stones from Greenland and Minnesota. *Smithsonian Miscellaneous Collections, 116*(3), 1–71.

Thornton, W. (1991). The Kensington Stone. In W. Thornton, *Fable, Fact, and History* (pp. 71–82). New York: Greenberg.

Time-Life Films (1973). *The Riddle of the Runestone.* (Also London BBC TV). Minnesota Historical Society, A-V Collection, A-34. St. Paul, MN.

Upham, W. (1910). The Kensington Rune Stone: Its discovery, its inscriptions and opinions concerning them. *Records of the Past, 9*, 3–7.

(1911). The Rune Stone of Kensington, Minnesota. *Magazine of History, 13*, 67–73.

Wahlgren, E. (1952). The Runes of Kensington. In *Studies in Honor of Albery Morey Sturtevant.* (pp. 57–70). Lawrence: University of Kansas Press.

(1958) *The Kensington Stone: A mystery solved.* Madison: University of Wisconsin Press.

(1959). The case of the Kensington Rune Stone. *American Heritage* (April), 34–35, 101–105.

(1982). American runes from Kensington to Spirit Pond. *Journal of English and German Philology, 81*, 157–185.

Wallace, B. L. (1982). Viking hoaxes. In E. Guralnick (Ed.), *Vikings in the west* (pp. 53–76). Chicago: Archaeological Institute of America.

Washburn, M. T. (1932). Were there fourteenth century Christian Europeans in the land that became the United States? *Journal of American History, 26,* 121–145.

Whittaker, J. (1992). The curse of the Runestone: Deathless hoaxes. *Skeptical Inquirer, 17,* 59–63.

(1993). Reply to Criticisms. *Skeptical Inquirer, 17*(3), 335–338.

Willson, C. C. (1917). A lawyer's view of the Kensington Rune Stone. *Minnesota History Bulletin, 2,* 13–19.

Yzermans, V. A. (1964). Our Lady of the Runestone. *Marian Era, 5,* 73–75.

Text Notes

1. It is almost an unstated principle with the Runestone that nothing is as clear as it first appears. From my text it can be read that there is direct evidence that the Stone was discovered on November 8, 1898. However, this is just one of several dates offered for the discovery, even by those who were there! Records taken close to the time of discovery very much favor the November time frame. However, in affidavits of 1909, even Ohman himself confirms that the discovery was made around August 1898. The latter unfortunately are documents in English, and it may well be that they were written by someone other than the deponent, and to what degree Ohman and others might have understood what was written is unclear. Further, it was ten years later, and memory is not perfect. Finally, there is a slight possibility that the Stone may have been "discovered" twice and such a possibility is very much bound up in the issue of fraud.

Websites

http://en.wikipedia.org/wiki/Kensington_Runestone
http://homepages.tesco.net/~trochos/krs1.htm
http://www.runestonemuseum.org/

6. THE VINLAND MAP

Source Materials

I think any modern study of the Vinland Map needs to start with two reference texts. First and foremost I would place Kirsten Seaver's *Maps, Myths, and Men: The Story of the Vinland Map*. It is an important resource and an essential point of departure. It is indeed a most interesting text, even if the reader does not specifically want to specialize in the Vinland Map. The story it tells is broader than this one artifact. However, the reader must realize that Seaver emphasizes her personal view on the issue of authenticity. What she presents is neither unchallenged nor undisputed (see also http://www.econ.ohio-state.edu/jhm/arch/vinland/vinalnd.htm). Similarly, the original work by Skelton, Marston, and Painter, *The Vinland Map and the Tartar Relation*, is a very important document to have at hand. From these one can branch out into specific facets of the controversy such as the issue of the ink, the dating of the parchment, and further exploration of Seaver's proposition concerning the creation of the map by a Jesuit Priest or more formally a member of the Society of Jesus. For critical comments on these textual observations, I found McCulloch's website a fascinating and insightful elaboration on the respective issues that have been raised. It also has the great advantage of being almost contemporary and periodically updated – the two featured texts often are not able to match. Reading this will provide useful understanding of why the issue remains contentious. It will not take too long to outstrip the content of the present chapter, but again the map is used here primarily as an example; this is not purported to be an exhaustive study. Like all of the other examples I have summarized, it is fully deserving of more detailed study in its own right. I have tried to provide a fairly comprehensive list of source materials to follow in such an endeavor. However, if one is to make an exhaustive study, one has to spend time at the Beinicke Rare Book Library at Yale. Primary sources are always paramount.

References

Andrews, P. (1974). A fictitious purported historical map. *Sussex Archeological Collections, 112*, 165–167.

cock, W. H. (1921). Recent history and present status of the Vinland problem. *ographical Review, 11*, 265–282.

e, A. D. (1974). The scientific examination of the Vinland Map at the horatory of the British Museum. *The Geographical Journal, 140*,

land voyages. *Transactions of the Royal Society of Canada*,

(2002). Analysis of pigmentary materials on the tion by Raman microprobe spectroscopy.

Vinland" on the world map in the ternational Map Collectors' Society,

R. A., Möller, G., Dutschke, D., & : New compositional evidence 59, 829–833.

port to the Yale University, y. (Also, *Time Magazine*,

Century Forgery. *Analytical*

s.

ytical Chemistry, 72*, R169–R188.

Crone, G. R. (1966). The Vinland map cartographically considered. *The Geographical Journal, 132*(1), 75–80. (Also Skelton's reply, pp. 336–339, and author's reply, p. 340).

Curtiz, M. (1940). *The Sea Hawk*. Hollywood, CA: Warner Brothers.

Davies, A. (1966). The Vinland Map and Tartar relation: A review. *Geography*, 259–265.

Donahue, D. J., Olin, J. S., & Harbottle, G. (2002). Determination of the radiocarbon age of the parchment of the Vinland Map. *Radiocarbon, 44*, 45–52.

Enterline, J. R. (2002a). Columbus Who? *Mercator's World, 7*(4), 9–11.

(2002b). *Erikson, Eskimos & Columbus*. Baltimore: Johns Hopkins University Press.

Fischer, J. (1903). *The Discoveriers of the Norsemen in America, with special relation to their early cartographical Representation*. New York: Burt Franklin. (Translation of 1902 German edition. Herder: London.)

Fitzhugh, W. W. (2005). A saga of wormholes and anatase. *Science, 307*, 1413.

Fitzhugh, W. W., & Ward, E. I. (Eds.). (2000). *Vikings: The North Atlantic saga*. Washington, DC: Smithsonian Books.

Fuoco, M. A. (2000). Continuing Vinland Map feud might make Musmanno smile. *Post-Gazette* February 29.

Garfield, S. (2013). *On the map*. Gotham Books: New York.

Gathorne-Hardy, G. M. (1921). *The Norse discoverers of America*. Oxford: Oxford University Press.

Graham, R. (2004). Vinland: An inky controversy lives. *Analytical Chemistry A Pages, 76*, 407A–412A.

Guthrie, J. L. (2000). Analysis of Douglas McNaughton's 'A World in Transition: Early Cartography of the North Atlantic'. *NEARA Journal, 34*, 11–14.

Guzman, G. G. (2004). Preliminary Comments on a *Speculum historiale* Manuscript in the Zentral- und Hochschulbibliotek, Luzern (Latin Ms P Msc 13.2° Vol. IV), *Vincent of Beauvais Newsletter*, Jan., Bradley University Department of History.

Haring, J. V. (1937). *Hand of Hauptmann*. New York: Patterson-Smith.

Haugen, E. I. (1942). *Voyages to Vinland*. New York: A. A. Knopf.

Haywood, J. (1995). *Historical Atlas of the Vikings*. London: Penguin.

Henchman, M. (2004). On the absence of evidence that the Vinland Map is m val. *Analytical Chemistry, 76*(9), 2674.

Hermannsson, H. (1936). *The problem of Wineland*. Ithaca, NY: Cornell U Press.

(1944). *The Wineland sagas*. Ithaca, NY: Cornell University Press.

Hovgaard, W. (1914). *The voyages of the Norsemen to America*. New Yo Scandinavian Publishing.

Hutchins, E. (1995). *Cognition in the wild*. Cambridge, MA: MIT P

Ingstad, H. (1963). Discovery of Vinland. *The Arctic Circular, 15,*

(1964). Vinland ruins prove Vikings found the new world. *N 126*, 708–734.

Jackson, M. H. (1966). The Vinland map and Tartar Relati *Cartographer, 3*(1), 14–17.

Lönnroth, L. (1997). Review of VMTR 1995, *Alvísmál, 7,*

Maddison, F. (1974). A skeptical view of the *Tartar Relation*. *The Geographical Journal, 140*, 187–191.

Mann, C. C. (2005). *1491: New revelations of the Americas before Columbus*. New York: Alfred A. Knopf.

Marston, T. E. (1966). The Vinalnd map/Dating the manuscript. *The Cartographer, 3*(1), 1–5.

McCrone, W. C. (1988). The Vinland Map. *Analytical Chemistry, 60*, 1009–1018.
 (1998). Choosing proper chemical problem-solving instrumentation. *American Laboratory*, 27–34.

McCrone, W. C., & McCrone, L. B. (1974). The Vinland Map ink. *The Geographical Journal, 140*, 212–214.

McCulloch, J. H. (2005). *The Vinland map: Some 'finer points' of the debate*. Retrieved October 21, 2011 from http://www.econ.ohio-state.edu/jhm/arch/vinland/vinland.htm

McNaughton, D. (2000). A world in transition: Early cartography of the North Atlantic. In Wm. W. Fitzhugh & E. I. Ward (Eds.), *Vikings: The North Atlantic Saga* (pp. 257–269). Washington, DC: Smithsonian Institution Press.

Menzies, G. (2002). *1421: The year China discovered the world*. London: Bantam Press.

Murad, E. (1997). Identification of minor amounts of anatase in kaolins by Raman spectroscopy, *American Mineralogist, 82*, 203–206.

Neilsen, L. (1936). *Danmarks Middelalderlige Haandskrifter*. København: Gyldendalske Boghandel Nordisk Forlag.

Newbrook, M. (2004). Zheng in the Americas and other unlikely tales of exploration and discovery. *Skeptical Briefs*, September.

NOVA/WGBH. (2005). The Viking Deception. Produced by Jonathan Dent for Granite Productions, February 8. Retrieved October 22, 2011 from http://www.pbs.org/wgbh/nova/schedule.html

Olin, J. S. (2000). Without comparative studies of inks, what do we know about the Vinland Map? *Pre-Columbiana, 2*(1), 1–10.
 (2003). Evidence that the Vinland Map is medieval. *Analytical Chemistry, 75*, 6745–6747.

Olson, J. E. (1913). Present aspects of the Vinland controversy. *Proceedings of the Society for the Advancement of Scandinavian Study, 1*, 147–156.

Painter, G. D. (1974). The matter of authenticity. *The Geographical Journal, 140*, 191–194.

Penrose, B. (1967). *Travel and discovery in the Renaissance*. London: Oxford University Press.

Perkins, R. M. (1974). Norse implications. *The Geographical Journal, 140*, 199–205.

Quinn, D. B. (1961). The argument for the English discovery of America between 1480 and 1494. *Geographical Journal, 227*, 277–285.

Quinn, D. B., & Foote, P. G. (1966). The Vinland map. *Saga-Book, 17*(1), 63–89.

Reeves, A. M. (1890). *The finding of Wineland the good*. London: Oxford University Press.

Reimer, S. P. (1998). *Manuscript Studies: Medieval and Early Modern*, Section IV.vii, "Paleography: Punctuation." December 2. Retrieved December 21, 2012 from http://www.ualberta.ca/~sreimer/ms-course/course/punc.htm

Reman, E. (1949). *The Norse discoveries and explorations in America*. Berkeley, CA: Greenwood Press.

Richey, M. W. (1966). The Vinland map. *The Journal of the Institute of Navigation*, 19(1), 124–125.

Robbins, M. W. (2003) Vinland Map, authenticated and debunked. *Discover*, 24(1), 44.

Saenger, P. (1998). "Vinland Re-read," review of *VMTR* 1995. *Imago Mundi*, 50, 199–202. Retrieved October 21, 2011 from http://www.maphistory.info/saenger.html

Seaver, K. A. (1995). The Vinland Map: Who made it, and why? New light on an old controversy. *The Map Collector*, 70, 32–40.

(1996). The mystery of the Vinland Map manuscript volume. *The Map Collector*, 74, 24–29.

(1997). The Vinland Map. *Mercator's World*, 2(2), 42–47.

(2000). Land of wine and forests: The Norse in North America. *Mercator's World*, 5(1), 18–25.

(2002a). Christopher Who? *Mercator's World*, 7(3), 54–57.

(2002b). Review of Enterline (2002a). *Mercator's World*, 7, 3.

(2002c). Goodbye Columbus. *Mercator's World*, 7, 5.

(2003). The Chart before the Norse. *Toronto Globe and Mail*, November 29, p. A26.

(2004). *Maps, myths and men: The story of the Vinland Map*. Stanford, CA: Stanford University Press.

Shailor, B.A. (1987). *Catalogue of medieval and Renaissance manuscripts in the Beinecke Rare Book and Manuscript Library, Yale University*, Vol. II: MSS 251–500. Medieval & Renaissance Texts & Studies, Binghamton, New York.

Skelton, R. A., Marston, T. E., & Painter, G. D. (1965). *The Vinland Map and the Tartar relation* New Haven, CT: Yale University Press. (*VMTR*). Reprinted in 1995 with new prefatory essays by Painter, Wilcomb E. Washburn, Thomas A Cahill and Bruce H. Kusko, and Laurence C. Witten II (*VMTR95*), but original pagination retained in body.

Snyder, J. P. (1993). *Flattening the Earth*. Chicago: University of Chicago Press.

Spalding, T. (2000–2001). *Vinlanda: The Vinland Map on the Web*. Retrieved June 20, 2012 from http://www.isidore-of-seville.com/vinland/index.html

Stensby, H. P. (1918). *The Norsemen's route from Greenland to Wineland*. Copenhagen: H. Koppel.

Thiele-Storm, G. (1889). *Studies on the Vineland voyages*. Copenhagen: H. Koppel.

Taylor, E. G. R. (1956). A letter dated 1577 from Mercator to John Dee. *Imago Mundi*, 13, 56–68.

Thordarson, M. (1930). *The Vinland voyages*. New York: American Geological Society.

Towe, K. M. (1990). The Vinland Map: Still a forgery. *Accounts of Chemical Research*, 23, 84–87.

(2004). The Vinland Map ink is NOT medieval. *Analytical Chemistry*, 76, 863–865.

Wallace, B. (2000). The Viking settlement at L'Anse aux Meadows. In W. W. Fitzhugh & E. I. Ward (Eds.), *Vikings: The North Atlantic saga* (pp. 208–224). Washington, DC: Smithsonian Institution Press.

Wallis, H. (1974). Introduction to a symposium on the strange case of the Vinland Map. *Geographical Journal, 140*, 183–187.

(1990). The Vinland Map: fake, forgery, or *jeu d'esprit? The Map Collector, 53,* 2–6.

(1991). The Vinland map: Genuine or false? *Bulletin du Bibliophile,* 76–83.

Wallis, H., Maddison, F. R., Painter, G. D., Quinn, D. B., Perkins, R. M. et al. (1974). The strange case of the Vinland Map. *The Geographical Journal, 140,* 183–216.

Washburn, W. E. (1971). *Proceedings of the Vinland Map Conference (PVMC),* held 1966, with contributions by Paul Fenimore Cooper, Jr., Armando Cortesão, Thomas E. Goldstein, Einar Haugen, Melvin H. Jackson, Gwyn Jones, Ib Rønne Kejlbo, Stephan Kuttner, Robert S. Lopez, Oystein Ore, John Parker, Konstantin Reichardt, Vsevolod Slessarev, Boleslav B. Szczesniak, Erik Wahlgren, and Laurence Witten, and extended commentary by the invited participants. University of Chicago Press, (*PVMC*).

Weaver, C. E. (1976). The nature of TiO_2 in kaolinite. *Clays and Clay Minerals, 24,* 215–218.

Wilford, J. N. (2000). Study casts disputed map as false link to Vikings. *The New York Times,* February 26.

Video

The Viking Deception: The truth behind the Vinland Map. Nova: WGBH Boston, 2005.

Websites

http://www.econ.ohio-state.edu/jhm/arch/vinland.vinland.htm
http://www.isidore-of-seville.com/vinland/2.html
http://www.pastpresented.info/vinland/

7. DECIDING ON DECEPTION

Source Materials

In this chapter I have contrasted what appears to be two different "camps" concerning the process of decision making. On the one side are those who look at rational decisions derived from logic and mathematics to try to specify first what "optimal" decisions are and second how and why people deviate from these optimal choices. Their paradigmatic approach requires that one sets up a world in which optimality can be specified. In essence, the right answer can be known. Then, one can explore the way people make their decisions and theorize on why we are sometimes so poor at making such decisions when evolution seems so intolerant of failure. The apparently "opposing" camp focuses on decisions "in the wild" – those that often have to be taken quickly and frequently concern navigation and high-level physical responses to challenges the world around us poses. No armchair mathematicians for this group of researchers! I look to show that, epitomized by Kahneman and Klein's paper, these are not opposing positions at all but rather are complementary in nature because they deal with different decision realms and different decision challenges. One might well be good at both or poor at one and good at another. Expertise is built up in both realms by the exercise of guided practice. Having advocated this reconciliation, I discuss in this chapter what each can tell us about deception, in both contemplative and fast-response situations.

References

Albrechtsen, J. S., Meissner, C. A., & Susa, K. J. (2009). Can intuition improve deception detection performance? *Journal of Experimental Social Psychology*, 45(4), 1052–1055.

Andrews, P. W. (2002). The influence of postreliance detection on the deceptive efficacy of dishonest signals of intent: Understanding facial clues to deceit as the outcome of signaling tradeoffs. *Evolution and Human Behavior*, 23(2), 103–121.

Bacon, F. (1620). Novum organum (*Idols of the tribe*, Aphorism, 46). In Spedding, J., Ellis, R. L., & Heath, D. D. (1863). *The works* (Vol. VIII). Boston: Taggard and Thompson.

Baron, J. (1994). *Thinking and deciding* (2nd ed.), Cambridge: Cambridge University Press.

Biros, D. P., George, J. F., & Zmud, R. W. (2002). Inducing sensitivity to deception in order to improve decision making performance: A field study. *MIS Quarterly*, 26(2), 119–144.

Campitelli, G., & Gobet, F. (2010). Herbert Simon's decision-making approach: Investigation of cognitive processes in experts. *Review of General Psychology*, 14(4), 354–364.

Caughlin, J. P., & Vangelisti, A. L. (2009). Why people conceal or reveal secrets: A multiple goals theory perspective. In T. D. Afifi & W. A. Afifi (Eds.), *Uncertainty, information management, and disclosure decisions: Theories and applications* (pp. 279–299). New York: Routledge/Taylor & Francis Group.

Chen-Bo, Z. (2011). The ethical dangers of deliberative decision making. *Administrative Science Quarterly*, 56(1), 1–25.

Collins, E. C., Percy, E. J., Smith, E. R., & Kruschke, J. K. (2011). Integrating advice and experience: Learning and decision making with social and nonsocial cues. *Journal of Personality and Social Psychology*, 100(6), 967–982.

Cook, M., & Smallman, H. (2008). Human factors of the confirmation bias in intelligence analysis: decision support from graphical evidence landscapes. *Human Factors*, 50(5), 745–754.

Cribb, A., & Entwistle, V. (2011). Shared decision making: Trade-offs between narrower and broader conceptions. *Health Expectations*, 14(2), 210–219.

Deniz, M. (2011). An investigation of decision making styles and the five-factor personality traits with respect to attachment styles. *Educational Sciences: Theory and Practice, 11*(1), 105–113.

Fischoff, B., & Beyth, R. (1975). "I knew it would happen": Remembered probabilities of once-future things. *Organizational Behaviour and Human Performance, 13*, 1–16.

Foer, J. (2011). *Moonwalking with Einstein.* New York: Penguin.

Fuller, C. M., Biros, D. P., & Delen, D. (2011). An investigation of data and text mining methods for real world deception detection. *Expert Systems with Applications, 38*(7), 8392–8398.

Ganis, G., & Keenan, J. (2009). The cognitive neuroscience of deception. *Social Neuroscience, 4*(6), 465–472.

Gladwell, M. (2005). *Blink: The power of thinking without thinking.* New York: Little, Brown & Co.

Grazioli, S., Jamal, K., & Johnson, P. E. (2006). A cognitive approach to fraud detection. *Journal of Forensic Accounting, 7*, 65–88.

Green, D. M., & Swets J. A. (1966) *Signal detection theory and psychophysics.* New York: Wiley.

Greenberg, I. (1982). The role of deception in decision theory. *Journal of Conflict Resolution, 26*(1), 139.

Hagmayer, Y., & Sloman, S. A. (2009). Decision makers conceive of their choices as interventions. *Journal of Experimental Psychology: General, 138*(1), 22–38.

Hancock, P. A., & Manser, M. P. (1998). Time-to-contact. In A. M. Feyer & A. M. Williamson (Ed.), *Occupational injury: Risk, prevention, and intervention* (pp. 44–58). London: Taylor & Francis.

Hancock, P. A., Masalonis, A. J., & Parasuraman, R. (2000). On the theory of fuzzy signal detection: Theoretical and practical considerations and extensions. *Theoretical Issues in Ergonomic Science, 1*(3), 207–230.

Helsloot, I., & Groenendaal, J. (2011). Naturalistic decision making in forensic science: Toward a better understanding of decision making by forensic team leaders. *Journal of Forensic Sciences, 56*(4), 890–897.

Hoffman, R. R. (Ed.). (2007). *Expertise out of context: Proceedings of the Sixth International Conference on Naturalistic Decision Making.* Boca Raton, FL: Taylor & Francis.

Johnson, P. E., Grazoli, S., Karim, J., & Berryman, R. G. (2001). Detecting deception: Adversarial problem solving in a low base-rate world. *Cognitive Science, 25*, 355–392.

Johnston, J. H., Driskell, J. E., & Salas, E. (1997). Vigilant and hypervigilant decision making. *Journal of Applied Psychology, 82*(4), 614–622.

Kahneman, D., & Klein, G. (2009). Conditions for intuitive expertise A failure to disagree. *American Psychologist, 64*(6), 515–526.

Kahneman, D., Slovic, P., & Tversky, A. (1982), *Judgment under uncertainty: Heuristics and biases.* Cambridge: Cambridge University Press.

Kimmel, A. J., Smith, N., & Klein, J. (2011). Ethical decision making and research deception in the behavioral Sciences: An application of social contract theory. *Ethics & Behavior, 21*(3), 222–251.

Klein, G. (1998). *Sources of power: How people make decisions.* Cambridge, MA: MIT Press.

(2008). Naturalistic decision making. *Human Factors, 50*(3), 456–460.

Kosnik, L. (2008). Refusing to budge: A confirmatory bias in decision making? *Mind and Society: A Journal of Cognitive Studies in Economics and Social Sciences, 7*(2), 193–214.

Kunde, W., Skirde, S., & Weigelt, M. (2011). Trust my face: Cognitive factors of head fakes in sports. *Journal of Experimental Psychology: Applied, 17*(2), 110–127.

Lakomski, G., & Evers, C. W. (2010). Passionate rationalism: The role of emotion in decision making. *Journal of Educational Administration, 48*(4), 438–450.

Le, J., Wu, X., & Cao, N. (2002). An assessment of decision-making in deception detection: A trial of Bayesian theory. *Psychological Science (China), 25*(6), 656–659.

Li, D., & Cruz, J. (2009). Information, decision-making and deception in games. *Decision Support Systems, 47*(4), 518–527.

Marewski, J. N., & Schooler, L. J. (2011). Cognitive niches: An ecological model of strategy selection. *Psychological Review, 118*(3), 393–437.

Masip, J., Garrido, E., & Herrero, C. (2006). Observers' decision moment in deception detection experiments: Its impact on judgment, accuracy, and confidence. *International Journal of Psychology, 41*(4), 304–319.

McAndrew, C., Gore, J., & Banks, A. (2009). Convince me: Modeling naturalistic decision making. *Journal of Cognitive Engineering and Decision Making, 3*(2), 156–175.

Merry, A. F. (2011). To do or not to do? – How people make decisions. Proceedings 2010 Perfusion Downunder Winter Meeting, August 5–8, 2010, Queenstown, New Zealand. *Journal of Extra-Corporeal Technology, 43*(1), P39–P43.

Nickerson, R. (1998). Confirmation bias: A ubiquitous phenomenon in many guises. *Review of General Psychology, 2*(2), 175–220.

Olekalns, M., & Smith, P. L. (2007). Loose with the truth: Predicting deception in negotiation. *Journal of Business Ethics, 76*(2), 225–238.

Oswald, M. E., & Grosjean, S. (2004). Confirmation bias. In R. F. Pohl (Ed.), *Cognitive illusions: A handbook on fallacies and biases in thinking, judgment and memory* (pp. 79–96). Hove, UK: Psychology Press.

Pinker, S. (2011). Representations and decision rules in the theory of self-deception. *Behavioral & Brain Sciences, 34*(1), 35–37.

Pleskac, T. J., & Busemeyer, J. R. (2011). Two-stage dynamic signal detection: A theory of choice, decision time, and confidence: Erratum. *Psychological Review, 118*(1), 56.

Simon, H. A. (1979). Rational decision making in business organizations. *The American Economic Review, 69*(4), 493–513.

Smith, N., Kimmel, A. J., & Klein, J. (2009). Social contract theory and the ethics of deception in consumer research. *Journal of Consumer Psychology (Elsevier Science), 19*(3), 486–496.

Steinel, W., Utz, S., & Koning, L. (2010). The good, the bad and the ugly thing to do when sharing information: Revealing, concealing and lying depend on social motivation, distribution and importance of information. *Organizational Behavior & Human Decision Processes, 113*(2), 85–96.

Traut-Mattausch, E., Jonas, E., Frey, D., & Zanna, M. (2011). Are there 'His' and 'Her' types of decisions? Exploring gender differences in the confirmation bias. *Sex Roles, 65*(3/4), 223–233.

Tversky, A., & Kahneman, D. (1974). Judgment under uncertainty: Heuristics and biases. *Science, 185*(4157), 1124–1131.

Websites

http://www.au.af.mil/au/awc/awcgate/milreview/ross.pdf

http://www.fs.fed.us/t-d/pubs/htmlpubs/htm95512855/page13.htm

http://www.truthaboutdeception.com/cheating-and-infidelity/why-people-cheat/decision-to-cheat.html

8. PILTDOWN MAN

Source Materials

In many ways, Piltdown is the most interesting of all the artifacts considered here from a scientific viewpoint. While the others largely appeal to lay constituencies, the now fully exposed Piltdown hoax was aimed squarely at the scientific establishment and in its function as a deception was eminently successful for many decades and outlived the life of most of the individuals involved. I am hesitant to recommend any specific texts since there are so many good sources available, including some intriguing novels presenting fictional but plausible accounts of the events now close to a century old. Uniquely, one can start either at the beginning and work forward in a chronological progression, and if one does that, the paper by Dawson and Woodward is the point of departure. One can also start in the middle; in this case, Weiner's classic 1955 text, *The Piltdown Forgery*, is essential reading. Finally, one can start at the end of the tale and reference modern work, and here primacy should be given to Oakley, who has been central to the controversy for a number of decades.

References

Aczel, A. D. (2007). *The Jesuit and the Skull*. New York: Penguin.

Andrews, P. (1953). Piltdown man. *Time and Tide, 12*, 646–647.

Ashmore, M. (1995). Fraud by numbers: Rhetoric in the Piltdown forgery discovery. *South Atlantic Quarterly, 94*, 591–618.

Berry, T. (1980). The Piltdown affair. *Teilhard Newsletter, 13*, 12.

Blinderman, C. (1986). *The Piltdown inquest*. Buffalo, NY: Prometheus Books.

Boaz, N. (1987). The Piltdown inquest. *American Journal of Physical Anthropology, 74*, 545–546.

Booher, H. (1986). Science fraud at Piltdown: The amateur and the priest. *Antioch Review, 44*, 389–407.

Burkitt, M. (1955). Obituaries of the Piltdown remains. *Nature, 175*, 569.

Chamberlain, A. (1968). The Piltdown forgery. *New Scientist, 40,* 516.

Chippindale, C. (1990). Piltdown: Who dunnit? Who cares? *Science, 250,* 162–163.

Clark, W. Le Gros. (1955a). Exposure of the Piltdown forgery. *Proceedings of the Royal Institute, 20,* 138–151.

Clark, W. Le Gros (1955b). Further contributions to the solution of the Piltdown problem. *Bulletin of the British Museum, 2*(6), 225–287.

Costello, P. (1981). Teilhard and the Piltdown hoax. *Antiquity, 55,* 58–59.

(1985). The Piltdown hoax reconsidered. *Antiquity, 59,* 167–171.

(1986). The Piltdown hoax: Beyond the Hewitt connexion. *Antiquity, 60,* 145–147.

Cox, D. (1983). Piltdown debate: Not so elementary. *Science, 83,* 18–20.

Dawson, C. (1913). The Piltdown skull. *Hastings & East Sussex Naturalist, 2,* 73–83.

(1915). The Piltdown skull. *Hastings & East Sussex Naturalist, 4,* 144–149.

Dawson, C., & Woodward, A. S. (1913). On the discovery of a Paleolithic human skull and mandible in a flint-bearing gravel overlying the Wealden (Hastings Beds) at Piltdown, Fletching (Sussex). *Quarterly Journal of the Geological Society of London, 69,* 117–151.

(1914). Supplementary note on the discovery of a Paleolithic human skull and mandible at Piltdown, (Sussex). *Quarterly Journal of the Geological Society of London, 70,* 82–90.

(1915). On a bone implement from Piltdown, (Sussex). *Quarterly Journal of the Geological Society of London, 71,* 144–149.

Dempster, W. (1996). Something up Dawson's sleeve. *Nature, 382,* 202.

De Vries, H., & Oakley, K. P. (1959). Radiocarbon dating of the Piltdown skull and jaw. *Nature, 184,* 224–226.

Eiseley, L. (1956) The Piltdown forgery. *American Journal of Physical Anthropology, 14,* 124–126.

Essex, R. (1955). The Piltdown plot: A hoax that grew. *Kent and Sussex Journal* (July–September), 94–95.

Gee, H. (1996). Box of bones 'clinches' identity of Piltdown paleontology hoaxes. *Nature, 381,* 261–262.

Gould, S. J. (1979). Piltdown revisited. *Natural History, 88,* 86–97.

(1980). The Piltdown conspiracy, *Natural History, 89,* 8–28.

Gregory, W. K. (1914). The dawn-man of Piltdown, England. *American Museum Journal, 14,* 189–200.

Grigson, C. (1990). Missing links of the Piltdown fraud. *New Scientist, 125,* 55–58.

(1991). Sir Arthur Keith and the Piltdown forgery. *Times Literary Supplement,* February 1.

Haddon, A. C. (1913). Eoanthropus dawsonii. *Science, 37,* 91–92.

Halstead, L. B. (1978). New light on the Piltdown hoax. *Nature, 276,* 11–13.

(1979). The Piltdown hoax: Cui bono? *Nature, 277,* 596.

Hammond, M. (1979). A framework of plausibility for an anthropological forgery: The Piltdown case. *Anthropology, 3,* 47–58.

Harrison, G. A. (1983). J. S. Weiner and the exposure of the Piltdown forgery. *Antiquity, 57,* 46–48.

Head, J. (1971). The Piltdown mystery. *New Scientist, 49,* 86.

Heal, V. (1980). Further light on Charles Dawson. *Antiquity, 54,* 222–225.

Heizer, R., & Cook, S. (1954). Comments on the Piltdown remains. *American Anthropologist, 56,* 92–94.

Hooten, E. A. (1954). The Piltdown affair. *American Anthropologist, 56,* 287–289.

Hoskins, C., & Fryd, C. (1953). The determination of fluorine in Piltdown and related fossils. *Journal of Applied Chemistry, 5,* 85–57.

Hrdlicka, A. (1913). The most ancient skeletal remains of man. *Annual Report of the Smithsonian Institute,* 491–552.

(1922). The Piltdown jaw. *American Journal of Physical Anthropology, 5,* 337–347.

(1923). Dimensions of the first and second molars, with their bearing on the Piltdown jaw and man's phylogeny. *American Journal of Physical Anthropology, 6,* 195–216.

Keith, A. (1913a). The Piltdown skull and brain cast. *Nature, 92,* 107–109, 197–199, 292, 345–346.

(1913b). Ape-man or modern man? The two Piltdown skull reconstructions. *Illustrated London News, 143,* 245.

(1913c). Piltdown: The most ancient skull in the world. *The Sphere, 53,* 76.

(1914). The significance of the discovery at Piltdown. *Bedrock, 2,* 435–453.

(1938–1939). A re-survey of the anatomical features of the Piltdown skull with some observations on the recently discovered Swanscombe skull. *Journal of Anatomy, 75,* 155–185, 234–254.

Langdon, J. (1991). Misinterpreting Piltdown. *Current Anthropology, 32,* 627–631.

Langham, I. (1979). The Piltdown hoax. *Nature, 277,* 170.

(1984). Sherlock Holmes, circumstantial evidence and Piltdown man. *Physical Anthropology News, 3*(1), 1–5.

Lowenstein, J. M., Molleson, T. I., & Washburn, S. L. (1982). Piltdown jaw confirmed as Orang. *Nature, 299,* 294.

Lyne, W. C. (1916). The significance of the radiographs of the Piltdown skull. *Royal Society of Medicine Proceedings, 9,* 33–62.

MacCurdy, G. (1913). Significance of the Piltdown skull. *American Journal of Science, 35,* 315–320.

(1914). The man of Piltdown. *American Anthropologist, 16,* 331–336.

MacCurdy, G. G. (1916). The revision of *Eoathropus Dawsoni. Science, 43,* 228–231.

Marks, P. (1987). *Skullduggery.* New York: Carroll & Graf.

Marston, A. T. (1936). Chimpanzee or man? The Piltdown canine tooth and mandible versus the human specific characteristics of the straight canine and fused alveolar-maxillo-premaxilliary suture. *Bristish Dental Journal,* 216–221.

(1952). Reasons why the Piltdown canine tooth and mandible could not belong to Piltdown man. *British Dental Journal, 93,* 1–14.

(1954). Comments on 'The solution of the Piltdown problem.' *Proceedings of the Royal Society of Medicine, 47,* 100–102.

Matthews, L. H. (1981). Piltdown man: The missing links. *New Scientist, 90,* 280–282; *91,* 26–28; *376,* 515–516, 578–579,647–648, 710–711; *785,* 861–862.

McCulloch, W. (1983). Gould's Piltdown argument. *Teilhard Perspectives, 16,* 4–7.

Millar, R. (1998). *The Piltdown mystery: The story behind the world's greatest archeological hoax.* Seaford: S. B. Publication.

Miller, G. S. (1915a). The Piltdown jaw. *American Journal of Physical Anthropology, 1,* 25–51.

(1915b). The jaw of Piltdown man. *Smithsonian Miscellaneous Collections, 65,* 1–31.

(1920). The Piltdown problem. *American Journal of Physical Anthropology, 3,* 585–586.

Moir, J. (1914). The Piltdown skull. *Antiquary, 50,* 21–23.

Montagu, M. (1954). The Piltdown nasal turbine and bone implements: Some questions. *Science, 119,* 884–886.

Oakley, K. (1949). Fluorine tests on the Piltdown skull. *Proceedings of the Geological Society of London,* 29–31.

(1950). New evidence on the Antiquity of Piltdown man. *Nature, 165,* 372–382.

(1960). Artificial thickening of bone and the Piltdown skull. *Nature, 187,* 174.

(1969). The Piltdown skull. *New Scientist, 40,* 154.

(1976). The Piltdown problem reconsidered. *Antiquity, 50,* 9–13.

(1979). Piltdown stains. *Nature, 278,* 302.

(1981). Piltdown man. *New Scientist, 92,* 457–458.

Oakley, K., & de Vries, H. (1959). Radiocarbon dating of the Piltdown skull and jaw. *Nature, 184,* 224–226.

Oakley, K., & Groves, C. P. (1970). Piltdown man: The realization of fraudulence. *Nature, 169,* 789.

Oakley, K., & Hoskins, C.R. (1950). New evidence on the antiquity of Piltdown man. *Nature, 165,* 379–382.

Oakley, K., & Weiner, J. (1953). Chemical examination of the Piltdown implements. *Nature, 172,* 110.

Osborn, H. F. (1921). The dawn man of Piltdown, Sussex. *Natural History (New York), 21,* 577–590.

Pycraft, W. P. (1917). The jaw of Piltdown man: A reply to Mr. Gerrit S. Miller. *Science Progress, 11,* 389–409.

Roberts, N. K. (2000). *From Piltdown man to point omega.* New York: Peter Lang.

Russell, M. (2003). *Piltdown Man: The secret life of Charles Dawson and the world's greatest archaeological hoax.* Stroud: Tempus.

Schmitz-Moorman, K. (1981). Teilhard and the Piltdown hoax. *Teilhard Review, 16,* 7–15.

Schwartz, I. (1994). *The Piltdown confession.* New York: Wyatt Book.

Shipman, P. (1990). On the trail of the Piltdown fraudsters. *New Scientist, 128,* 52–54.

Smith, G. E. (1913a). The controversies concerning the interpretations and meaning of the remains of the Dawn-man found near Piltdown. *Nature, 92,* 468–469.

(1913b). The Piltdown skull. *Nature, 92,* 118–126.

(1913c). The Piltdown skull and brain cast. *Nature, 92,* 267–268, 318–319.

(1914). On the exact determination of the median plane of the Piltdown skull. *Quarterly Journal of the Geological Society of London, 70,* 93–93.

(1916). The cranial cast of the Piltdown skull. *Man, 16,* 131–132.

Spencer, F. (1990). *Piltdown: A scientific forgery.* London: British Museum.

(1990). *The Piltdown papers.* New York: Oxford University Press.

Straus, W. (1954). The great Piltdown hoax. *Science, 119,* 265–269.

Thacker, A. G. (1916). The significance of the Piltdown controversy. *Science Progress, 8,* 275–290.

Thackeray, J. (1992). On the Piltdown joker and accomplice: A French connection? *Current Anthropology, 33,* 587–589.

Thomson, K. (1991). Piltdown man – The great English mystery story. *American Scientist, 79*, 194–201.

Tobias, P. (1992). An appraisal of the case against Sir Arthur Keith. *Current Anthropology, 33*, 243–293.

(1993). On Piltdown: The French connection revisited. *Current Anthropology, 34*, 65–67.

Underwood, A. S. (1912). The Piltdown skull. *British Dental Journal, 56*, 650–652.

Vere, F. (1959). *Lessons of Piltdown*. London: Ensworth, AE Norms.

Wade, N. (1978). Voice from the dead names new suspect for Piltdown hoax. *Science, 202*, 1062.

Walsh, J. E. (1996). *Unraveling Piltdown*. New York: Random House.

Washburn, S. (1954). The Piltdown hoax. *American Anthropologist, 55*, 259–262.

(1979). The Piltdown hoax: Piltdown 2. *Science, 203*, 955–957.

Waterson, D. (1913a). Discussion on Piltdown. *Quarterly Journal of the Geological Society of London, 69*, 150.

(1913b). The Piltdown mandible. *Nature, 92*, 319.

Weiner, J. S. (1955). *The Piltdown forgery*. Oxford: London.

(1979). Piltdown hoax: New light. *Nature, 277*, 10.

Weiner, J. S., Clark, W., Oakley, K., Claringbull, G., Hey, M. et al. (1955). Further contributions to the solution to the Piltdown problem. *Bulletin of the British Natural History Museum (Geology), 2*, 225–287.

Weiner, J. S., & Oakley, K. (1954). The Piltdown fraud. *American Journal of Physical Anthropology, 12*, 1–7.

Weiner, J. S., Oakley, K. P., & Le Gros Clark, W. E. (1953). The solution to the Piltdown problem. *Bulletin of the British Natural History Museum (Geology), 2*, 141–146.

Winslow, J. H., & Meyer, A. (1983). The perpetrator at Piltdown. *Science, 83*(4), 32–43.

Woodward, A. S. (1913). Note on the Piltdown man. *Geological Magazine, 10*, 433–434.

(1914). Note on the Piltdown excavations. *Nature, 94*, 5.

(1917). Fourth note on the Piltdown gravel with evidence of a second skull of *Eoanthropus dawsonii*. *Quarterly Journal of the Geological Society of London, 73*, 1–10.

(1933). The second Piltdown skull. *Nature, 131*, 242.

(1948). *The earliest Englishman*. London: Watts & Co.

Wright, W. (1916). The endocranial cast of the Piltdown skull. *Man, 16*, 158.

Zuckerman, S. (1990). A new clue to the real Piltdown forgery. *New Scientist, 128*, 16.

Websites

http://www.clarku.edu/~piltdown/pp_map.html

http://www.donsmaps.com/images3/piltdownexcavation.jpg

http://news.bbc.co.uk/2/shared/spl/hi/pop_ups/03/sci_nat_piltdown_man0_unmasking_a_hoax/html/1.stm

http://www.talkorigins.org/faqs/piltdown/piltmap2.gif

9. THE SHROUD OF TURIN

Source Materials

With the Shroud, in one sense, one is spoiled for choice. There is certainly no lack of opinions and now there is even a fairly substantive level of contributions in the accepted scientific journals. In this sense, the Shroud continues to weave its magic. Although spoiled for choice, one has to pick one's way carefully through this prospective minefield. It is not always easy to distinguish solid information from slippery persuasion, and some advocacy groups have a way of encapsulating their belief-driven agenda in a shroud of what can easily appear to be mainstream information. In this I have been most grateful to be guided by Joe Nickell who has spent much time and effort navigating these respective pitfalls. He has pointed to numerous sources that have, I hope, lent intelligibility to my present account. The battle over the Shroud continues, and I can only be sure that by the time this appears there will have been a new revelation. Perhaps the miracle we all look for is a final resolution to the argument. Don't look for it any time soon. But do look through a selection of the following references to get a flavor of the area and feel free to dive in if you want to specialize in this particular artifact.

References

Allen, N. P. L. (1993) Is the Shroud of Turin the first recorded photograph? *The South African Journal of Art History*, 11, 23–32.

(1993) *The methods and techniques employed in the manufacture of the Shroud of Turin.* Unpublished D.Phil thesis, University of Durban-Westville.

Barber, M. (1982). The Templars and the Turin Shroud. *The Catholic Historical Review*, 68(2), 206–225.

Bennett, J. (2001). *Sacred blood, sacred image: The Sudarium of Oviedo, new evidence for the authenticity of the Shroud of Turin.* San Francisco: Ignatius Press.

Bortin, V. (1980). Science and the Shroud of Turin. *The Biblical Archaeologist*, 43(2), 109–117.

Brooks, E. H., II., Miller, V. D., & Schwortz, B. M. (1978–1981). *The Turin Shroud: Worldwide exhibition.* Northbrook, IL: Shroud of Turin Presentation Inc.

Bruce, R., & Wilson, I. (1982). *Jesus and the Shroud: A reserve book for religious studies.* Eastbourne, UK: Holt, Rinehart, & Winston.

Damon, P. E., Donahue, D. J., Gone, B. H., Hatheway, A. L., Jull, A. J. T., & Litflick, T. W. (1989). Radiocarbon dating of the Shroud of Turin. *Nature, 337*, 611–615.

Di Lazzaro, P., Murra, D., Santoni, A., Fanti, G., Nichelatti, E., & Baldacchini, G. (2010). Deep ultraviolet radiation simulates Turin Shroud image. *Journal of Imaging Science and Technology*, 54(4).

Doyle, L. R., Lorre, J. J., & Doyle, E. B. (1986). The application of computer image processing techniques to artifact analysis as applied to the Shroud of Turin study. *Studies in Conservation*, 31(1), 1–6.

Drews, R. (1984). *In search of the Shroud of Turin: New light on its history and origins.* Totowa, NJ: Rowman & Allanheld.

Fanti, G., Botella, J. A., Di Lazarro, P., Heimburger, T., Schneider, R., & Svensson, N. (2010). Microsopic and macroscopic characteristics of the Shroud of Turin image superficiality. *Journal of Imaging Science and Technology, 54*(4), 40201.

Favaro, O. (1978). *The Holy Shroud in the light of the gospels and of modern science: The way of the cross.* (Trans. P. Rinaldi). Torino: Sac. Valentino Scarasso.

Fazio, G. G., & Mandaglio, G. G. (2011). Stochastic distribution of the fibrils that yielded the Shroud of Turin body image. *Radiation Effects & Defects in Solids, 166*(7), 476–479.

Fazio, G. G., Mandaglio, G. G., & Manganaro, M. M. (2010). The interaction between radiation and the Linen of Turin. *Radiation Effects & Defects in Solids, 165*(5), 337–342.

Frale, B. (2004a). The Chinon chart: Papal absolution to the last Templar, Master Jacques de Molay. *Journal of Medieval History, 30*(2), 109–134.

(2004b). *The Templars: The secret history revealed.* New York: Arcade Publishing.

Freer-Waters, R. A., & Jull, A. J. T. (2010). Investigating a dated piece of the Shroud of Turin. *Radiocarbon, 52*(4), 1521–1527.

Gove, H. E. (1996). *Relic, icon or hoax: Carbon dating the Shroud of Turin.* Bristol, UK: Institute of Physics Publishing.

Heller, J. H. (1983). *Report on the Shroud of Turin.* Boston: Houghton Mifflin.

Hoffmann, R. J., & Larue, G. A. (Eds.). (1986). *Jesus in history and myth.* Amherst, NY: Prometheus Books.

Humber, T. (1974). *The fifth gospel.* New York: Pocket Books.

(1978). *The Sacred Shroud.* New York: Pocket Books.

Jonathan, A. (2005). The Turin Shroud. *Physics Education, 40*(1), 67–73.

Kersten, H., & Grober, E. R. (1995). *The Jesus conspiracy: The Turin Shroud and the truth about the resurrection.* New York: Barnes and Noble Books.

Killmon, J. (1997–1998). The Shroud of Turin: Genuine artifact or manufactured relic? *The Glyph: The Journal of the Archaeological Institute of America, San Diego, 1*(10); (11); (12).

Knight, C., & Lomas, R. (1997). *The second Messiah: Templars, the Turin shroud, and the great secret of freemasonry.* Gloucester, MA: Fair Winds Press.

Marion, A. (1998). Discovery of inscriptions on the Shroud of Turin by digital image processing. *Optical Engineering, 37*(8), 2308–2313.

Meacham, W. (1983). The authentication of the Turin Shroud: An issue in archaeological epistemology. *Current Anthropology, 24*(3), 283–295.

Monreno, G.-H., Villalaín Blanco, J.-D., & Rodríguez Almenar, J.-M. R. (1998). *Comparative study of the Sudarium of Oviedo and the Shroud of Turin.* Turin: III Congresso Internazionale di Studi Sulla Sindone Turin.

Nickell, J. (1983) *Inquest on the Shroud of Turin.* Buffalo, NY: Prometheus Books.

(2001). Scandals and follies of the 'Holy Shroud.' *Skeptical Inquirer, 25*(5), 17–20.

(2005) Claims of invalid 'Shroud' radiocarbon date cut from whole cloth. *Skeptical Inquirer, 29*(3), 14.

(2007). *Relics of Christ.* Lexington: The University Press of Kentucky.

(2009). *Real or fake: Studies in authentication.* Lexington: The University Press of Kentucky.

Oxley, M. (2010). *The challenge of the Shroud: History, science and the Shroud of Turin*. London: Author House.

Pickett, T. J. (1996). Can contamination save the Shroud of Turin? *Skeptical Briefs*, June, p. 3.

Picknett, L., & Prince, C. (1994). *Turin Shroud: In whose image? The truth behind the centuries-long conspiracy of silence*. New York: Harper-Collins.

Polidoro, M. (2010). The Shroud of Turin duplicated. *Skeptical Inquirer*, 34(1), 18.

Rahmani, L. Y. (1980). The Shroud of Turin. *The Biblical Archaeologist*, 43(4), 197.

Rinaldi, P. M. (1979). *When millions saw the Shroud*. New Rochelle, NY: Don Bosco Publications.

Rogers, R. N. (2005). Studies on the radiocarbon sample from the Shroud of Turin. *Thermochimica Acta*, 425(1/2), 189–194.

Scavone, D. C. (1989). *The Shroud of Turin: Opposing viewpoints*. San Diego, CA: Greenhaven Press.

Stevenson, K. E., & Habermas, G. R. (1981). *Verdict on the shroud*. Wayne, PA: Banbury Books.

Thurston, H. (1903). The Holy Shroud and the verdict of history. *The Month*, 51, 17–29.

Walsh, J. (1963). *The Shroud*. New York: Random House.

White, J. (2008). The Easter mystery solved. *Journal of Spirituality & Paranormal Studies*, 31(3), 149–153.

Wilcox, R. K. (2010). *The truth about the Shroud of Turin: Solving the mystery*. Washington, DC: Regnery Publishing.

Wilson, I. (1978). *The Shroud of Turin: The burial cloth of Jesus Christ?* Garden City, NY: Doubleday & Company, Inc.

(1998). *The blood and the Shroud*. New York: Simon & Schuster.

Wilson, I., & Miller, V. (1986). *The mysterious shroud*. Garden City, NY: Doubleday.

Wuenschel, E. (1953). *The holy Shroud of Turin*. Bronx, NY: Redemptionist Fathers.

Zugibe, F. T. (1989). The man of the Shroud was washed. Centro Internazionale Di Sindonology, Torino, Italy. *Nuova serre*, 1(1), 171–177.

Websites

http://www.factsplusfacts.com/shroud-of-turin-blood.htm

http://news.yahoo.com/s/ap/eu_italy_shroud_of_turin

http://news.yahoo.com/s/nm/20091005/sc_nm/us_italy_shroud

http://www.pbs.org/wnet/secrets/previous_seasons/case_shroudchrist/interview.html, and see also: http://de.wikipedia.org/wiki/Mechthild_Flury-Lemberg

http://www.shroud.com/pdfs/rogers8.pdf

http://www.shroudstory.com/faq-pray-manuscript.htm

http://www.skepticalspectacle.com/history06.htm

http://www.tqnyc.org/2006/NYC063363/turin/leon1.htm

http://www.uthscsa.edu/mission/spring96/shroud.htm

http://www.world-mysteries.com/sar_2.htm

❖❖❖

10. DECEPTION REDUX

Source Materials

In this chapter I aim to provide a summary and a synthesis of the general principles that have emerged from a consideration of the psychology of cognitive deception and an examination of those principles in action in the various stories recounted. Thus, my source materials come from both the specific stories but also some classic works such as those of Francis Bacon and Jean-Jacques Rousseau, each of whom were very aware of the frailties and fallibilities of man. I point out that it is these weaknesses that have been exploited in war and conflict ever since we humans have been writing about such issues, as well as underlying events as modern as Bernie Madoff's Ponzi scheme. It is apparent that deception is a persistent part of nature and, as we ourselves are only just one more expression of nature, we place our own peculiar human twist on deception's story.

References

Abe, N., Suzuki, M., Mori, E., Itoh, M., & Fujii, T. (2007). Deceiving others: Distinct neural responses of the prefrontal cortex and amygdala in simple fabrication and deception with social interactions. *Journal of Cognitive Neuroscience*, *19*(2), 287–295.

Benz, J. J., Anderson, M. K., & Miller, R. L. (2005). Attributions of deception in dating situations. *The Psychological Record*, *55*, 305–314.

Buller, D. B., Strzyzewski, K. D., & Comstock, J. (1991). Interpersonal deception: I. deceivers' reactions to receivers' suspicions and probing. *Communication Monographs*, *58*, 1–24.

Carlson, S. M., Moses, L. J., & Hix, H. R. (1998). The role of inhibitory processes in young children's difficulties with deception and false belief. *Child Development*, *69*(3), 672–691.

Chaline, E. (2010). *History's greatest deceptions*. New York: Metro Books: New York.

Colligan, M. J., Pennebaker, J. W., & Murphy, L. R. (Eds.). (1982). *Mass psychogenic illness: A social psychological analysis*. Hillsdale, NJ: Lawrence Erlbaum Associates.

Cremer, S., Sledge, M. F., & Heinze, J. (2002). Male ants disguised by the queen's bouquet. *Nature*, *419*, 897–898.

DePaulo, B. M., Lanier, K., & Davis, T. (1983). Detecting the deceit of the motivated liar. *Journal of Personality and Social Psychology*, *45*(5), 1096–1103.

DePaulo, B. M., Lindsay, J. J., Malone, B. E., Muhlenbruck, L., Charlton, K., & Cooper, H. (2003). Cues to deception. *Psychological Bulletin*, *129*(1), 74–18.

Ekman, P. (2009). Why Lies Fail…Part 1. *Reading Between the Lies*, *2*(1).

Ekman, P., & Friesen, W. V. (1974). Detecting deception from the body or face. *Journal of Personality and Social Psychology*, *29*(3), 288–298.

Fetzer, J. H. (2004). Disinformation: The use of false information. *Minds and Machines, 14,* 231–240.

Gombos, V. A. (2006). The cognition of deception: The role of executive processes in producing lies. *Genetic, Social, and General Psychology Monographs, 132*(3), 197–214.

Granhag, P. A., & Hartwig, M. (2008). A new theoretical perspective on deception detection: On the psychology of instrumental mind-reading. *Psychology, Crime & Law, 14*(3), 189–200.

Hill, M. L., & Craig, K. D. (2004). Detecting deception in facial expressions of pain: Accuracy and training. *Clinical Journal of Pain, 20*(6), 415–422.

Hyman, R. (1989). The psychology of deception. *Annual Review of Psychology, 40,* 133–154.

Lewis, M., Stanger, C., & Sullivan, M. W. (1989). Deception in 3-year-olds. *Developmental Psychology, 25*(3), 439–443.

Lubow, R. E., & Fein, O. (1996). Pupillary size in response to a visual guilty knowledge test: New technique for the detection of deception. *Journal of Experimental Psychology: Applied, 2*(2), 164–177.

Mann, C. C. (2005). *1491: New revelations of the Americas before Columbus.* New York: Knopf.

Mann, S. A., Vrij, A., Fisher, R. P., & Robinson, M. (2008). See no lies, hear no lies: Differences in discrimination accuracy and response bias when watching or listening to police suspect interviews. *Applied Cognitive Psychology, 22,* 1062–1071.

McHugh, L., Barnes-Holmes, Y., Barnes-Holmes, D., Stewart, I., & Dymond, S. (2007). Deictic relational complexity and the development of deception. *The Psychological Record, 57,* 517–531.

Millar, M., & Millar, K., (1995). Detection of deception in familiar and unfamiliar persons: The effect of information restriction. *Journal of Nonverbal Behavior, 19*(2), 69–84.

Moomal, Z., & Henzi, S. P. (2000). The evolutionary psychology of deception and self-deception. *South African Journal of Psychology, 30*(3), 45–51.

Nielsen, R., & Wolter, S. F. (2006). *The Kensington Rune Stone: Compelling new evidence.* Evanston, IL: Lake Superior Agate Publishing.

Park, H. S., Levine, T. R., McCornack, S. A., Morrison, K., & Ferrara, M. (2002). How people really detect lies. *Communication Monographs, 69*(2), 144–157.

Porter, S., Campbell, M. A., Stapleton, J., & Birt, A. R. (2002). The influence of judge, target, and stimulus characteristics on the accuracy of detecting deceit. *Canadian Journal of Behavioural Science, 34*(3), 172–185.

Porter, S., Juodis, M., ten Brinke, L. M., Klein, R., & Wilson, K. (2009). Evaluation of the effectiveness of a brief deception detection training program. *The Journal of Forensic Psychiatry & Psychology,* 1–11.

Porter, S., & ten Brinke, L. (2009). Dangerous decisions: A theoretical framework for understanding how judges assess credibility in the courtroom. *Legal and Criminological Psychology, 14,* 119–134.

(2009). The truth about lies: What works in detecting high-stakes deception? *Legal and Criminological Psychology, 15,* 1–21.

Rousseau, J. J. (1776). *Reveries of a solitary walker.* Cambridge: Hacket Publishing.

Shermer, M. (1997). *Why people believe weird things.* New York: W. H. Freeman.

Sokal, A. D. (1996). Transgressing the boundaries: Towards a transformative herme-neutics of quantum gravity. *Social Text, 46/47,* 217–252.

Spence, S. A. (2008). Playing devil's advocate: The case against fMRI lie detection. *Legal and Criminological Psychology, 13,* 11–25.

Stanley, J. T., & Blanchard-Fields, F. (2008). Challenges older adults face in detecting deceit: The role of emotion recognition. *Psychology and Aging, 23*(1), 24–32.

Strömwall, L. A., Granhag, P. A., & Landström, S. (2007). Children's prepared and unprepared lies: Can adults see through their strategies? *Applied Cognitive Psychology, 21,* 457–471.

Sun Tzu (1910 Trans.). *The Art of War by Sun Tzu – special edition.* (L. Giles, Ed, 2005), El Paso, TX: Norte Press.

ten Brinke, L., & Porter, S. (2015). Discovering deceit: Applying laboratory and field research in the search for truthful and deceptive behavior. In *Applied issues in investigative interviewing, eyewitness memory, and credibility assessment* (pp. 221–237). New York: Springer.

Vendemia, J. M. C., Buzan, B. F., & Simon-Dack, S. L. (2005). Reaction time of motor responses in two-stimulus paradigms involving deception and congru-ity with varying levels of difficulty. *Behavioral Neurology, 16,* 25–36.

Walczyk, J. J., Schwartz, J. P., Clifton, R., Adams, B., Wei, M., & Zha, P. (2005). Lying person-to-person about life events: A cognitive framework for lie detection. *Personnel Psychology, 58,* 141–170.

Waller, J. (2009). Looking back: Dancing plagues and mass hysteria. *The Psychologist, 22*(7), 644–647.

Whittaker, J. (1992). The curse of the Runestone: Deathless hoaxes. *Skeptical Inquirer, 17,* 59–63.

Websites

http://www.mnc.net/norway/LeifErikson.htm
http://en.wikipedia.org/wiki/Bernard_Madoff
http://en.wikipedia.org/wiki/Sokal_affair

11. SUMMARY: HOAX SPRINGS ETERNAL

Source Materials

This final chapter looks more toward the future and uses some sources that derive from the burgeoning neurosciences in this area of research. It reiterates that while the present examples come largely from historic cases, such deceptions are prac-ticed and perpetrated on the Web every day of the week. It references the con-cept of memes, which is the notion that ideas persist in a somewhat similar way to genes. Like genes, there are advantageous, adaptive ones and others that are less so. I finish here by commending three texts that I have especially enjoyed and thus recommend them to the reader for their further perusal and pleasure. In no particular order they are: Trivers, R. (2011). *The folly of fools*. New York: Basic Books; Gigerenzer, G., Todd, P. M., & the ABC research Group. (1999). *Simple heuristics that make us smart*. Oxford: Oxford University Press; and finally, Macknik, S. L., & Martinez-Conde, S. (2010). *Sleights of mind: What the neuroscience of magic reveals about our everyday deceptions*. New York: Holt & Co. If you read these, you may not be absolutely proof against deception but you will certainly know enough to be both informed and warned.

References

Ben-Shakhar, G., & Elaad, E. (2003). The validity of psychophysiological detection of information with the guilty knowledge test: A meta-analytic review. *Journal of Applied Psychology, 88*(1), 131–151.

Bond, C. F., & DePaulo, B. M. (2008). Individual differences in judging deception: Accuracy and bias. *Psychological Bulletin, 134*(4), 477–492.

Caddell, J. W., & U.S. Army War College. (2004). *Deception 101: Primer on deception*. Carlisle, PA: Strategic Studies Institute, U.S. Army War College.

Caspi, A., & Gorsky, P. (2006). Online deception: Prevalence, motivation, and emotion. *CyberPsychology & Behavior, 9*(1), 54–59.

Coad, J. G. (1970). *Hailes Abbey*. London: HMSO.

Deceiving the law [Editorial]. (2008). *Nature Neuroscience, 11*(11), 1231.

Einav, S., & Hood, B. M. (2008). Tell-tale eyes: Children's attribution of gaze aversion as a lying cue. *Developmental Psychology, 44*(6), 1655–1667.

Ekman, P., & O'Sullivan, M. (1991). Who can catch a liar? *American Psychologist, 46*(9), 913–920.

Farquhar, M. (2005). *A treasury of deception*. London: Penguin.

Fox, M. J. (2002). *Lucky man*. New York: Hyperion.

Frank, M. G., & Ekman, P. (2004). Appearing truthful generalizes across different deception situations. *Journal of Personality and Social Psychology, 86*(3), 486–495.

Frankfurt, H. G. (2005). *On bullshit*. Princeton, NJ: Princeton University Press.

Gigerenzer, G., Todd, P. M., & the ABC research Group. (1999). *Simple heuristics that make us smart*. Oxford: Oxford University Press.

Gouzoules, H., & Gouzoules, S. (2002). Primate communication: By nature honest, or by experience wise? *International Journal of Primatology, 23*(4), 821–848.

Gregg, A. P. (2007). When vying reveals lying: The timed antagonistic response alethiometer. *Applied Cognitive Psychology, 21*, 621–647.

Horn, A. (2007). Deconstructing animal deceit. *Ethology, 113*(2), 207–208.

Innes, B. (2005). *Fakes and forgeries*. Pleasantville, NY: Reader's Digest.

Jones, M. (Ed.). (1990). *Fake: the art of deception*. London: British Museum.

Leal, S., & Vrij, A. (2008). Blinking during and after lying. *Journal of Nonverbal Behavior, 32*, 187–194.

Luber, B., Fisher, C., Applebaum, P. S., Ploesser, M., & Lisanby, S. H. (2009). Noninvasive brain stimulation in the detection of deception: Scientific challenges and ethical consequences. *Behavioral Sciences and the Law, 27*, 191–208.

MacDougall, C. D. (1958). *Hoaxes*. New York: Dover Publications.

Macknik, S. L., & Martinez-Conde, S. (2010). *Sleights of mind: What the neuroscience of magic reveals about our everyday deceptions.* New York: Holt & Co.

Malcolm, S. R., & Keenan, J. P. (2005). Hemispheric asymmetry and deception detection. *Laterality, 10*(2), 103–110.

Mann, S., Vriji, A., & Bull, R. (2004). Detecting true lies: Police officers' ability to detect suspects' lies. *Journal of Applied Psychology, 89*(1), 137–149.

Mertens, R., & Allen, J. J. B. (2008). The role of psychophysiology in forensic assessments: Deception detection, ERPs, and virtual reality mock crime scenarios. *Psychophysiology, 45*, 286–298.

Mitchell, R. W., & Thompson, N. S. (1993). Familiarity and the rarity of deception: Two theories and their relevance to play between dogs (*Canis familiaris*) and humans (*Homo sapiens*). *Journal of Comparative Psychology, 107*(3), 291–300.

Orne, M. T., Thackray, R. I., & Paskewitz, D. A. (1972). On the detection of deception: A model for the study of the physiological effects of psychological stimuli. In N. S. Greenfield & R. A. Sternbach (Eds.), *Handbook of psychophysiology* (pp. 743–785). New York: Holt, Rinehart & Winston.

Osman, M., Channon, S., & Fitzpatrick, S. (2009). Does the truth interfere with our ability to deceive? *Psychnomic Bulletin & Review, 16*(5), 901–906.

Pavlidis, I., & Levine, J. (2002). Thermal facial screening for deception detection. *Proceedings of the Second Joint EMBS/BMES Conference*, 23–26.

Pavlidis, I., Eberhardt, N. L., & Levine, J. A. (2002). Seeing through the face of deception. *Nature, 415*, 35–37.

Rook, T. (2002). *Roman baths in Britain.* Princes Risborough, UK: Shire Archeology.

Rothwell, J., Bandar, Z., O'Shea, J., & McLean, D. (2006). Silent talker: A new computer-based system for the analysis of facial cues to deception. *Applied Cognitive Psychology, 20*, 757–777.

Rousseau, J. J. (1979 [1776]). *Reveries of a solitary walker* London: Penguin.

Schuiling, G. A. (2004). Deceive, and be deceived! *Journal of Psychosomatic Obstetrics & Gynecology, 25*, 170–174.

Sporer, S. L. (1997). The less travelled road to truth: Verbal cues in deception detection in accounts of fabricated and self-experienced events. *Applied Cognitive Psychology, 11*, 373–397.

Sporer, S. L., & Schwandt, B. (2007). Moderators of nonverbal indicators of deception: A meta-analytic synthesis. *Psychology, Public Policy, and Law, 13*(1), 1–34.

St. Clair Baddeley, W. (1960). *Hailes Abbey.* London: National Trust.

Stieger, S., Eichinger, T., & Honeder, B. (2009). Can mate choice strategies explain sex differences? The deceived persons' feelings in reaction to revealed online deception of sex, age, and appearance. *Social Psychology, 40*(1), 16–25.

Talwar, V., & Lee, K. (2008). Social and cognitive correlates of children's lying behavior. *Child Development, 79*(4), 866–881.

The Global Deception Research Team. (2006). A world of lies. *Journal of Cross-Cultural Psychology, 37*, 60–74.

Trivers, R. (2011). *The folly of fools.* New York: Basic Books.

Vrij, A., Akehurst, L. Brown, L., & Mann, S. (2006). Detecting lies in young children, adolescents and adults. *Applied Cognitive Psychology, 20*, 1225–1237.

Vrij, A., Akehurst, L., Soukara, S., & Bull, R. (2004). Let me inform you how to tell a convincing story: CBCA and reality monitoring scores as a function of age, coaching, and deception. *Canadian Journal of Behavioural Science, 36*(2), 113–126.

Vrij, A., Fisher, R., Mann, S., & Leal, S. (2008). A cognitive load approach to lie detection. *Journal of Investigative Psychology and Offender Profiling, 5,* 39–43.

Vrij, A., & Mann, S. (2001). Who killed my relative? Police officers' ability to detect real-life high-stake lies. *Psychology, Crime & Law, 7,* 119–132.

INDEX

CPSIA information can be obtained
at www.ICGtesting.com
Printed in the USA
FFOW03n1555200215
11274FF